Music Industry
management & promotion

second edition

Dedication

To Jill, Hayley, Jodie and Christian

Music Industry
management & promotion

second edition

Chris Kemp

elm publications

This second edition of *Music Industry: management and promotion* is published December 2000 by ELM Publications, Seaton House, Kings Ripton, Huntingdon, PE28 2NJ, telephone 01487 773254, Fax 01487 773359, www.elm-training.co.uk

Printed by St Edmundsbury Press, Bury St Edmunds, Suffolk, England. Bound by Woolnough Bookbinding, Express Works, Church Street, Irthlingborough, Northamptonshire, England.

ISBN 1 85450 285 9

British Library Cataloguing-in-Publication Data

A catalogue record for this publication is available from the British Library.

Contents

List of Figures and Photographs

Figure

Photographs are by Chris Kemp and are copyright to him,
except for Figure 1: 8 by Mark Catanach.

Acknowledgements

Many people have assisted in different ways in the writing of this book. Some have produced chapters, others have given up their time to be interviewed and others have just been there when I needed their support. I would like in particular to thank Tony Platt, David Walker-Collins and Bob Carpenter who have contributed chapters to this book. I would also like to thank Stuart Galbraith from SFX, Paul Allen from Morning Press, Mike Dewdney from ITB, Gem Howard and Andy Black from Music For Nations, Ian Sales from Helter Skelter, Nick Peel from MPI, Martin Tibbets from Revolution, James Delanoy an independent radio promoter, Bill and Tim from Northampton, the Milton Keynes Borough Council Environmental Health Department, and, see page ix, Darryl Franklin, who all allowed me to interview them.

Philip Windsor and Simon Teesdale from Milton Keynes Borough Council Environmental Health Department gave permission for much of the concert detail from venues used throughout this book. Phil was most helpful to me at events, always giving advice when it was needed. I worked with him on a number of occasions, including concerts for Mettallica, Bon Jovi and Guns'n Roses. Phil is also an exceptional lecturer, inspiring my students with his insight into health and safety at events.

Contributors

Paul Allen is the Director of Morning Press.

Robert Carpenter is a director of Apex Stages.

James Delanoy is an independent radio promoter.

Mike Dewdney is an Agent with ITB.

Darryl Franklin, see page viii, is Vice President, Business and Legal Affairs, Interscope/ANM/Geffen Records, Universal Music.

Stuart Galbraith is a Partner and Director of SFX

Gem Howard and Andy Black are Directors of Music For Nations Record Company.

Nick Peel is an Agent with Miracle Prestige International.

Tony Platt is a Producer and Sound Engineer responsible for, among others, albums with Iron Maiden, Def Leppard, Buddy Guy and AC/DC.

Ian Sales is an Agent with Helter Skelter.

Martin Tibbets is Head of Film Promotion at Revolution Promotions.

David Walker-Collins is a Manager at The Stables, Wavendon.

Philip Windsor is the Chief Environmental Health Officer for Milton Keynes Borough Council.

About the authors

Chris Kemp has been active in the music, arts and entertainment business for the past twenty years. His enthusiastic and innovative development of the Pitz club at the Woughton Centre in Milton Keynes, as a promoter and venue manager, turned a musical desert into one of the highest profile club venues in the country. The constant development of all genres of music kept the venue in the limelight for many years. Chris not only promoted and marketed musical acts but also theatre, dance, mime, comedy and opera, initiating comedy at the Clock Inn, a successful Sunday night club also in Milton Keynes. Acts such as Iron Maiden, The Pasadenas, Joan Armatrading, The Stranglers, The Royal Shakespeare Company, DV8 Physical Theatre, Ian Botham and Viv Richards, Eddie Izzard and The Cranberries were among the three thousand acts that Chris promoted over a twelve year period.

After graduating from York St John's PE College in 1982 with twelve years of every conceivable sport behind him, Chris took a post as Assistant Manager at a sports and arts centre in Thame. During this period he became Artistic Director of Rococo Dance Company and took the company on tour to several venues in England, including The Barbican in London and the Adelphi Hotel in Liverpool. During his work at the sports and arts centre, Chris took a further degree in Arts Administration at City University in London. With this degree Chris left Thame and moved to a new job as Arts Manager at the Woughton Centre in Milton Keynes. In Milton Keynes Chris was promoted twice, ending up as Area Arts and Entertainment Officer for Buckinghamshire County Council.

In 1993 Chris left the Woughton Centre to take up a lecturing post at Buckinghamshire Chilterns University College. After leaving the Centre, he continued to promote at a number of venues around the country in a music partnership called Atlantic Music Promotions. He is now Head of the Department of Leisure at the University College.

Over the past five years Chris has created and developed both an undergraduate and masters degree in Music Industry Management. The course has already had two cohorts of graduates who have entered the industry. The majority of students have gained employment with music based companies, including the MCPS, Sony, Anglo Plugging, Virgin and the PRS. The course has been a great success and has now diversified into four separate strands in specific aspects of the music industry. Chris is still active within the music industry, and assists with his wife's Dance Promotions, acts as a DJ and participates in a number of other projects, including a record company which he set up at the University College. Currently Chris is in the final stages of a Doctorate at Liverpool University's Institute Of Popular Music which considers the classification of genre within music, concentrating specifically on punk and hardcore.

David Walker Collins ran the Noise Factory for some years and worked as a freelance promoter and tour manager for companies, including MCP. He also managed London Astoria 2.

Tony Platt runs Platinum Tones productions and ia most sought-after producer. He has worked with Testament, Buddy Guy, Iron Maiden, Def Leppard and AC/DC, as well as many other artists.

Dr Robert Carpenter has worked in the live outdoor concert industry for many years and is the Director of Apex Staging.

Introduction

Although much of this book is a personal account written by those with music close to their hearts, it does give an insight into the workings of the industry itself. It has been written in simple language without ceremony to give a clear picture of many of the difficult structures that often defy understanding within this ever-changing industry. It gives a no-nonsense look at, not only the management and promotional systems within music, but also at some of the smaller areas often overlooked by general music books. This book includes many of the people working within music who rarely get a voice, thus making sure that every angle possible has been taken into consideration.

The book is written as a Club[1] overview. It may be said that larger venues and stadium promotions are similar, but on a much larger scale. The author has not attempted to comment on these, feeling that they are best left to hardened and experienced professionals.

This book is not the music management bible, and some people in the music business may disagree with parts of it. But, it answers many of the questions posed by students and those wanting to know more about the industry as new or would-be promoters. It is a guide written by people within the industry who have amassed a great deal of knowledge and informed opinion over the last twenty years. It contains opinions from a wide range of protagonists, including crew members about the bands that they mix with and the experiences of record company executives, each of whom have valid and important points to contribute.

If we look closely at the world of music management, it becomes apparent that we are working in a world in constant flux. New

---

[1] Club in this context refers to indie, rock and pop promotions on the small-scale club circuit, and not dance promotions.

technological developments and constant business growth are shown in each area of the music business.

But, none of this would be possible if it were not for the rich history and development of musical genre over the last century. Music is a part of everyone's life. From the car radio to supermarket music, it is with us throughout the day. It brings joy to many and sadness to others. It reminds us of past times – good and bad. It forms the rich fabric of experience whilst we are growing up and follows us to our graves at funeral services. It marks both christenings and weddings. It fills our leisure time with products and services related to music. In its own way it is a ubiquitous entity. Some of us are gifted with the ability to create music, whilst others can only appreciate it. But, we are all able to buy music in its numerous forms: CD's tapes DATs, mini discs, vinyl, sheet music, instruments and computers can all be purchased to either create or to appreciate musical form and content. Today's fast freely-flowing music technology has enabled non-playing musicians to create music without being able to read music; it has enabled programmers to create beautiful works that we thought at one stage or another would not be possible without years of musical study.

Behind this musical development there is a management system that enables music to be heard, produced, developed and assimilated through a complex system of business deals and management manœuvres. The legal, financial and political issues of this system do not normally affect the punter, unless they influence the price of the product or service offered. The punter is normally concerned with the finished product only and as long as that is available he or she has little time for the way in which music is managed or promoted. Subconsciously, though, everyone plays his or her part in music's development. Adverts on the TV, film music and radio airplay influence each and every one of our buying choices. The industry controls, through gatekeepers, what is released and these developments are then taken up by retailers and marketeers to try to get us as consumers to buy the product or service offered. It is this underlying music business that this book is concerned with. The development of this business means that hundreds of thousands, if not millions, of people are employed in some manner working with music.

This book primarily aims to give an insight into the management and administration of the various sectors of club music and the general business of music. Owing to the special relationship that the author has with many of the contributors, this book is written without frills and is straight to the point. All areas discussed have been carefully documented from true-life situations and, therefore, this book is not only an insight into the music business, but also reflects personal touches from each contributor.

The book takes the reader to the very heart of music promotion, introducing the promoter, who, in the terms of the Oxford Dictionary, *is one who is financially responsible for an ... event.* It focuses on the commercial aspects of promotion as well as the promoter and the people with whom he comes into contact when putting on an event. The book also makes the reader aware of other industries that are important in the music business, primarily those that are product related. The record industry, studio production, venue management, PA and lighting companies and the agency are all scrutinised in great detail, giving the reader a great insight into how these areas are managed and controlled, and how they relate to the artist and event.

Many hours of work have gone into the production of this book and the authors and all concerned hope that you have as much fun reading it as we did, not only writing it but being in the music business.

The material is relevant for NVQ, HND and undergraduate degree work in all aspects of the music management and promotion industry.

ALL REFERENCES TO 'HE' THROUGHOUT THIS BOOK SHOULD BE TAKEN TO APPLY TO BOTH **HE AND SHE,** EXCEPT WHERE INDICATED TO THE CONTRARY.

Chris Kemp, October 2000

Chapter 1

Selecting an Artist and the Role of the Promoter

Introduction

Profit is usually the motive behind a promoter's choice of artist. Will the artist generate enough income for the promoter to be able to pay the fixed costs and overheads and, thus, make a profit?

The philosophy behind the decision to promote an artist is far more complex. When a promoter enters into the process of selecting an artist, there are several crucial decisions that must be taken. These are often linked to the promoter's philosophical or economic experiences within the music industry.

- What takes precedence over any other factor is gut-feeling and awareness. Has the promoter ever heard of the artist? This statement is one that is often exploited by the agent if the artist is new and creating a buzz, but has no significant punter loyalty. The agent, in theory, may prey on the unsuspecting promoter, lulling him or her into a false sense of security and thus off-loading the artist at a vastly over-inflated price. However, as the promoter grows in confidence and creates a network of contacts, the problem of awareness is alleviated. A promoter may develop networks of contacts in record shops, in other venues and with promotion companies, which the promoter will contact when offered a band that he or she is unsure of. By surrounding himself with these contacts, the promoter cuts down the problem of exploitation by the agent.

1

- The artist's economic viability is important. The promoter has to ask himself whether the artist will sell. This is often a difficult question and the promoter may need to carry out market research into the viability of the artist. The contacts detailed above are often important in establishing this. If an artist has recently had a high sell-through of albums or has sold well in the area at another venue, this information may be sufficient to ensure that the promoter will book the artist.

- Musical Genre. Does the promoter feel that this is the right genre of music to put into the venue or area that he is promoting in? In many cases promoters have failed when promoting genres of music in either an unsuitable venue or in a place without a reputation for the type of music promoted. This often happens when a promoter wishes to change the genre of music promoted in a club. People are creatures of habit and it takes a period of time to change the average punter's view of a venue. If a club has a reputation for playing rock music and a promoter tries a soul night, the soul night will almost certainly fall flat as the audience will not consider the venue appropriate for the show. It takes time to develop reputations and atmospheres, and these are essential to the presentation of the show.

The idea of promoting an artist and a style of music that the promoter enjoys is one of those leading philosophical, ethical, and moral questions often discussed in music circles. It is seen partly as a duality with little compromise or, at times, it has been seen as an extravagant loss-leader for the promoter. You, as a promoter, should be led by market forces and punter needs rather than by personal taste and choice.

Personal choice is a temptation that you must overcome. The institution of personally-based artist promotion decisions have resulted in the demise of many promoters and promotion companies, especially in an economic climate where the promoter has to be very careful about the viability of each attempted promotion.

When selecting an artist in each different musical genre, the same rules apply. A great deal of thought and research should go into the final decision on whether to promote an artist or not. Figure 1:1, page four, shows some of the factors that affect the promoter's decision when selecting an artist. The decision has to be based on several key factors.

- Has the artist been around long enough to have built up an audience large enough to sustain a tour of the length planned?

- Has the artist been around long enough to attract a reasonable fan base to ensure that the promotion is economically viable?

- Is the artist at present a new club favourite?

- Has the artist attained cult status?

To make value judgments, the promoter must first find out as much information as possible. This will come from the agent, record shops, other promoters and the music press.

The type of information needed by you, as a promoter, includes the number of dates planned for the tour. If only five dates are planned, and the artist is reasonably popular, it may not matter too much about a reduced local fan base. This is because if only a few dates are planned, an audience will travel to see the artist in question. Linked with this is the amount of publicity that the artist is receiving at that moment. You need to establish whether the current publicity will be sufficient in the run up to the concert to ensure a capacity audience. If the artist has already built up a large following, you should ascertain whether or not there are too many dates on the tour to ensure an audience that will cover the costs of the promotion. These dates may include some areas in close proximity to the venue in which your promotion is taking place. This may militate against the audience coming to your promotion. If this is the case, then further negotiations with the agent may be necessary to ensure:

- That your concert is the only one in the area, and

- That there are not too many dates on the tour.

If it is impossible to negotiate on these matters, then another artist or venue might be a better alternative.

An aspect that is often overlooked during a promotion is propoer estimation of the total amount of real costs incurred. Romantic as it may seem, promoting is not an easy task. It is made up of several hard economic facts. The first is that, on the surface, a promoter looking at an event from a romantic rather than an objective viewpoint may feel that he can afford to do the promotion. However, underneath this facade, the general economics of the whole event may not seem so viable. An event consists of not only the artist costs, but also hall/venue hire and associated expenses, which may include public address systems (PA), lighting, staffing, crew, hospitality and security.

Figure 1:1 Some of the factors affecting the promoter's decision when selecting an artist

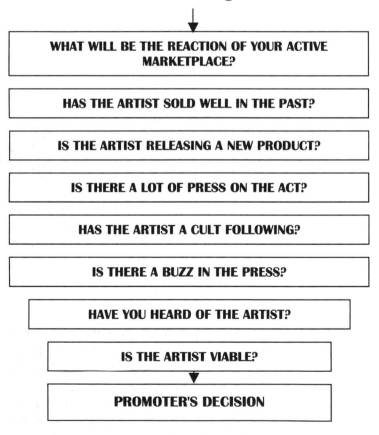

WHAT WILL BE THE REACTION OF YOUR ACTIVE MARKETPLACE?
HAS THE ARTIST SOLD WELL IN THE PAST?
IS THE ARTIST RELEASING A NEW PRODUCT?
IS THERE A LOT OF PRESS ON THE ACT?
HAS THE ARTIST A CULT FOLLOWING?
IS THERE A BUZZ IN THE PRESS?
HAVE YOU HEARD OF THE ARTIST?
IS THE ARTIST VIABLE?
PROMOTER'S DECISION

There are also marketing, promotion, ticket and press costs that may not be included in any original calculation for an event. The sum total of these costs may be well above the amount that the promoter can afford to pay out for the show. The fact is, if the promoter does not make enough from ticket sales and extraneous income to cover the costs, he will make a loss. Any promoter must make sure that he has done his homework carefully, and knows the costs of the promotion down to the last penny. A contingency budget should be included in case of error or oversight.

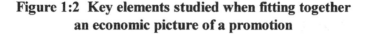

Figure 1:2 Key elements studied when fitting together an economic picture of a promotion

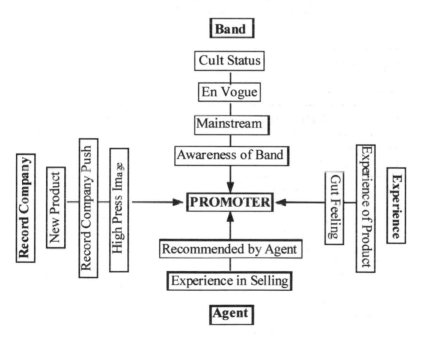

The promoter must be aware of the music category that an artist fits into, i.e., its genre. He must also know the magazines and periodicals that pertain to this genre, as well as radio and television programmes. Fitting together an economic and media picture of the artist is essential. This alone could be a key reason for making a choice. A telephone call to several local record shops will show how the artist is performing with CD sales and help to judge viability. Calling other promoters around the country to get their ideas on the artist or a skim through the last two months' major music magazines can all help to build up a picture of an artist's economic viability for promotion. The music business is very transient, and few people really know what is going to happen within the industry. If the artist is selling a high number of CDs in Britain or another country, or the record company is about to pour X million pounds into a promotional drive, it may be a good time to book the artist.

Another key area of musical logistics to examine is whether new product will be released before the artist goes on tour. New product may mean increased sales for the promoter, provided it is in the right time frame. This would span four weeks to two months before the artist is due to tour. The tour would specifically coincide with the product release for two reasons:

- The consumer who purchases the product may want to see the artist live.

- The tour may encourage consumers, once they have seen the artist, to purchase the product.

A tour immediately after the release of new product may only increase ticket sales if the record company, agent and promotional marketing machine are fully behind the artist. This type of tour is called a piggy-back tour, where the artist tours on the back of product. Figure 1:2 shows four of the vital areas that the promoter can consider when making his final decision on whether to book a artist or not.

Hard to define, but important is gut feeling. When I promoted the band Therapy, I had heard their last album and read their press and it seemed to me that they were bubbling just under chart success. Knowing that they were bringing a new single (Teethgrinder) out six weeks before my show, I took a gamble and promoted them. Luckily the single made the charts and the press gave them a high profile. The show did very well.

In another instance I was not so lucky. I predicted success for Little Angels much earlier than they actually attained it, losing out on a concert just before they hit the big time, accompanied by a rush of publicity.

The choice of artist genre can often be affected by geographical area and demographics. For instance, it is known that heavy metal and rock sells well in some places but struggles in others. Therefore, a seasoned promoter will have built up an audience profile over a number of concerts to try to establish what types of music best serve a community.

Figure 1: 3, page eight, shows a graph constructed from information collected from a market research project carried out over five events at the Pitz in Milton Keynes. The information was obtained very easily by asking members of the audience three questions:

- Where did you travel from?

- How old are you?

- How did you find out about the show?

The Steve Hacket concert showed a large majority of the audience came from the local area, or within the three counties of Buckinghamshire, Northamptonshire and Bedfordshire, whereas the audience for Skyclad travelled from further afield. Both Greek and Wolfsbane attracted relatively local audiences but Annihilator, who were appearing in only two venues in the country, attracted an even spread of audience from around the areas researched. This sort of information can be used to build up a generic profile and is also useful when promoting these or similar artists on future occasions.

Figure 1: 4, page eight, shows the way in which the audience found out about the shows. For the two rock/thrash artists, Skyclad and Annihilator, the majority of the audience found out about the gig from the heavy metal and rock magazine *Kerrang*. For local favourites, Steve Hacket, Greek and Wolfsbane, audiences found out about the show from the local press. The graph also shows the benefit of different genre mailing lists, especially for Greek, Wolfsbane and Annihilator. The former is a theatre production and the other two are a rock artist and a thrash artist respectively. When the two graphs are combined with an audience age range graph, a client profile can be produced which makes it much easier to market and to promote concerts. Market research is discussed further in Chapter 4.

Figure 1: 3 The differing audience catchment profiles for five events at the Pitz in Milton Keynes

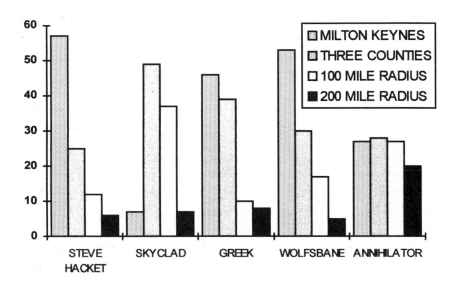

Figure 1: 4 Awareness vehicles for the Pitz in Milton Keynes

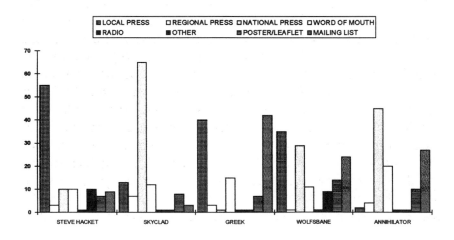

Depending on the press, popularity and longevity of an artist, the catchment area for the venue will change. For example, a local artist will probably pull a crowd from only within their town or city. A national artist may pull from an area of forty miles (65 km). However, an international artist, or an artist of specialised genre, may pull from all over the country and even from Europe and America. Figures 1:3 and 1:4, page eight, show this well, with Annihilator being the only international event in the five selected for market research. Low population in certain areas may make the promotion of nationally renowned artists impossible.

The agent–promoter relationship is a symbiotic one; they rely on each other to survive. So, agents tend to deal with promoters whom they know and trust. Therefore, the most likely combination for a first-choice promoter will be one in a major city and one that the agent has used to good effect on a number of occasions.

It can be hard to weigh up these economic and philosophical questions for those promoters trying to make ends meet whilst also trying to provide a quality service for the punters. If the punters do not receive a quality service, then the promoter and venue will suffer in the long term. A series of venues have closed recently, due in part to cutting corners and the reduction of a mainstream quality service.

It may not be the promoter who finally selects an artist. Sometimes the artist will ask their agent if they can play at certain venues. These venues may be where they have been treated well in the past or where the artists know that they will be marketed properly. If this happens, then there is a little leeway in the pricing of the artist. Negotiations with the agent could result in a reduced fee because the artist may agree to drop the price in consideration of the service given on prior visits. It sometimes happens that, if a venue persists with an artist who does not pull in a lot of punters initially but then becomes a large crowd puller, the artist remembers and will ask to play at the venue in recognition of the loyalty during their rise to fame. In a way it is giving the promoter and the venue a little of the success that the artist has gained over the years. If a promoter has the magic touch, whereby every choice that he makes does really well, then an agent may give that promoter better-known artists in return for him taking a chance on some of the agent's up and coming acts.

The average 'shelf' life of an artist today is much shorter than in the past. Some artists appear in the music headlines for only a matter of weeks, fading into obscurity, perhaps without even releasing a CD. Gauging the right time to promote this style of artist, usually part of the genre known as indie (which took its name originally from a artist signed to an independent record label rather than a major label), is very difficult and is often a 'hit and miss' affair. It takes an up-to-date knowledge of the whole of this genre and how it works to be able to promote this type of music successfully. This must include meticulous research and constant press updating on the artists to try to cause a stir in the club scene at the right time.

Selecting an artist is the hardest part of any promoter's existence because a wrong decision can be very costly. ITB's (International Talent Booking) Mike Dewdney, one of Britain's finest agents, responsible for, among others, Pearl Jam, Rage Against The Machine, Little Angels, Tori Amos and The Spin Doctors, made an engaging comment during an interview: *The agent really is just like a glorified double-glazing salesman.* The double-glazing salesmen I have met have always been sharp and cut-throat; is it the same with agents? This very point is expanded in Chapter 2.

To con or not to con – the economics of truth

Promoters have the potential to lie to record companies, agents and managers alike.

The promoter is out on a limb and the other parties in this business rely very much on his honesty. An increase in hall capacity on the night, a falsification of accounts, a reduction in security or a change in bar take percentages are all areas where it has been known for promoters to be a little economic with the truth. The falsification of ticket manifests and other promotional documentation has been tried, sometimes successfully and sometimes not. It has even been known for a promoter to abscond with the evening's takings, hotly pursued by the tour manager and security. The question always is, why? The answer usually is, because the promoter has not thought carefully enough about:

a) the reasons behind the promotion, and/or

b) the planning of the event.

If a promotion has only been created for the money and short-term gain, then forget it! Short-term gain only leads to cutting the quality of the events and can eventually end in a loss for the promoters concerned. It may not be just monetary loss, but the loss of a licence or an appearance in court because of a slap-dash attitude which led ultimately to tragedy. For instance, the death of a punter because safety standards were not complied with.

The honesty of the promoter has always been paramount in the success and quality of venues and the scale of promotion.

Small exaggerations of facility costs and staff time and the presentation of a promoter's profit within the accounts are part and parcel of the promoter's art of survival. However, an increase in audience numbers at venues over and above the limit set by the Environmental Health Department, not only breaks the law and puts the punter in danger, but also betrays the trust of the other interested parties. It must be remembered that all the other parties in this business want to survive. When a promoter is dishonest or rescinds part of an agreement, word soon gets around. This can cause untold problems because agents tend not to place artists with dishonest promoters again.

Promotion is a risk business. The promoter takes the risk but always has the chance to refuse an act. Whatever an agent or a record company says, the promoter can still refuse without losing face. The partnership between agents and promoters is based on mutual trust and the cementing of this bond over a number of years can be beneficial to both parties. Keeping in close contact with agents is not a difficult job and its inherent benefits far outweigh the sometimes tedious telephone calls to the office when the promoter is told that the agent is in a meeting. Constant communication keeps the promoter in the agent's

11

mind, especially useful when a tour is being planned. However, constant communication is not always a good thing as a nagging promoter may be put at the bottom of an agent's pile. Communication is a balance of neither being too keen nor stand-offish. Relationships between promoters and agents can lead to other benefits. For example, having dealt with Paul Bolton from Helter Skelter for many years, I received a phone call at the University asking me if I needed new lecturers or guest lecturers for the music degree course. Paul offered me Aubrey Nunn the bassist and manager from Faithless who was taking a year out and was interested in lecturing to students. Aubrey is now presenting guest lectures on the degree course.

Gaining confidence

The surest way to gain confidence as a promoter is to build the business steadily and not to be too greedy. Many of the most successful promoters started by promoting local artists for a long time or were in student unions as entertainment officers. When they had enough confidence and had established some sort of core musical audience, they began to promote smaller national artists, and then moved up the scale. Some promoters even founded huge promotion companies like MCP and SJM.

Promotion is a methodical step-by-step process, where everything must be prepared meticulously in advance. It takes many years to finely hone those skills and, without them, promotion is extremely difficult, if not impossible. Nothing must ever be left to chance, and the promoter must always have contingency if anything goes wrong. Figure 1:5, page 13, shows a number of major considerations for a promotion. These are many and have to be carefully balanced for a successful outcome.

The promoter is like a juggler with all the balls in the air at the same time, until the promotion takes place. The majority of events run smoothly, but there are a number where problems emerge which the promoter has not been able to prepare for. These problems are such that it is not always possible to plan for them, even with the tightest promotion and management system in the world. Several examples that I have come across have left me with a feeling of total lack of control.

Figure 1:5 Some major considerations taken into account during a promotion

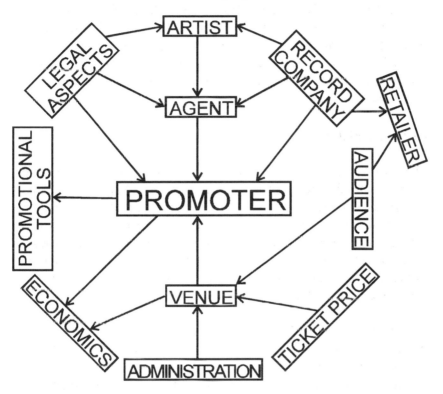

One example was with a thrash metal act called Acid Reign. The road crew took bags of polystyrene balls up onto the gantry above the artist and caused an artificial snowstorm during one of the songs. Although the effect was simply stunning, the cost of cleaning up after the event ran into hundreds of pounds. This was an expense that I, as a promoter, could have well done without. The balls were still turning up in the PA and on the gantry for over a year after the concert.

A second example of this took place at a concert with the band Blur. The guitarist threw his guitar into the audience. The guitar unfortunately injured a member of the audience who was taken to hospital to recover. As a relatively hot-headed youngster, I banned the band from playing at the venue. In hindsight, this was probably not advisable as the incident made many of the national papers and all the music press. Had I been seeking adverse press, it would have been fine, but unfortunately the story ran and ran and still occasionally appears in newspaper articles and books. Owing to the very nature of musical genres, this type of activity would not happen at classical, blues or jazz concerts but many stunts do take place in the world of rock, pop and indie.

A good idea for any promoter is to prepare a promotional plan or event information sheet that sets out all the things that are needed. This plan also has a space for dates where the promoter can mark the time, place and reason for the action. Figure 1:6, pages 16-17, shows an example of this plan, which can be used by the promoter to detail each area of the event. Although all of the areas may need more detail than this, it is a good starting point. Tight plans are essential, especially for the timing and use of promotional tools, where all deadline dates must be known in advance for your publicity machine to work effectively.

Promotional confidence is something that is learned. The promoter should always take time to talk to people at agencies and record companies, and should always have time for journalists. Above all, remember that contacts made today could be your lifeline tomorrow. If you make good contacts with agencies and record companies and a special event comes up, you may be contacted to promote the artist as a special favour. A quality service in promotion stems from integrity, care, communications and sound relationships, all which must be first class. The music business is very incestuous, and the same tour managers, crew, lampies[1] and technicians keep turning up regularly but, quite unexpectedly, with different artists.

During the recession many new promoters and venues folded, owing to the added pressures and higher costs. When starting up a promotion business or opening a new venue, a great deal of work has to be done

---

[1] Lampies are lighting technicians, crew and designers.

on the potential customer base and the established catchment area. The potential customer base can be procured from the local council, which usually has census or market survey reports on demographics in the county/district/city/town.

For instance, it would be pointless to set up a large club venue in an area with a small population, especially if most of the population are over 50, live in a depressed area where unemployment is high, and there are poor road and rail communications. To promote rock, indie and pop in such an area would be futile, unless it was close to a large town or city, or the venue was large enough to promote acts that would draw from an immense catchment area.

During the recession, when artist prices were higher than normal and available money was lower, each promotional risk element became higher. The risk element is often outweighed by factors out of the promoter's control. Many promoters have been offered artists that they would love to promote, but know in their hearts that there is not a large enough audience to make it viable. In some cases, the challenge can outweigh common sense. Often this ends in disaster, either because the promoter has not got the physical resources to promote the artist properly or because there is very little interest in the promotion. Some promoters are renowned in the business for being a soft touch.

Promoters are easily closed down on a deal for an artist. An agent can, at times, make it very difficult for a new promoter to refuse the artist that he is selling. These are things that a promoter must be aware of and will learn about whilst gaining confidence in the business. Eventually the promoter knows which agents and managers are to be trusted and which are unscrupulous. However, unscrupulous agents and managers may, on occasions, become unstuck. The wise promoter will spot good deals and take only those artists from that agent that he knows are winners.

Promoters should never be afraid to ask for help. In the business help is always on offer, from record companies, agents, artists and magazines – who all want to see their product sell as much as the promoter does.

Figure 1:6 Event Information Sheet

AREA 1
A. BOOKING
Name of Artist.. ....
Name of Support Act..
Date Booked..
Agent..
Contact Number ....
Venue..
Contact...
Contact Number ....

AREA 2
A. TECHNICAL DETAILS
Get in Time ....
PA..
Lighting ....
Sound Check Time...
Arrival Time of Gear...
Arrival Time of Artist...

B. RIDER
(The rider contains hospitality, sound, lighting and other special requirements)
Contract Received   ..../..../....
Contract Returned   ..../..../....
Rider Received   ..../..../....
Rider Returned   ..../..../....
Special Rider Agreements ....
....
....

C. STAFFING
Security Number...
Security Firm..
Crew Number ....
Crew Firm..
Front of House Staff ....
....
Rep ....
Other Staff...
....

D. INFORMATION
To Staff ..../..../....
To File ..../..../....
Accommodation...

E. TICKETS
Number ....
Type...
Agents to be used..
....
When Ordered ..../..../....
When Arrived ..../..../....

F. TIMES
Doors Open...
Support Times...
....
Main Artist..
Interval...
Suitable for Children   YES/NO
Age Bar...
Duration of Show..
Finish Time ....

G. SPECIAL DETAILS
Hospitality Required   YES/NO
In House   YES/NO
Hospitality Provider...
....
....
Contact Number ....
Merchandising Split...
Type of Settlement   CASH/CHEQUE
Payment on Night   YES/NO

H. SHORT PUBLICITY SPECIFICATION
Posters   YES/NO
Flyers   YES/NO
Local ads   YES/NO
National ads   YES/NO
Record Co ads   YES/NO
Local editorial   YES/NO
Other..

THE PHILOSOPHY OF PROMOTION

What is promotion? The Oxford Dictionary's definition is *to publicise or sell a product.*

> *If for the purposes of economic analysis we consider a live performance to be a commodity, we are immediately struck by the fact that, unlike most commodities offered for sale in our society, this commodity is not standardised. It is not machine made. It is a hand-crafted item.* P Toffler, quoted in Hirsch (1990)

This statement encapsulates the very essence of promotion; the promoter is selling a unique experience, and no two promotions are the same because of this. In a world rife with competition for the pound in the pocket the promoter is constantly having to fight to bring an audience to his promotion. With the advent of dance music, the way in which promotions are marketed has changed. The punter has become more discerning and is looking to the promoter to provide a total experience. If one promoter can show that he is providing a better service than other promoters in the area or is offering added value and more of an experience at a particular venue, this will inspire customer loyalty.

Promotion has to be looked at from two different angles, the first of which places promotion in an objective mode as something a person does to promote a concert. This could be the placing of posters on billboards or gaining editorial space in a newspaper. From another angle promotion means the presenting of an artist before an audience. Oh, that it was this simple! Promotion relies on many constituent parts: it needs an artist, a record company, an agent, managers, a venue, security, crew, staff, tickets, licences, lighting, PA, food, drink, changing facilities, car parking, punters, T-shirts, posters, programmes, newspapers, radio, CDs, uniforms, logos, flyers, handouts, fan clubs and many other factors too numerous to mention. The complication is that all these constituent parts must fit together to ensure a smooth running and exciting promotion (see Figure 1:5, page 13). To take away the elements of risk and satisfaction is unthinkable as these are integral parts of the promotion itself. To promote music without an interest in it is very difficult, but many successful promoters have done just this. This type of promotion is for monetary gain only, and the total satisfaction in such a promotion is this one goal. Most promoters are genuinely interested in music and the music business, which becomes part of their lives, even the central core. Although promotion at club level is not a glamour business, and the venues are often referred to as toilets, it does have several advantages over a nine-to-five job. Promoters meet people of a like mind in artists, other promoters, journalists and the entourage of an artist. Through this great network, friendships are often fused, and favours are always being done. For example, if a promoter is friendly with an agent and wishes to see another artist on the agent's books, the agent may provide tickets for a specific gig. Another great bonus for the honest promoter is word of mouth. In some cases artists stipulate that they will play certain venues only if their chosen promoter promotes the show. Artists talk to other artists and the promoter's name and the name of the venue will spread.

The satisfaction gained from a first class promotion is manifold: the artist and entourage enjoy themselves, the promoter and his workforce have a good night and, above all, the punters enjoy themselves. If the punters enjoy themselves, there may be spin offs.

- They will come back.

- They will tell others about the promotion.

- The promoter has created a committed attendee.

A major factor in successful promotion is the ability of the promoter to keep punters attending his concerts; to create a cadre of regular customers. The motivation for such *attenders* is that the promoter or the venue is providing them with a service that they are happy with and relate to. This creates customer loyalty.

If market research is carried out into the habits and pastimes of attendees, areas where people of similar tastes and demographics congregate may be targeted. The promoter may thus encourage those who would have attended the concerts, but did not know that the concerts were taking place, to attend. The *intenders* are those people who always intend to come, but are unable to do so because of numerous factors, including ignorance or a stigma regarding a venue or an artist. *Impassives* are people are those who do not really care about the venue or the promotions and travel to other places to see artists. However, if the type of artist that they like does appear, or there is a promotion of their favourite beer, then these extraneous factors may attract impassives to the venue.

There are also people who are *hostile* (Diggle, 1984) to the venue and the promoter, for example, people who do not go to the venue because it presents only folk music and not classical music. It will take a radical change in the venue or the promotions to make these people attend. The hostility may be towards the venue and the hostile punter may still refuse to go, even if the promotions are changed. The style of promotion may differ depending on how the promotion is approached. For instance, the philosophical reasons behind why a promoter promotes and why the artist and record company promote are quite different.

Figure 1:7 Types of attendee at a concert

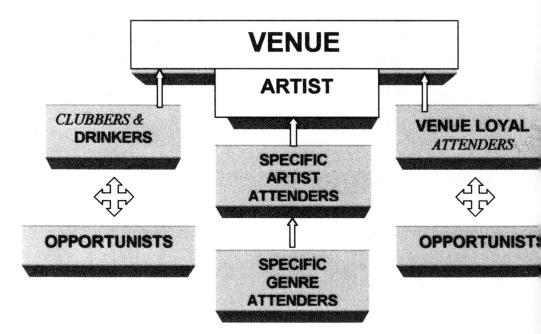

On any tour, whilst the promoter concentrates generally on the awareness of the venue and its reputation for a style of music, hoping for a profitable promotion, the artist and record company have quite a different outlook. The artist concentrates on an improvement of style. She needs to give a good performance, improve her technical mastery and to provide the audience with a credible display, thus enhancing her profile in the music business. The artist may also want to sell as much merchandise as possible, because there are artists who survive solely on the sales of T-shirts, hats and other merchandise.

For the record company, the artist may specifically tour to sell product units. Each unit sold brings payment towards the cost of the product, the production, and the tour (if tour support[2] has been provided). Where a record company agrees to fund a tour, it has its own interests at heart. The bigger the profile that the company can give an artist, the more people will go to see that artist on tour. Thus, the more potential product unit sales there will be. In the present climate of record company management there have been several instances of artists being refused release dates for new material because the material is not commercial enough. This compromises the artist's standing, and reverberations are felt around the world. One example of this is George Michael's High Court battle with Sony. Sam Brown is another artist who was more concerned with the validity of her music than the amount of recorded units that it would shift. Is it not the music that counts and not its saleable value? Having worked with Sam Brown on many occasions, her whole musical and management structure is first class, offering quality rather than compromise.

It can be clearly seen that there are four main strands of promotion cutting right across all sections of the music industry.

- Creating awareness
- Selling a product/Service
- Making a profit.
- Customer care/Quality

---

[2] Tour support is the provision of money to a touring artist by the record company.

These areas are paramount to the success of any of the music operations dealt with in this book

Presenting a quality service

> *Achieving quality standards within organisations is about attitude at all levels. Quality is not just about systems, it is not just about using specific techniques and tools ... Quality is about the attitude of mind of all the individuals within organisations, it is about winning the hearts and minds not only of them but also the customer who must come to believe that the organisation produces goods and services which meet their specific requirements.*
> Collard (1990a)

The quality of the promotion presented is of paramount importance, not only to the external customer but also to the internal customer. Internal customers are all those people involved with the promotion itself, from the cleaners and crew to the agents and managers. External customers are the punters, those people for whom you are creating the concert or event.

> *Not only is quality perceived by attitude but also by good management, total involvement and training of the staff.*
> Collard (1990b)

Each person in the chain of promotion is as valuable as the next. Without the crew the event cannot be set up, without the agent the artist will not be sold to the promoter. Quality service within the internal client environment stems from three major concerns:

• The communications between all internal clients must be efficient and well organised. A promotional plan may be instituted which tells everyone on every level what is happening. From the artist's standpoint, the tour manager liaises with the promoter to sort out the finer details of the performance. These details are exchanged at an interface between the tour manager and the promoter and are submitted on an event information sheet (Figure 1:6, pages 16-17). To gain the specific information the promoter must have set up a good communication network with the venue, the technicians and the security personnel. It is futile for the promoter to lie on the information sheet because, if something is agreed in the document by both parties and the promoter fails to keep his end of the bargain, then the tour manager has every right to demand that the promoter provides the service stated. Once the sheet has been signed, a copy will be forwarded to the venue and a copy will be given to the staff who will be on duty on the night of the concert.

- In many venues the liaison between the promoter and the venue manager is fragile as they each have a different view of the way that the concert should or should not be run. But, in most venues the relationship is a good one, especially if the venue manager is also interested in the care of his customers. If the concert is a joint promotion between the venue and the promoter, once the two parties have decided who is providing which concert attributes, the staff are contacted. Close liaison between all levels of staff may be provided through a concert plan, with a meeting held several weeks before the event. If there is a discussion several weeks in advance, with minutes marked for action, possible difficulties can be highlighted. Last-minute problems may be brought to light at another meeting a week before the event. If everyone is kept informed, then the staff working on the evening will do so efficiently, and the event will go as smoothly as hoped. Any problems with other internal clients, such as the record company, or arguments over the rider, should be kept away from the venue staff so that they do not become personally involved. If you, as a promoter, expect a problem on the night, always brief staff in advance.

- The meeting of the internal and external customers is always important. A key point is that, even if the promoter has had many problems throughout the day and nothing has gone right, the external customers do not care. They are at the venue only for one thing: the total experience – to see their favourite artist, to meet their friends, to buy the T-shirt, to socialise and drink alcohol, etc. Whatever has happened during the day is of no concern to the external customer and the internal customer must remember this. Everything on the night must run like clockwork, or seem to do so even if it does not. If something is wrong or the artist is going to be late, let the punters know. They have paid money to be entertained and they expect a quality service. An announcement of a delay, and the reasons for it, from the stage or over the tannoy, usually placates those who are anxious. If the punters are not informed, trouble can start as tempers fray and drink starts to play a role.

• There are many marketing tools which can be employed to make the promoter more customer friendly. Before punters arrive at the venue they have to purchase a ticket. A way of endearing an audience to planned promotions is to offer special discounts. This may work to the advantage of both parties. It is known that people will buy tickets for a show that they are only marginally interested in if they are discounted. By doing this the customer feels that he is being well looked after. The promoter may be discounting the tickets only because the show is not selling very well. Therefore, the promoter is also benefiting by selling extra tickets, even if at a slightly discounted price. For instance, if a promoter has a run of three concerts and expects two of the concerts to sell well but is uncertain about the third, he could offer buyers of tickets for the first two gigs a discount on tickets for the third. This may encourage a larger audience at the third gig, but it may also encourage further sales of the other two gigs because punters now wish to go to all three concerts.

Everyone involved with the gig must be involved at all times. The promoter must devolve duties and responsibilities so that the staff feel part of the promotion. Members of staff given training and development are more likely to be loyal to the promoter.

In the venue itself, a fast and friendly bar service, and a disco before, between and after the artists, often prove winners. In the case of well-established clubs, an all night club after the gig is often better attended than the gig itself. Careful planning of the vending stall and customer-friendly security are also important for the customer to feel at ease in the venue. Security is often a problem. If the security staff are not well trained, efficient and friendly, then things can go badly wrong. At a concert I promoted with the Blue Aeroplanes several years ago, the head of security tried to eject the dancer, who is an integral part of the Aeroplanes' performance, from the stage. tempers became heated and I had to intervene to calm things down. On another occasion, during a concert with the thrash band Exodus, a Japanese photographer was bodily hurled from the stage into the audience by an over-zealous security person because she had stayed by the stage for longer than the allotted photography time. A cutting write up in *Kerrang* ended in the sacking of the security staff involved and the initiation of a training scheme. To reiterate, the punters have paid to see a show and they do not care how many hours it took to set up the promotion, or what problems the promoter is having on the night; the problem is not their concern. Every effort has to be made to welcome the customer. A good promoter talks to the audience to find out what they like and dislike about the night or the venue. From this, you can change those things that, in the consensus of people's opinion, are wrong.

British promotion has several entrenched attitudes that prevent the smooth running of a performance. One of these is the acceptance of shoddy workmanship, accepted because it is *always someone else's job* (Collard, 1990c) to put it right. When American and European artists tour Britain, they expect a high level of workmanship. If they do not get this, then the promoter gets a rough ride. The promoter always tends to blame others rather than accepting the blame himself. The problem always seems to shift from the promoter to the staff, the venue or the crew, and many promoters fail to take responsibilities for their own actions. This is often picked up by the Americans who retort that it is the promoter who hires the crew, the venue and the staff. It is, therefore, the promoter's responsibility to make sure that everything is of the highest standard.

Many promoters have a resistance to change. They book the same acts year in, year out because they have always sold well in the past. This style of promotion tends to miss out on new and exciting artists, reducing the quality of service to both the internal and external customers, and gradually reducing the base number of artists as bands split up or no longer tour.

Many promoters regard quality as an unacceptable expense. Others put an emphasis on short-term results, quickly cashing in, but not establishing a base for the future. Such inflexibility has cost promoters dearly with falling audiences and falling income.

Figure 1:8 Ashton Liburd, from Two Tribes, on stage at the Woughton Centre. © *Mark Catanach photograph for Chris Kemp*

Promotion review

Links with other promoters in the industry are of great value. There are several key problems that can be solved by integrating with others.

A problem that often occurs when promoters work totally independently of each other is that of clashing. This is a promoter's nightmare when, in a town of 20,000 inhabitants, two or even three promoters have the same type of music on the same night. The audience will be divided and everyone will lose out. Constant contact with other promoters in the area may alleviate this problem, and even the forming of a programme consortium where the promoters meet every month to discuss programmes may be helpful. This not only sorts out the clashing problem, but also makes the promoters feel that they are not out on a limb. I used to meet with my nearest 'rival' on a regular basis and built up a strong friendship through the promotion of artists. We used to ring each other to find out if agents were playing off our venues against each other. This was very helpful as we could discuss the appropriate action to take. What we discussed at these meetings was in everyone's interests. Meetings held between promoters who promote different genres are also beneficial. If clashes do occur, there may be mileage in putting on two different musical genres in the same town on the same night as each genre would appeal to a different type of audience. Other factors that can be brought to an open forum include the prices of artists, agents' ideas, collaborations and ticket prices. For instance, some promoters openly discuss with other promoters the price they have been asked for by artists to see if they are getting a good deal or not from the agent. This comparison is sometimes complicated by the size of the venue and the previous loyalty and record of the promoters concerned.

In some cases, where a large number of promoters meet from month to month, they may present a comprehensive gig list which will include all the promotions in a given area or a composite poster of the same artist appearing at several gigs. The advantage of this is that all the promoters end up paying less for their advertising. There is also the Concert Promoters Association (CPA) which meets on a regular basis to discuss pertinent facts and problems in the promotion industry at club level.

MCP - A STORY OF SUCCESS

MCP Promotions was formed in 1978 during the Punk music boom. Its original clients included the Sex Pistols, The Clash and many of the

Two-Tone (the first SKA label) artists. The company quickly took a lead in music promotion and branched out into other areas, two of which were heavy metal and comedy. In the mid 1990's MCP Promotions was promoting something in the region of 400 to 500 indoor and two to 12 outdoor shows each year, which was probably more than any other company in Britain at the time.

The company was formed from a partnership between Tim Parsons and Maurice Jones. Maurice Jones had worked in the music business for 30 years, and in 1977 there was an inherent need for a promoter who could deliver a quality service with the back-up of paper work. 1977-78 was the Punk era; there were many Punk promoters who did not deliver the quality to the client or to the artist. There were no accounting systems, gigs did not take place, and unscrupulous promoters ran off with the takings.

MCP's success started with the comedian Jasper Carrott. After this, AC/DC took the company into the field of heavy metal. Although the company did a lot with Punk artists and artists such as The Police, and the early shows with Dire Straits, it rapidly grew in size and in 1978 started promoting outdoor shows with the now famous Monsters of Rock. Outdoor shows were attempted because the company identified that there was a requirement in the market for them. On the back of Monsters of Rock, the company became more of a heavy metal promoter. Stuart Galbraith joined the company in 1984. He was Leeds University's social secretary and had done some shows before with MCP. At this time Tim Parsons was concentrating on pop artists and Stuart was brought in to supplement him. In 1987 Stuart Galbraith became a director, shareholder and partner in the company. Today Stuart and Tim do most of the promoting, as Maurice has a primary interest in running Donington Park and another of the MCP group of companies called 2/4 Sports. Today Maurice Jones pursues a number of other business interests.

In the 1990's MCP had four directors, two senior and two junior. The company had expanded dramatically over the years and, at the time, employed 21 staff split into various departments. Publicity work is done by an internal subsidiary company which is responsible for all the artwork, print and advertisement layout. It is an origination company. It is much better to have a department like this rather than to send out of house for posters, flyers and adverts as there is more control over timing, design and speed of delivery. Another bonus is that no courier charges are incurred.

The production, or tour management department, consisted of two full-time members of staff. One member stayed in the office whilst the other toured. This worked well as one of the staff was available to answer messages and sort out details with managers and tour personnel whilst the other was working in the field. A secretary was assigned to the office.

A time came when, because of the volume of work that the company was handling, the directors did not have enough time to put in the leg work, get biographies and photographs out to the press, put competitions into newspapers, and deal with the media requirements for shows. The company felt that it was not giving the full promotional service that it should. One new member of staff was brought in initially, to set up a press and promotion department, but after two to three years it became evident that another member of staff was needed to cope with the volume of work. This department also takes on public relations (PR) and marketing work from other areas which makes it an income generator. Examples of outside work are Kiri Te Kanawa at the ITC for IMG, and film tours for AC/DC and Kate Bush. They handle the PR for Midge Ure and are about to take on press and promotions for Radio 1 Sound City.

The accounts department consisted of a book-keeper and a credit controller. The rest of the staff were secretaries, administrators, telephonists and receptionists.

Three of the four directors and one other member of staff were responsible for generating business. The company assessed its position in the market and decided that the directors had lost touch with the punter on the street and that the company was not competing on the lower promotional levels. This was purely and simply because there were not enough hours in the day. The directors then took the decision to bring someone in to book the smaller indie artists. This was not because the company thought that the way ahead was to deal with smaller indie acts, but was a company investment for the future: out of these smaller acts will come the artists who will play the arenas over the next five to ten years. The company is not in the field necessarily to be a major player but to pick up acts which will guarantee them longevity in the music business. The company chose a clever promoter for the job and allowed him to work in his own way. Working as an indie promoter in an indie style gave the company credibility at street level. The intention was to generate relationships with new indie artists.

It is this long-term view that has kept MCP at the top of the industry, sacrificing short-term gains for long-term prosperity. The company has promoted Oasis, Rollins and Echobelly, which by 1998 were acts worth a great many punters.

Company philosophy

The directors and staff at MCP enjoy what they do but, to be blunt, the philosophy like that of any private company is to make money. The company is very thorough, everything is committed to paper, nothing is left to chance, whether it is an aspect of a concert or ensuring that tickets are going to sell in advance. At the larger venues promoters have to be proactive rather than reactive. They have to lead the promotion, particularly if they are using arenas. There is no marketing set-up at arenas or at outdoor shows. It is virtually the same, apart from the scale, to set up a concert for 800 people as it is to set up a concert for 100,000 people. This includes a television deal, a radio deal or an Adshel (a type of bus shelter) campaign. As a company, MCP likes to think that it is innovative in the way that it promotes shows. MCP was one of the first companies to use independent local radio (ILR) promotion, and the first company to use Radio 1 as a promotional vehicle. It is difficult to promote a small gig with an ILR deal, a huge fly posting campaign, or a huge mail-out because of financial constraints. It is word of mouth, flyers and press editorial that promote small shows. MCP uses all these methods for the larger shows as well, but the most exciting area of promotion now is the mail shot – direct promotion to a captive audience. At first it can be phenomenally expensive with a small return, but used properly on the right target markets, such as previous clients, it can be very financially rewarding. For example, the last time that Guns 'n' Roses played at Wembley, prior to the tickets going on sale, MCP did a mail shot to all previous customers. They pre-sold 12,500 tickets before they were offered to the general public. When Simply Red toured in the UK in the mid 1990's, it was a three-part tour, the first and third parts indoors and the second part outdoors. By the time the artist reached the third part of the tour, MCP had a mailing list of 35,000 people. The artist was very popular at the time, but it was the speed of the ticket sales that was staggering. The artist sold 200,000 tickets for the tour in two and a half weeks. MCP knew how to get to the audience because of market research on the previous two tours. The company did not waste money on peripheral advertising. Big adverts were placed where they were needed, and one 30,000 mail-out was sent. The marketing was very focused.

MCP does particularly well when promoting Australian or South African artists, for example, INXS, Midnight Oil, Johnny Clegg, Crowded House and Hunters and Collectors, mainly because it knows how to reach the markets. There are ways of going through embassies and deals can be done with airlines. The philosophy is to make money and to deliver a promotion service that cannot be bettered by any other company. MCP has worked with 95 per cent of its acts, in terms of their live career, since each act's first show. Simply Red, for example, did their first ever show with MCP. In June 1985 they had their first show at Manchester International, which sold 750 tickets, and since then every show has sold out. Deliberately, the company uses its expertise to develop artists and to help them to achieve their goals, whether that includes playing arenas, or city halls or clubs. The perception of what the artist wants to be will change as they develop. This gives both the company and the artist a lot of satisfaction in what they do.

Forward planning

This is partially dictated by the artists. The company has had a strategy for five years which does not include just music. Over the years MCP has moved into many areas as it has diversified. They have not only promoted music but also WWF wrestling, Gladiators and The Chippendales. The company keeps looking for the next idea to emerge. and tries to explore as many new areas as possible. It has promoted the world climbing championships, films, motor sport and the British Motorcycle Grand Prix. MCP is a group of companies that owns a print company and a transport company (to bus people to gigs). Through 2/4 Sports it has promoted motor racing at Donington and other circuits around the country. No one else promotes motor racing as a sport. The company has looked at many new areas – indoor motor cross at the NEC, indoor wind surfing and indoor rally cross. It feels that it must keep up with the rest of the field.

Country music is a very large growth area and MCP has made a big effort to get involved with it. In 1995 the company did a fifteen-date country tour linked in with ILR stations with strong country programmes. New Country music is almost underground, with a small audience which is slowly growing.

The company needs a firm financial footing as far into the future as possible and, therefore, has various investments. There is a company pension scheme. MCP owns three buildings in Walsall. The company offices are in one while the other two have been turned into offices to rent, since office space is at a premium in the area. MCP also runs a nursing home in Burton and is looking to take on another two in the near future. The nursing home was taken on because the company saw a requirement for it and not because of any knowledge about running the home. But, they knew a man who did! The home opened in September 1993 and already has a good reputation. It is pleasing for the company that it is not financially dependent on the music industry and that it has so many other businesses that other firms do not have. But, other firms do have different areas of development – for instance, Kennedy Street have a publishing company, Mcintyres has comedy and Torville and Dean. This diversification does wonders for the stability of a company.

MCP rarely co-promoted as it did not see the point of giving away 50 per cent of the profits or of bearing 50 per cent of the loss. If it had the confidence to promote an act, it might as well go the whole way. Even so, in today's promotion climate it is sometimes pertinent to split tours with one or two other promoters.

At the moment there are many more split tours with different promoters taking on two or three shows each. The profit margins are much smaller. Tours have been vastly reduced from what they were. The annual return from concerts is much less than it was, and many smaller companies have gone out of business. For those with all their eggs in one basket, one poor tour can destroy the company. The profits are much smaller, but the risks are still high.

Financial systems

Cash flow must be good and it is the responsibility of the company's financial director to ensure that any of the cash that the company has is working to earn as much as possible. Her remit is to deal with the day-to-day money, playing the money markets around the world. The money is shuffled around to where and when it is needed, for example, venue deposits, artist deposits. She is responsible for all departments when money is coming in; for example, large amounts of ticket money from promoters or ticket offices, and for making sure that nothing is missed. Shows are accounted for on a quick, prompt and accurate basis. Credit control does not tolerate too many large debts at any one time. If the company carries a large debt for a number of weeks, it will be chased and recovered.

Ticket income is dealt with in the tightest way possible. Ticket figures are obtained bi-weekly. The company knows at any time how many tickets have been sold for each event. Whenever the company can it draws advanced money on ticket sales. This is not applicable to club or college shows as this takes up more time than it is worth. If there are 10,000 tickets on sale at £12.50 each and the show sells out in advance, there is a large amount of money which can be banked before the show. The company never delay payment. The philosophy behind this is quite simple: if someone provides a service, and the company has agreed to pay for that service, then the service should be paid for as quickly as possible. For example, Monsters of Rock had expenses of £900,000. Within two weeks of the show nearly every bill had been settled. Other companies tend to delay the paying of bills for as long as possible. Ultimately MCP has a better working relationship with supply companies because they know that if they provide a service they will immediately be paid.

Development plan

MCP does not know if it can go much further in musical spheres. One of the primary aims of the company is to provide its employees with a living, but a living which is enjoyable. Since 1990, the fun has started to go out of the business. The culture was loose and fun, but now it is harder nosed and the old ways of working have almost been eradicated. There are less people to trust today, and everything has to be given in writing. There is still a lot of satisfaction in watching an artist from the side of the stage, whether it is in front of 200 or 100,000 people. Bringing another promoter into the company to deal with the smaller indie artists will prolong the life of the company.

Tim Parsons and Stuart Galbraith aim to bring in six new acts a year, but these need to be acts with some sort of longevity. Cross-over pop acts come within this category. The big money in music is in the large arena shows and this is where a company like MCP gets the money to promote smaller acts. 1994 was a very lean year for arena concerts, whereas 1993 had a plethora of events. In 1994 more festivals took place than ever before. This not only had a detrimental effect on a lot of festivals, due to saturation, but also sorted out those with pulling power which will survive.

The larger the venue, the higher the ticket price. For example, the ticket price goes up from £6 for a club event to £9 for a city hall to £30 for a stadium. Although the risks and outgoings increase with larger events, the profit margins, if it is successful, are larger.

Today there are huge radio road shows with 30,000 people at them. There is no safety element and many of them are badly run. Soon there will be an accident if the promoters are not careful. The difference is clear: MCP holds a licensed event and has the knowledge and expertise

34

to promote it. Everything is scrutinised down to the last detail. It is a sign of the times that the new companies are now bringing in MCP to run some of their events, which is another way in which the production department can become income generating. The company does not offer this service to other promoters as this would educate them sufficiently to set up in competition. The company is now looking at shopping centre entertainment programmes, new kids' cartoons or films. MCP comments that the problem with British leisure and recreation is that it is not high enough on people's agenda. A great many things that work in America will not work here. People's lives do not have the same orientation. In America, a town the size of Walsall would have a 12,000 capacity arena. A town the size of Leicester would have a 100,000 capacity stadium. There are so many forms of entertainment in America which are more widely accepted. The Americans have a different philosophy on life.

The company no longer intends to progress with indoor climbing, and London Weekend Television decided to promote the Gladiators themselves. Indoor American Football and motocross will progress and MCP is hoping to bring Monster trucks into the country. The company hopes to team up with the American company SMGI to run motosport events in this country. Although linked with American entertainment and companies, MCP prefers to work in Britain as it knows the market better.

Turning points

In general, the economic climate in the music business in the 1980s was very prosperous but, in the recession money, became tight. Groups find it harder to get shortfall – the adverse difference between earned income and real expenditure on a tour – out of record companies, and so they squeeze agents who, in turn, squeeze promoters. Promoters then squeeze venues and money becomes ever tighter. In the upper reaches of the business, although the promoter's profit margins have tightened, artists' profits have increased. Owing to the recession, all areas of the business have had to tighten up financially.

It can clearly be seen that MCP is an exceptionally successful company. This has been brought about by meticulous forward planning and an ability to ignore short-term temptations while working for long-term profits. A company with such depth and an ever-expanding programme heralds promotion in the future.

Two and a half years ago, around the time of Maurice Jones' retirement from MCP, another member of staff, an indie promoter of up-and-coming bands, also left. Two of the three remaining directors, Tim and Stuart, reassessed the direction of the company to see if working with small bands was profitable. An analysis of the accounts at that time indicated that, with the exception of Oasis, the company had not made any financial progress with the promotion of small-scale bands. The indie booker was not replaced and the two directors decided to break four or five new bands a year.

Examples of bands broken in recent years include the Stereophonics, Muse, Top Loader and Slipknot. At the same time as Maurice's retirement and the departure of the indie booker, the consolidation of the US music industry started, with a major company, SFX buying most of this type of business. It became clear to MCP that this consolidation was pivotal and the directors had about 18 months to put MCP in a position to be a potential acquisition for a large company such as SFX.

This development rapidly came to fruition. On 20th September, 1999 SFX acquired MCP in a multi-million pound deal which ensured that MCP became part of a multi-national consolidation in the music industry. SFX is the only multi-national able to use national auxiliary income in sponsorship, marketing and ticketing, and is likely to survive in an industry undergoing unprecendented change now and in the next few years. MCP's acquisition by SFX has also given the company access to extensive financial resources to enable them to develop many projects which they have started but, as yet, have been unable to continue. These include internet ticketing, affinity club cards (a joint venture with MBNA Bank) and the ultimate freehold development of Donnington Park Race Circuit to become a leading Formula One race location.

> *The section on MCP was produced at an interview with Stuart Galbraith, a director of the company, and is reproduced with MCP's kind permission.*

Conclusion

It can be seen clearly from this chapter that the promoter is a key player in the development of live music promotion. The promoter is the person who takes the risk and often the person who loses money on a show or event. In Chapter 2, we will look at the agent whose relationship with the promoter is vital, not only to the success of an event, but in the origins of the event itself.

Chapter 2

The Agent

Introduction

The agent is the middle man between the promoter and the artist. The agent sells an artist to a promoter on behalf of an artist, a manager or a management company. The artist gains exposure to his/her audience through live performance or personal appearance. Today an agent also plays other roles but, this book concentrates on the main one, that of live music promotion.

Figure 2:1 Terrorvision on stage at the 'Big Day Out'
© Chris Kemp, photograph

This chapter looks at four different agents and the way that they work within the music industry. The agents selected are four of the most influential figures on the club circuit today. They are Ian Sales with Helter Skelter, Mike Dewdney from International Talent Booking Agency (ITB), Nick Peel from Miracle Prestige International (MPI) and Martin Tibbets formerly of Solo ITG and now with Revolution Productions.

Acquiring the band

One of the first questions that must be answered is how does an agent pick up a band? There are many ways:

- Agents are sometimes recommended to bands by people in the music industry. Nick Peel suggests that there is a very good bush telegraph system. If a band are not happy with their current agent, word gets around very quickly. This is bad news for the current agent but good news for the agent who is recommended.

- Agents talk to artist and repertoire (A&R) departments of record companies to get an awareness of new bands that are breaking through.

- Agents build relationships with managers. For instance, the manager of That Petrol Emotion asked Martin Tibbets (formerly of Solo ITG) to represent Bitty Mclean. This agent-manager relationship had been built up over a number of years.

- Agents visit show cases, where bands who are looking for agency representation play.

- Agents read the music papers, go to see bands and then offer their services.

What is an agent?

An agent is a salesperson who sells a band to the promoter. The agent's basic responsibility to the band lies within the symbiotic relationship with the promoter. The agent decides which promoter to use and in which cities the bands will play, although these decisions also include the band and the record company. The agent negotiates the venue, the costings and the ticket price.

The right venue for a band is particularly important. Does the band play a club or a college? What are the relative merits of each? A college may not have a public licence and, therefore, many people are excluded. Many bands will not play college venues because of this. But, bands often need college dates in the tour to contribute to touring expenses. In the past, agents have been able to extract large sums of money from college promoters, cashing in on their inexperience. Today colleges are more practised and, in some cases, employ a full-time professional to book the entertainment. The manager at Norwich UEA (University of East Anglia) has been there for many years and knows the business well.

'Territories' are not exclusively the agent's decision as they are booked in consultation with the band's manager. For instance, at MPI it was not Paradise Lost's agent who said that the band must play in Slovenia, as the country was not on the band's last tour itinerary. It was the band's plan to play as many countries as possible and to build up a fan base. The first time the band played Slovenia they played to 300 people in a small club on the Italian border; two tours later they played to 1000 punters in Ljubljana. Paradise Lost had a lot of airplay on MTV (Music Television). There are many people in Slovenia who have MTV and this helped with marketing the band. For the agent, Ljubljana is a convenient stopping-place between Italy and Austria and playing there saves having a day off. Touring overseas has many problems. One of the worst aspects of touring in Europe is if the bus driver has to work for sixteen hours without a break. It is not only dangerous and against the law, but also causes a great deal of tension and friction amongst everyone else on the trip. The agent has to bear this kind of detail in mind when planning a tour.

The promoter and agent need each other to survive. The agent needs the promoter to sell product to, the promoter needs the agent to buy product from. Without each other, the whole club promotion circuit would not exist. The success of an agent depends on two things:

- The reputation he acquires from the way that he treats his bands.

- The ability to convince the promoter that the band that he is offering is a good buy.

Can the agent make the band sufficiently appealing to the promoter to convince him to promote it? Is the price reasonable? Does the promoter feel that he can sell the band to the punters in the catchment area? Can the promoter make enough profit margin on the promotion to make it worthwhile?

All these points have to be considered by both the agent and the promoter. If an agent continually sells a promoter a bad deal, then the promoter will use other agents. Many agents accept that ITB and Helter Skelter are the biggest agencies in Britain. Other agencies have adopted different approaches and methodologies to ITB so that they can stay sufficiently different and, thus, survive in an extremely competitive world. Nick Peel from MPI, a combination of the Miracle agency and the Prestige Talent agency, feels that MPI has invented a new concept within agencies. Usually an agent tends to represent a lot of bands and he looks for turnover and profit margin on that turnover. MPI's philosophy is different. The company has agents who each represent a small number of bands, and they work these in a very personal way. This can provide a better all-round service than if the agent were looking after twice as many bands. The ratio of bands to agents at MPI is quite low.

Prestige Talent was an agency predominantly operating in the rock field. It had quite a lot of well-established artists who had been around for a long time. Miracle agency worked almost exclusively with independent music, which was very strong at the time of the merger. The merger worked well, combining new, fresh, independent talent with older, more-established bands, giving the new company a wide portfolio of acts. It was a mutually beneficial merger and has paid dividends.

Mike Dewdney, a very successful agent with ITB, who, amongst others, looks after Rage Against the Machine, Tori Amos and Pearl Jam, has a very philosophical outlook on promotion. He feels that an agent is there to book live shows with all the extraneous parameters organised. Are the CDs there? Is the press hot? Is the vibe there? Everything leads to something else. Historically, an agent was called a booking agent. Mike has a saying: 'out of every hour, it takes five minutes to book a show and fifty-five minutes to administer it'.

The first thing an agent must do is to establish himself by building up a client base known as a *roster*. An agent working on a commission basis only makes a living when his bands are touring. An agent cannot afford to just book date after date – he has to be selective and the tour has to be routed properly. If a band plays a venue and then plays the same town two weeks later, that would defeat the object of trying to sell the band. The agent's job entails a lot more than just booking the date. He needs to make sure that a vibe is kept going on the band, that it is playing the right venues, not underplaying nor overplaying.

Helter Skelter, as an agency, tends to lay excellent grounding for its bands and is conscious of the venues that they choose. An example of this is that the agency places artists at Buckley Tivoli, because it is a well-established club with a large rock audience and covers the whole of the North West area. Helter Skelter take a lot of time and effort to nurture bands continually as they play the club circuit, until they are big enough to play the halls. Bands should never be put into a place that is too big for them or it could destroy the band, by either demoralising the members or by exposing the artist to poor audiences. An artist who is pushed into big venues too early does not have time to develop an audience profile.

The agent often changes the venues used within a city. For example, over the past twenty years, venues like the Marquee Club and The Rainbow closed and new venues like The Borderline and The Brixton Academy have come into favour. The agent has a choice of venues to play in London and this depends on capacity, availability and the particular promoter.

It is well-known that music continually moves in cycles. 1960's music has appeared in the 1970's, 1980's and 1990's. Punk has re-appeared in a number of guises, as has glam and heavy metal. It is the same with venues in cities. Only a small number of mainstream venues can continue to survive. As stated above, many of the major venues of the 1980's and 1990's have closed, to be replaced with other new venues.

The punters must be satisfied when going to a show, because this ensures repeat visits to both the band and the venue. Dealing with a live product is quite difficult. Bands are successful if they can build up a live following that sells CDs. This is how bands made it to the top years ago, by getting out there and playing, giving themselves exposure. Today, getting out there and playing does not have the same effect because 'the circuit' in its former sense no longer exists and often artists are not willing to put the work in at the lower levels. This means that their fan base does not become consolidated and, if they move quickly into larger audience venues, they are not able to sustain audience development and they fail to make the next crucial step.

The agent also acts in a supportive role. He is the person to contact if a show is not selling well. Rather than cancel, the agent helps the promoter as much as possible to re-sell the show or to create more of a buzz about it.

Mike Dewdney feels that it takes four to eight weeks to promote a show successfully. Sometimes bands get a lucky break or a tour hits at the right time, but no-one can sit and become complacent. If the time period is too tight, there are what are called in the business 'dartboard tours', where dates are not booked in a logical tour sequence but they make sure that the band have somewhere to play. Mike often has new bands that he wants to get bookings for, but they must be the right dates at the right time. It gives the agent a lot of satisfaction to watch a band grow from obscurity, for example, the Gin Blossoms. It took four months from their first date in Britain for them to create a buzz. Recognition takes time to develop. It could be someone from a radio station seeing a show or it could be a re-packaging of a CD single. A DJ could say that he has seen a band or that he has heard the CD single, likes it gives it another spin. A few factors come together with a little bit of luck and the band can break. An agent has then got to keep the artist in the public eye by making sure that the artist gets the correct tour profile, and plays in the right places at the right time.

The agent has to get to the clubs to see the bands and make trips abroad to sign up bands with promise. The agent builds up new relationships with new managers who keep him informed of new bands.

He still has to fight for the band – any good manager will be able to name a string of agents who are after his band. But, out of every band that is successful, there are nine that are not. If an agent telephones a manager because he likes the band's CD, obviously the agent wants to see what the manager can deliver. The agent is not just going to sit back and expect it to be a hit; then book the act. He has to do something. It has often been stated that *Guns 'n' Roses were the ultimate marketing machine*. Their policy was to market themselves. They were so well known that, in their heyday, their faces and achievements stood out more than those of any other band in the world.

To start a band's career, live shows are the most important events. If the band tours, the record company can use the tour as a catalyst to start everything else moving. The press are invited to the concerts to start promoting the band. Here, personal contact is best, rather than dumping a record or a photograph and a video on the reporter's desk. A video could sit on the desk for three months without being seen. The band need action and they need it now.

To repeat, the relationship between the agent and the promoter is symbiotic, one cannot exist without the other. The agent needs the promoter to produce the live shows for the band and the promoter needs the agent to supply him with a constant flow of artists to be promoted through live shows. A good dialogue between the two often leads to trouble-free promotions and a smooth working relationship. Whereas the promoter takes a risk with a promotion but can often make a good profit, the agent receives a percentage each time one of his bands plays a live gig. The agent will insure a show against loss of commission, just as the promoter will insure against cancellation.

Agreements and working with artists

At MPI all bands are taken on only if they sign an agency agreement, as it is no longer possible to make an agreement on the basis of a handshake. It also makes for a more professionally run business with an obligation on both sides, i.e., it makes the artist and the agent more responsible for delivering the goods.

There are a number of agents who work exclusively with certain record companies. Nick Peel does a lot of work with Music For Nations (MFN), because a lot of his acts are rock bands and MFN are one of the leaders in the independent rock field. Some agents prefer to work with only one promoter in each country while some like to work with many different promoters. They tend to work with people with whom they get on well, like and, above all, trust. Sometimes the decision is down to location and the services that a venue or a promoter can provide. Many promoters only operate in major cities for various reasons, such as captive audience and catchment quotas. Many of the major tours tend to play only the major cities, with a widening tour moving into secondary markets in other cities and towns when necessary. Remember that the agent does not have the only say in where a band plays. Some bands only wish to play major cities on a small tour, where they will get maximum exposure. On these tours, other promoters in other areas will not get a look in. Often a band on a large tour proposes to the agent the venues that they would like to go back to because previously they have been treated really well. Thus, the way that a promoter or venue treats a band does pay dividends one way or another. Some places are not classed as major markets but the agent will feel that, from time to time, it is important to play there because the band needs to build up a fan base in that area.

Promoters in the major cities tend to get the bulk of the bands because a band has to play London, Manchester, Leeds/Bradford, Wolverhampton, Nottingham, Bristol, Hamburg, Munich etc. Other shows can become a luxury, especially if the tour is losing money. Many shows cost bands money when the subsidy from the record company does not cover the show's shortfall. Milton Keynes is a prime example of a secondary market which one day may become a primary market. Agents are also aware of how promoters work. If they see a promoter taking cash out of a venue in the short term, and not putting anything back in, then they are, in some cases, less likely to work with them. Working with a promoter comes down to how they treat the agent, their own staff and the bands that come into the venue. If the promoter has no interest in the punter or the music, the main point is for monetary gain. The main aim should be to maximise profit, whilst maintaining high customer service.

One promoter of the Princess Charlotte in Leicester was a huge music fan. He wanted to promote every night. He made money by selling beer, and the more punters that he brought into the pub to see live music, the more beer he sold. That is called reinvesting. He invested money into his music and bands. The venue gave people in the area a chance to see things they might otherwise have missed.

There are a lot of American artists breaking at the moment. ITB still represents a large percentage of American acts, some of which did have American agents to start off with but switched to ITB because of its reputation. Some of the American agents really struggled, trying to book Paris and Glasgow back-to-back. It may look a short distance on the map, but is just not feasible in transport terms. American agents are put under severe strain when they try to book their smaller bands over in this country. They need to package the band so that several acts of varying degrees of popularity come over together. When these introduced bands come back to Britain with tours of their own, then they introduce other bands to the British audience.

Small bands are the agents' bread and butter. The big acts in Britain and America, such as Dire Straits and Status Quo, will book themselves on their reputation. Once a band has played Wembley, where do they go? As an artist becomes bigger, managers, lawyers and accountants have more of a say in major decisions. This may result in the lawyers or accountants advising the artist through the manager that they could get a better deal by changing their agent. Although managing a big artist can be profitable, it is often very stressful and precarious.

Financial trends and staff

The agent, as Mike Dewdney rightly points out, is a broker, convincing people to promote their bands. But, the agent has to believe in his product to be able to do this. He is the man in the middle. If he telephones someone and he does not believe in the product, how is going to get that person to believe in it? All the pieces of the promotional jigsaw have to be in place or the promotion will not work. This is especially true of rock and indie bands. There is only a limited amount of time before something new comes along and the press, record company money and hype are transferred to it. There have been times where a record company has put £60,000 to £70,000 into a band and then pulled their support because the band has sold only 6000 to 7000 CDs. Rather than nurture them or develop their strengths, the company has withdrawn funding and dropped the band. Some agents try to build their bands by constant club touring. This builds up a fan base, then the band can be gradually elevated to larger halls. It is stupid to push a band straight into a large hall, especially if they are a one-hit wonder, as it will destroy all credibility if the band plays to 300 people in a venue that normally holds 3000.

The agent is as powerful as his bands. The people who make the most money are those deemed to be at the top. An agent might not have the most aspiring roster in the world with all the most influential bands on it but, if he has established bands that still do good business, he will still make money.

Mike Dewdney's roster may be rather topical but it earns him only one-third the income of some agents with more established acts. One day, with luck and good judgment, if these acts are still around and established, then Mike will be in a position to earn much more money. A tour for ZZ Top will earn more money for one agent than another agent's total tours in a year. It is a fact of life that the money for doing one open-air show will be astronomical compared with that for doing two nights at Brixton Academy with its 4000 capacity.

Figure 2:2 A typical agency hierarchy chart

DIRECTORS

AGENTS

BACK UP STAFF

ASSISTANTS

As an agent develops, she grows out of some tasks, such as filling in the contracts. This is delegated to her personal assistant (PA) or a member of the support staff. Delegation can also shield agents from inconvenient and menial jobs. For instance, if there is someone she does not want to talk to, or someone just dropping in ticket figures, then the PA can deal with this. But, to be able to do this, the PA must be briefed very carefully and always kept abreast of what is going on. This is quite hard to do as, in this business, things can change from minute to minute. The secretarial staff are responsible for the paperwork which is tedious but essential.

Agents have to develop a personal involvement with the artist so that they can let promoters know of any problems or special needs that the artist requires. Good relations with other agents are a must. For instance, if Mike Dewdney needs to book five shows in three weeks for a new artist, he telephones other agents to see what they have going out in the next three weeks and to ask if they will put the artist on with any of their shows. Agents within the same agency meet often to discuss what is going on and when it is going out. At this meeting, agents can ask for help on a variety of issues. For instance, the agency may be about to lose a band unless a support tour is found for them; another agent may be able to offer them a support tour. Sometimes the agent may be under heavy pressure to get dates for a band, but it may be impossible to do this.

A lot of agencies have problems meeting costs; any respectable agency incurs costs of £300,000 to £500,000 per year. To cover that sort of money, the agent would have to gross over £5 million. A combination of acts cover these costs – new acts, long running acts, stadium acts, and club acts all piece together in this financial jigsaw. Bands come and go, but agents stay, although they may move from agency to agency. Agents lose bands to other agents all the time, for a better deal or for a new image. Some agents take it personally, but it is a fact of life in the music business.

At MPI agents tend to work on their own, because agents always build up their own stable of artists. In some agencies people work together more than in others. In MPI there is quite a lot of co-operation but, by definition, the agent for each band is the person responsible for that band who will do the most work for them. The agents at MPI are not really operating in competing areas. At any agency it would not be in the agency's interest for more than one agent to go after and try to procure the same act. Each agent at MPI negotiates his own deals. It is fairly common practice for an agent to be on a guaranteed salary with, once a threshold has been reached, bonuses attached to it. Some agents are paid on a commission-only basis where they take a percentage of their turnover with the balance going to the company.

Case Studies

Rage Against the Machine

Two of Mike Dewdney's most successful bands are Rage Against the Machine (RATM) and Pearl Jam. Rod Macsween, one of the directors of ITB, saw the two bands at Lolapolooza in America. They were on stage together playing *Rockin' in the Free World*. The director thought that they were excellent. The agent and the management were checked out. ITB moved in, hustled and pushed the manager, and got the band contract for the agency. They were in the right place at the right time. Then ITB put RATM on the Suicidal Tendencies' tour. RATM were so good live, it all just clicked. The band came straight back and did a headline tour. Two months later the CD single came out, and the band gradually built up a very good reputation.

Spin Doctors

The Spin Doctors did ten London shows in two years. They were beginning to build a profile in the American Billboard charts. They toured America extensively and then came back to Britain, after they had sold one million albums in the USA. *Two Princes* received non-stop radio play. Mike heard them, found the record company number and kept on hustling until he got the band.

Eve's Plumb

For one of Mike's bands, Eve's Plumb, success did not come easily. The band supported the Manic Street Preachers and the Spin Doctors on tour. Radio DJs hated the band but the press and television eventually started to show an interest in them. Many thousands of dollars were spent on shortfall for singles and touring. They needed a little luck. Mike looked at summer festival options and thought about putting in ten key dates. This would present the band to a much wider audience. But, every slot on a festival has about 20 bands competing for it. This is where the power of the agent can help. If an agent has a band that is on the top of the bill, the promoter will look favourably at that agent's bands for the foot of the bill. Eve's Plumb did not get the festival dates they needed, and the band, after much work from the agent, failed to make the big time.

An agent cannot compromise his position with an artist. He might get a better cut if the new band is supporting another of his bands. If the new band makes it more quickly than it otherwise would because of the bands that they are supporting, then in the long run it will be far more profitable for the agent concerned. If an agent forces something on a band and it is wrong, he could lose them and, if they have potential, then this benefits someone else. An agent needs to have good communications with the members of the band. Even if they are not working, he still needs to stay in touch with them, and to tell them what is happening. For a lot of American bands, their agent is their eyes and ears in this country and can become like a manager to them. He can give them their midweek position in the charts, or whether they have a review in *Kerrang*.

It is difficult to comprehend the frequent disparity between ticket sales and product sales. Nick Peel says that an band's size in terms of ticket sales and product sales cannot be directly correlated. For example, in Britain Jools Holland has a very successful live career with his band. In 1993, MPI had 96 shows in the UK with Jools Holland, all of which sold very well, yet his product sales are in the region of 15,000 to 20,000 units. Jools is definitely a 'live' phenomenon, which has not yet translated effectively into recorded material. When this book was first published, MPI's major client was Sting; other major clients were Jeff Beck and Black Sabbath. The Spanish act Heroes Del Silencio are huge in Europe but not yet in Britain. ITB looks after more than 150 acts, whereas MPI concentrates on 50 or so.

The American connection

Many companies have an American connection. Some agencies can be owned by an American company, some have amalgamated with American companies, whilst others have an agency agreement. As ITB is an extremely strong company, it does not need an American company for any of these purposes.

If you were to buy ITB, what would you buy? Your assets are your agents and your offices. If the agents all go, then the bands will follow them. There is a tendency for companies to merge to form larger companies – this is the nature of survival in the music business today. ICM merged with Fair Warning and, later, a further merger/demerger created Helter Skelter.

Today, many companies in the music industry have merged. The larger agents, promotion companies and record companies have also merged to form huge conglomerates. This has totally changed the face of the musin industry. In some cases, agents, promotion companies and venues have merged to form companies that provide a wide range of services.

Many of these mergers are pan-European or Euro-Atlantic. This has meant two things: firstly, the music industry has become much smaller; secondly, it has become polarised with a myriad of smaller companies and a few big companies, with nothing much in between. The effect is yet to be fully felt.

In the early 1990s, Solo merged with ITG. The Solo ITG agency was owned on a 50 per cent each share between the American and British arms of the company. Solo ITG was owned by BCL, the L of this being Labatts. There was mutual respect between the agencies and it made the booking of American acts into Britain and British acts into

America a formality. Neil Warnock of The Agency set up his own operation in America. Owing to these developments within the bigger agencies, many of the smaller agents have disappeared.

Prestige Talent felt that a merger would make it more competitive in the market place in relation to bigger agencies. There is a strong feeling that only the bigger agencies will survive and Miracle wanted to be up there with them. This was part of Prestige Talent's thinking when it joined with Miracle to form Miracle Prestige International (MPI). But, MPI does not have any direct, formal tie with an American agency. Nick Peel feels that, if an agency works exclusively with only one American agency, this will preclude to some extent meaningful relationships with other American agencies. Relationships between British and American agencies are not always straightforward, and it can make life more difficult if people do not understand the nature of an agent's relationship with his American partner.

Several years ago an American company started to book acts direct with British promoters. This caused some controversy in the business. The American company decided that, rather than form an allegiance or take over a European agency, they would go it alone, take a band and book them directly into Europe. The major reason was financial. The American company could make more money by booking a band direct into Europe than they would through a European agent. A lot of agents in Britain became upset about this, but the agent succeeds on the quality of service it gives its own bands. There seemed to be a lack of quality in the promotions directly from America. It was an easy way for unscrupulous promoters to act unfairly towards the band as the only direct lines of communication were the telephone or fax. If the rider was wrong or the specification not up to standard, it was hard for the agent to advise the band and tour manager because he had no physical presence on the spot. If a major catastrophe happens with a show in Europe, a British agent can be there in a couple of hours and can attend to it personally.

New markets

Agents are constantly looking for new markets: South Africa, the Baltic States, Romania and the Czech Republic are all new areas opening up, but breaking into them is still difficult. In the spring of 1995, I spent some time researching in the Czech Republic. The marketing and promotional system is still quite primitive with most local music using word-of-mouth to front their promotional drives. The enthusiasm of the promoters and bands is exceptional and they would think it nothing to play for fifteen dates on the trot just for beer and some food. When interviewing the master violinist Kliment Navratil, he stated that he never played for a fee but enjoyed the music so much that hospitality was enough for him. Hopefully this kindred spirit will not be knocked out of such wonderful people by the rise of capitalism. But, on a recent visit to the Czech Republic in 1999, it became apparent that the promotion system is much more advanced. Parky, a promoter with Interkoncerts, related that the promotion system is now almost on a par with other western European countries, but the venues and their electric and safety systems still leave a lot to be desired. Finland is an example of developed promotion with a two-tier promotion system. On the first tier there is a system like the UK where major artists are promoted through central agents and big efforts are made on marketing but, on the second level, most of the promotion is carried out through the bands and most of the marketing is word of mouth.

There are still major artists who do not use an agent. The former manager of Dire Straits, Ed Bicknell, used to book the band directly with promoters; he is an agent with the expertise to do it. This also cuts out the agent as the middle-man and saves money, because there is no agent's commission to pay.

Agent philosophy

There are some unscrupulous agents who are not bothered about putting promoters out of business, but there are those that do care. If a promoter feels that he has negotiated a deal wrongly, then he can always ask to have the deal renegotiated. Before a deal is made, the promoter always has the right to refuse an act. Very often it is the promoter's, not the agent's, fault that a show does not sell, because sometimes promoters do not market and promote an event fully. Time and time again, when letting halls to outside promoters, I was appalled at the lack of forethought in promoting events and the lack of contact with essential parties. Many of these events would be poorly attended and promoters would then try to renegotiate the hall hire fee with the venue and the artist fee with the agent. An agent or venue manager would often be sympathetic, if every effort had been made to plan and to promote the show carefully and appropriately. But, if the promoter had failed to do the sums correctly, then the deal would not be reviewed. It is possible to spot in advance if a promoter is not totally in control of an event. For instance, if a promoter has booked a venue which holds 1000 for a very big artist, is paying over the odds to get that artist and has a high percentage break-even, they have a problem. Once spotted during negotiation, the agent will see that the deal is not feasible. It is sometimes impossible to put more punters into a venue because of health and safety regulations, but promoters often disregard this.

Nick Peel at MPI has the following approach: he chooses to represent a band because he believes in them. He takes the view that the band will bear fruit for a long time. He could lose money for two to three years before the band start to make him money. This is why agents now insist on only handling bands with contracts. These can be three- to four-year contracts: if a band make it after three years, then the agent who has stuck by them will benefit the next year.

When agents deal directly with venues there can be problems. Council-run venues are sometimes hard to deal with. They tend to want everything for nothing and sometimes refuse to provide beer and food for the band. The typical response from such a venue is that they *are not running a restaurant*. Since 1990, a lot of the problems have been ironed out. Compulsory Competitive Tendering resulted in a more professional approach from venue managers. This meant that the venue needed the promoter's custom to survive and this bolstered the venue-promoter relationship. Now that CCT has almost stopped and venues are often run by either management committees or trusts, the system is a little different. But, having such a management structure at such venues alleviates problems with payment to agents from promoters.

The agent often recommends a tour manager, but the decision ultimately rests with the band's management. There is a pool of tour managers to choose from. Many that I dealt with appeared often in any given year. The more experience a tour manager has with bands the easier a promotion is, as we both quickly got to know each other 's expectations.

In Britain a band is best exposed by radio play. The band need to release the right CD for radio, to have a great image, to be able to come across well to a live audience, and have a little luck. If the band have a show in London one week after their single has appeared on the chart show or on MTV, then they will have a good response. MTV is revered in America. If a band makes MTV, they are usually successful. MTV is very strong in Europe, but not in Britain as yet. MTV has great power if a band appear on their A and B play listing: the single or track is played in very frequent rotation. This works well in some ways, but it can also be destructive as the power of television can dictate popular taste and leaves the control of a major influencing industry to programmers. (A and B play lists are those most regularly played by radio and television stations.)

Programmers are the people who make the decisions on what they feel people want to hear. If a band get a single in the top 40, they are halfway there; yet a number-one single does not a band make, a number-one album does. If a band wish to tour throughout March, but the product does not come out until April, there is no point in touring clubs without the support of that product. It is fine to start a tour the week before the product comes out, because the press and promotion have already started. The agent has got to be careful and should liaise with the record company for the best plan.

Agent finances

An agent makes money as a broker. He takes a percentage of what the band earns in money paid by the promoter to the band. On the tour, the agent is usually the bank for the band. The agent takes the deposits for the tour, which are held in an escrow account (money is deposited with a solicitor until the contract is fulfilled, when it is released to the payee), and the band members are advanced money as they need it. The deposits are sent to the agent as the middle-man. The money in the account is paid to the band on successful completion of the show or tour. A promoter keeps his side of the bargain by investing money in the band. If the band do not play the show, the agent is legally bound to send the money back to the promoter. The agent knows how much the band will be getting during the tour, so he cuts the deal accordingly. If the band are getting a much better deal than he is, then he may be able to renegotiate the deal. If the band are big, it may be like a *show deal*. The agent will receive a set fee, plus a percentage, depending on what he and the band management have negotiated. As the amount the band make increases, so the agent's value of the percentage increases accordingly.

The amount that you, as an agent, can make varies greatly. One year, when all your artists are successful, you could make £200,000. In another year you may make only £20,000. All this depends on the artists that you have and how well they do. If you move from one agency to another, what is the transfer fee? Is it based on the acts that you bring with you and whether you represent unknown acts and are giving them three to four years to become known. An agent is rarely paid more than he brings in. Very often a new agent will not make money for two to three years and is brought in as a booker for one of the more successful agents or directors of the agency.

Sometimes an artist can go completely wrong, for instance, RPLA. This band were heavily pushed as a rock act. They made the front page of *Kerrang*, but was it the wrong front page? Should it have been *New Musical Express (NME)* or *Vox*? It takes some bands two to three years before they are offered the front page of *Kerrang*, so it was an opportunity not to be missed. It was like putting a Take That advert in *Kerrang* – it did not work. With Tori Amos, one advert in *The Evening Standard*, when she first appeared, pulled in 100 punters. At the end of that tour, one advert in *Time Out* pulled in 400 punters. It is all about knowing the market and who and when to hit. A Tori Amos advert on Capitol Radio now would sell out the show. Her singles are always heavily played on this station. Marketing is risky; if you get it wrong the first time, it is difficult to change. Let the band play, get the press down early. If you usually get a better response from one newspaper than another, then ensure that the best possible press are represented.

Tour administration

For a full European tour, the band have to be supplied with an itinerary of dates, venues, capacities, promoter's and financial details. This is backed up by the contract. An accountant's knowledge is very useful because the tax laws in each country are different, for example, rates of tax and the reduction of liability vary. The accounting procedure makes sure that all the deposits are in, that cash flow is good, that the ledger is filled in and that the balance is carried forward. Passport details for the band and crew must be checked. The agent must liaise with the manager and the record company to make sure everyone is on top of things and know what they want.

- Has all the relevant tour information been passed on?

- Has the record company done the press announcement?

- Have the press promotional packages for the tour gone out to the promoters?

- Is everything that should be happening in fact happening?

The agent is there to administer the whole tour. There can be a lot of paperwork but, in the end, this makes the show successful. The contract has to be sent to the band, signed and exchanged. Exchange very rarely happens these days. In twelve years of promoting over 3000 bands and acts I only ever received back half a dozen contracts signed by the artist. But, with major shows, contracts must be exchanged before the promoter will part with his deposit. The agent must be able to tell the band and management their offer, with the withholding and/or other taxes deducted.

Mike Dewdney worked for three months on the Spin Doctors' tour, which was still not ready as they could not decide which was the best way around to do it, which venues they were going to play, or which bands were going to support. With any tour, until the major shows are put to bed, the rest of the tour will just float. But, as soon as the major decisions are made, the rest of the tour will be booked up within a week. An agent may put a tour together two or three times before it is right. Options have to be kept open and alternative tours planned. Other parameters often come into play. For example, the American single release may be put back, making it wiser to play Europe first, where the single has been released, and then to play America on the second leg of the tour, when the single is out. It is not always best to say 'yes' to everything. If the agent wants the band to tour before the single is released, he must put up good reasons to the record company and they might change their minds.

If a single comes out after a tour and is a big success, then the tour is wasted and the band are in limbo land until their next tour. Their next tour may coincide with a flop single, and the tour is again wasted. It is all down to luck and good timing. Each time a band tours, they must play to more people or they are only playing to established fans. But, the power of the press can also turn the tide. One person's opinion in rubbishing a band can destroy their reputation.

Business interests and assets

Companies like MPI have other business interests. This is similar to the case study of MCP Promotions in Chapter 1, where a company does not rely solely on one business, but has assets in other areas. One of the partners in MPI is Miles Copeland, who was Sting's manager when this book was first published and who is also a director of EMI records. There was a publishing company called Bugle Songs, run by Torquil Creavey, which did all the publishing for Miles Copeland's artists. There were other companies too. One of the more interesting ones was the retailing company that developed a new concept for retailing CDs. It developed a CD vending machine after research showed that a large percentage of people were frightened of going into record shops and buying CDs. The idea behind the development was that some people felt more comfortable buying a CD from a machine than going into a retail outlet. These machines, which take cash or credit cards, were strategically placed in airports, supermarkets, shopping malls and other places for everyday users. There are test sites throughout the country.

Marketing perspectives

The marketing of a band by the agent can sometimes depend on the strength of the record company. Marketing the band is not necessarily the agent's role. That is mainly to negotiate the fees for a live performance. Most agents tend to work closely with the record company, public relations (PR) companies and independent press agencies. In terms of actual marketing, the agent tends to market the band or artist to promoters and festivals. The agent makes up brochures and sends them to people that she thinks might be interested in a promotion of the band or artist, but is careful not to step on the toes of the PR company. If the band do not have a PR company or the PR company is not doing its job, then the agent will work with the band. An agent does a number of things that are outside her brief, but which she does to help the promoter or her own career. Most agents do not have formal sales training; it tends to be picked up by experience, but it is an enormous benefit to many promoters and agents. It is a big benefit if a record company can target a sales and marketing campaign specifically around the dates and in the cities played on a tour. When marketing, the agent has a peripheral rather than central role.

Other duties

An agent has other duties to fulfil. Artists visiting Britain need Foreign Entertainment Unit (FEU) papers so that tax can be deducted from the total paid to them. The Foreign Entertainment Unit is a specialist department of the Inland Revenue. If a foreign artist does not obtain FEU clearance, then tax still has to be deducted at source and the promoter will be responsible for deducting the tax from the artist's payment. If the artist plays, then the promoter is liable for the taxes incurred. Some agents handle FEU applications for American artists, but many do not. FEUs are also discussed in Chapter 8.

An agent is sometimes responsible for the application to the Department of Employment for work permits for foreign artists. Without a work permit, it is illegal for a foreign artist to perform in Britain. There have been occasions where bands or artists without work permits have been halted at the airport and sent home on the next plane. These permits can take up to eight weeks to come through.

In Sweden, driving permits are needed and special passes are required to get trucks into places in cities where they are not normally allowed. Driving permits are not usually needed in EU countries, but in Germany and Switzerland a Sunday Driving Permit has to be obtained to drive heavy vehicles on a Sunday.

The tax laws of each country must be known and although, this is not the responsibility of the agent, a good agent will perhaps offer this knowledge as part of his service. It is a beneficial for an agent to have a broad knowledge of the law and to be able to advise on tax liabilities. In many cases an accountant is employed to find this out. Deduction of tax is a problem all over Europe. In the UK it is 25 per cent of gross, Germany 17 per cent, Austria 20 per cent. This makes a major hole in the touring budget. The tax laws regarding double taxation treaties are quite complicated and best handled by accountants.

Conclusion

It can be seen that the job of an agent is a complicated and many-faceted role which influences an artist's rise or their niche within the market. This role is of prime importance as is that of agencies in the promotion of live music and the development of a band through record sales and public relations. The next chapter will deal with the printer and the way in which the promoter obtains new publicity material to promote concerts.

Chapter 3

Managing Publicity

Introduction

Over a period a promoter accumulates a large amount of knowledge which enables him to judge just how much an artist is worth. From trial and error and informed opinion, the promoter is also able to evaluate the constituents that make up a good or fair deal. Eventually the promoter has extensive knowledge of the economic viability of each of the services that he is buying in for each concert promoted. These services include publicity, advertising and marketing. In this chapter we concentrate on publicity.

One of the best ways of judging the services that are used is to obtain a series of quotes from other companies, providing the same service to the same specification. The promoter can then compare these prices. The major problem with using such a system is that a cheaper quote does not necessarily mean a comparable or quality service and the promoter may find that, by using a different or cheaper supplier, the quality of service gained is not as good as services used in the past.

One area where savings can be made is in printing. This chapter outlines the sections of the printing trade that are useful in the promotion of concerts. Large promoters, such as MCP, have their own in-house printing companies but, as a rule, the average promoter has to rely on the local printer for all his printing needs. Paul Allen at Morning Press in Milton Keynes, a first rate, quality printer with a first class service, has provided much of the information in this chapter. Although other firms may work in a slightly different way, Paul gives an insight into the processes, staffing and systems of a printing firm.

He gives an in-depth understanding of where the money goes, and tips on how to save money when having your printing produced.

Printing for publicity

The first steps and costing

The first step for the printer is to find out what the promoter requires and what he will accept in paper quality and weight. The variation in the cost of paper is very wide: one type of paper can cost three times as much as another, changing the cost from, say, £30 to £90. If the promoter is shown a number of different papers at different prices and thicknesses, he can make up his own mind with informed advice on the best paper to use for the job required. The normal rule of thumb is that the cost of the paper represents one third of the total job costs, not including art work and VAT. But, these costs are only for a single colour print job, as an increased number of inks increases the price. The number of posters or leaflets to be printed also increases the cost. The more posters or leaflets printed, the higher the cost, but the cost per unit decreases proportionately to the quantity printed on the same print run. For example, the cost of printing 2000 posters will be less than double the cost of printing 1000 posters.

The next cost to consider is for the printing plates, which are the printing machine's register of your image. Printing plates are made of aluminium, which is very light and durable. They are easily fitted to the press as they are very thin and bend to fit the rollers. Prepared art work is transferred to the plates by the printer. The plates are then attached to the machine and the paper is run over the plates, leaving the image of the art work on the paper in ink. The cost of the plates depends upon their size, which is the same size as the poster or flyer to be printed. The size of the plates depends on the job to be run. For instance, if the job consists of one small flyer, the printer may decide to print it on double crown size paper, which is the same size as a cinema poster. Therefore, the plate that is made will have a large number of reproductions of the same flyer cut into it. This double crown paper ,when run through the machine, will print perhaps twenty copies of the flyer on each sheet of paper. This will cut down on the number of sheets of paper needed and, thus, the paper costs, but will mean that the paper has to be cut several times to obtain the small flyers.

An increase in price can also occur as a result of the type of image required. A printing job will cost more if it has a photograph or a full-out solid printed on it. A full-out solid occurs where there is a reversal of the printing. This means that, instead of a white poster with coloured writing, the poster is coloured with the writing appearing in white. Most of the poster is, therefore, covered in ink.

A poster or leaflet with a photograph also costs more because the photograph has to be scanned first. A solid photograph in colour uses much more ink than printing words in the same area, and this increases the printing cost.

There are factors which dictate the type of press that the job will be printed on. These factors include the size of the posters and length of the print run. Morning Press have two sizes of printing machines, A2 and A3. Paul has an A3 Rotaprint, two Heidelberg A3s and a Heidelberg A2. An A2 press runs paper that is twice as big as that on an A3 press (and an A3 press runs paper that is twice the size of a standard A4 sheet). A printing job on the Rotaprint costs less per hour for the same job than on any of the other machines. The Heidelberg A3 and A2 machine charges are more than for the A3 Rotaprint purely because the set up time on those presses is much longer. To *make ready* means the time taken on the press to clean, set up and wash down on each job. The plates for each press differ in price. An A3 plate is cheaper than an A2 plate, which is twice the size. A problem arises on occasions when a client supplies art work which is not produced properly or in the correct way. In such a case, the printer has to shoot a negative of the art work and then contact into a positive to be able to use it. The printer then needs to make a set of positive plates for the printing machine. It costs a great deal more to prepare the art work this way. Therefore, if the artwork is prepared properly, the cost incurred by creating a new positive is avoided.

The next printing costs to examine are the consumables or chemicals. For example, five kilos of black ink can be bought for £20, whereas five kilos of another colour could cost £100, depending on which colour is chosen. The printer will normally have a *Pantone booklet* which shows hundreds of strips of colours. From these you can chose shades that you feel are right for your job, but that shade may be made up of different ink mixes. The printer then has to establish the four or five different pigments that go into making up that mix. These pigments have to be weighed accurately so that the exact colour can be reproduced. If the printer incorrectly weighs one of those pigments, then the colour that is produced will not be the colour that you have chosen. This will mean that all of the pigments mixed have been wasted and the printer may have to start the job all over again. Another complication is that different types and colours of paper show the ink up in different tones. Therefore, the printer has to take this into consideration when mixing the pigments. This can often mean that there have to be fine adjustments made to the mix before the colour requested is ready to go into the machine.

The type of paper that the ink goes onto will, in two out of ten cases, still alter the finished colour of the ink. This has to be tested before the print run is started. Another difficulty facing the printer is that, when he buys paper stock it may be more absorbent than the last consignment. In such a case, the paper will change the colour of the ink. This is often due to the humidity of the atmosphere which affects the paper.

There are many makes of ink and these are divided into two categories, oil-based and rubber-based. Rubber-based inks dry more quickly than oil-based inks. But, one of the major problems with rubber-based ink is that, on a long print run, the ink may dry on the machine rollers. It does not dry totally, but in patches, which stop the image printing properly.

When the print run is finished, the printer has to allow the ink a certain amount of time to dry. This again is affected by the atmosphere. If a print run on one day takes 50 minutes to dry, this does not necessarily mean that this is the norm for each day. If the printer re-runs the job on the next day and the humidity of the air is different, it may take 12 hours to dry. It is possible to add dryers to the ink to accelerate the drying time, but the printer has to be careful when doing this because these dryers can alter its colour and possibly ruin the print job.

Once the paper and the inks have been chosen and the job run, another possible cost of a complicated job is a *finished fold*. Many venues produce programmes of events and these are very glossy and folded in many weird and wonderful ways. The folding of a programme or flyer can add a great deal to the price. The cheapest basic fold is A4 to A5 (see Figure 3:1 for size details), a single fold. The more folds that a programme has, the more expensive it is. If it is a very complicated fold, it is even more expensive, and the programme has to be sent out to a finisher who has the required type of folding machine. It takes the operator more time to set up the machine for each extra fold.

As previously mentioned, the cost of a printing job increases as the number of colours to be printed increases. For a single colour job, there is only one printing plate, one make ready, one wash up and one run. For a four-colour job, each of these operations is carried out four times, which increases the price, not only for the number of inks used but also for the machine time and the other associated jobs involved. Any sort of one- to four-colour line work will not be as expensive as doing a one- to four-colour process because a photograph, for example, has to be sent to a trade scanning house. Very few printers have their own scanning facilities; the cost of a scanner is in the region of a quarter of a million pounds. The laser within the scanner breaks down the photograph into four colours so that the photograph can then be replicated exactly onto the print job. Any colour job is printed using red (magenta), blue (cyan), yellow and black. Most other colours are tints or pigment mixtures. Occasionally a fifth colour may be required, which may be a silver or a gold. This fifth colour may be a particular corporate colour which you are not happy to have produced using the four colour process.

Figure 3:1 Paper sizes. A6 is half A5, which is half A4, which is half A3, which is half A2.

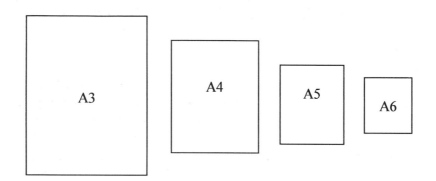

Planning and special effects

When the scan has been produced, it has to be planned up. Many printers get trade planning houses to do this. They have to be accurate because one minute dot of one colour has to register perfectly with the minute dots of other colours. If the planner does not get it right, then what results is what is called a *moray effect*. This is where the printed photograph overlaps on all the colours, causing distortion.

Special effects can be done but they increase the price substantially. But, there are some good, but cheap, effects that can be substituted for those more complicated and expensive, keeping the price of the job containable. The effectiveness of the finished job is important, because the effects used in it affect the way in which your audience view the venue and the promotion.

•   **Thermographing** The machine minder takes the print job when it is still wet and puts it through a special powder. The powdered paper is put through a heater which fuses the powdered resin and makes the treated print rise off the paper.

- **Duo toning** A mono photograph is printed, then a second colour is scanned onto the first with the screen angle changed. This gives the photograph a three-dimensional effect. It seems to lift the image off the paper because the two images are not exactly matched up. This process will be successful, depending on the second colour used, for example, a red is more effective than a blue.

- **Blind embossing** A male and female die of an image or a logo are made and the paper is literally squeezed through under pressure, which raises the paper up. This process does not physically print but pushes the paper up between the two halves of the die. The embossed image can be printed as well, which gives a raised and printed image on the paper. The dies are usually cast out of metal.

- **Gloss and matt varnishes** These can be run on a press to make parts of the paper shiny or dull. These print formats usually follow a trend. A printer will get a spate of jobs being run with a gloss varnish on a matt paper or at other times a matt varnish on a gloss paper. This process gives a shiny or a dull surface on areas that are printed on.

Some print jobs need to be aqua sealed, especially if there is a large area of solid ink colour present. When a job with a large area of solid is trimmed, where the pressure of the blade cuts along the edges of the poster or leaflet, the reverse side will have a halo effect around the edge. It does not matter how sharp the blade is, or how few posters or leaflets are cut at any one time, or how long the ink has been left to dry, this halo still appears. The trick is to aqua seal the job. Aqua seal acts like a varnish and when it dries it does not affect the texture or the colour but it stops the ink forming the halo effect.

As a general rule, most leaflets are A5 and most posters are either A2 or A3. The cinema industry uses double-Crown posters as does the record industry and fly-posting companies. These are bigger and create much more of an impact, but there are very few shops, theatres or businesses that have room to take such large posters. A4 is the standard paper size (210 mm x 297 mm), used for day-to-day business letters. A5 is the size of an A4 single folded sheet (210 mm x 148 mm). Double Crown is 1620 mm x 5080 mm.

For most posters there is no need to consider aqua sealing because they will be displayed indoors on walls or in halls, and to carry out this process would add to their general cost. But, it may be worth using this process on a classy leaflet, where you, as a promoter, are trying to attract a more discerning client to your event.

Producing the job

The cheapest poster a printer can produce

The printer will try to establish which typeface you, as a promoter, prefer for the text on the poster. The poster in the chosen text is then generated (most likely on a computer). The job is then proof read by you. Any changes which are the your fault are usually charged for. But, any mistakes made by the printer are corrected without charge. It is a good idea for you to get a third party to check the copy as well; no matter how many times you read copy, you may miss something very obvious. The printer will normally ask you to *sign off* the art work, to show that you are happy with the spelling, the look and everything else that goes into the final proof. The printer and you then discuss the type of paper and the type of ink or inks that you require. On a poster, the printer would not recommend to go below 100 gsm (grams per square metre) in paper weight. Some people do go up to 200 gsm, depending on the quality that they want. When a leaflet is printed on both sides, too thin a paper will result in *show through*. If a leaflet is printed on one side, then the lowest paper weight recommended for a quality print job is 115 gsm. If you go lower than this, you get very thin flyers which are great to give away outside clubs, but are useless for other marketing purposes. When it comes to the larger, more-prestigious, concerts a thicker flyer is necessary.

For a programme, 135-150 gsm paper is used because, for psychological reasons, when a person receives a programme, the more stylish and well produced it is, the more likely they are to read the events advertised and the more it gives them an expectation of the quality of the show. The last thing that a promoter wants to happen is for the punter to throw the leaflet or flyer straight into the bin without even looking at it. If it feels good, the prospective punter will keep it; this fact might be difficult to qualify or quantify, but it seems to be true. Consider your own reaction: if you get a black on white leaflet on a flimsy paper, which is badly photocopied, you are more likely to throw it away than a similar leaflet printed on a thicker stock and in a bright colour. As a promoter, approaching the printer with this sort of knowledge and information, you can make sure that you are getting the print and paper in the correct proportions, and that you are not having the wool pulled over your eyes about the price of the product. From the printer's point of view the job price is kept down by:

- using the right paper, inks and colours for the job;

- making sure that the client is aware of what the finished product will look like; and

- making sure extraneous costs are not incurred by a client suddenly changing his mind or adding last minute details.

Approaching the printer

The general way in which clients approach a printer is by a request for a quote. Most promoters produce a specification and tout it around three or more printers for quotes. The printer used tends to be the one who gives the cheapest quote for the specification given. But, the promoter must make sure that all the costs are included in the quote and that new specification charges, plate costs and VAT do not suddenly crop up.

Tricks of the trade

One of the tricks of the trade that the promoter must watch out for has just been mentioned above. When you telephone for a quote, the printer has to get as much information as possible from you over the telephone so that he can prepare a quote as near to your specification as possible. Having done this, the printer will give you a quote. But, when your get the bill for the job, the printer may have charged extra for the plates. The quote does not always include the films and plates, but the printer does not always tell you this. You must make sure that the quote given by each printer contains both the film and plate costs so that each of the quotes can then be properly compared. Of course, this is not normal practice and printers of the calibre of Morning Press would not think of compromising their clients in this way.

The quote can alter because, in many cases, the client may change his mind before or during the actual printing process. If it is not too big a change, then the printer may not mind a small extra cost being added to his actual costs. If a print job changes to something very different to the original specification and it is impossible to complete the change without extra cost to the client, the printer will have to re-quote.

If you have been charged for printing plates (and you have paid the printer's bill), the plates are your property and the printer is obliged to release them to you. If you request the plates from a printer to get a reprint done with another printer, the original printer should be able to release the plates to you, unless they have been thrown away. In a professional printing business the plates and films are usually stored in job bags and are referenced, so that a printer can immediately retrieve a job when the plates are requested. Printing plates have a life expectancy of two years, if they are gummed up properly. They must have a coating of gum Arabic on them to stop them oxidising. After about two years that gum will break down. A plate may last 100,000 impressions before the image starts abrading away.

The printer's staff

Within any printing business an administrative post is needed. The administrator sees in the work, raises the relevant paperwork and takes on such tasks as administering the buying in of the paper at the right price. Printers usually have paper merchants' price lists to hand, and they can negotiate the price of the paper with these merchants, depending on the quantity of paper that they require.

Morning Press has a receptionist who deals with all telephone calls and callers, and also deals with the day-to-day administration of the business. A paper buyer is employed who, once he has negotiated with the merchant, passes the relevant paperwork to the administrator to process. A print estimator and an artist are also crucial to the smooth running of a printing business with a busy studio. The estimator gives a client the price that it would cost the print shop to do the job that the client has specified. An artist designs art work for those clients who request it. Some of the art work will be free-hand drawing and the remainder will be created on a computer. Art work does not just consist of pictures, but also text and different textual forms.

A plate maker who is conversant with the dark room is also employed. Years ago there was a plate maker and a camera operator. But, owing to cut backs, these two roles have been combined in most print shops.

On the print floor a machine minder (operator), a foreman or overseer, and a finisher are all specially trained for these extremely demanding positions.

Each one of these people is a specialist, but Morning Press try to train each employee in as many aspects of the printing trade as possible. This has been done so that, if someone within the business is on sick leave or on holiday, another member of staff can step in and take over from them competently whilst they are away.

The finisher has an extremely important job, cutting the work to size and folding it, among many other tasks.

For each job, a *job sheet* is filled out. When a new job is started, the job sheet is taken out of the file, and the relevant details noted. The paper is then taken from stock and trimmed down to fit the machine. Printing is always done on over-size sheets so that the finisher can trim it down to the right size without damaging the finished product. One of the reasons for this is that, if the job is too near to the edge of the sheet, the printing machine will not print the job properly. On the paper there are cut marks, registration points and colour bars which are a complicated system that a minder can understand. These detail the ink coverage, and the densities of ink running in the machine. The minder can also tell whether his colours are dirty from the colour bars at the side of each sheet of paper. For example, when printing yellow, which is the most difficult colour to print, any pigment left on the rollers will turn the yellow to green or discolour it in some way. If producing a four-colour job, a change in one of the ink colours could be a disaster. In the normal scheme of printing, the machine minder washes up the press three or four times before printing the yellow ink. Black ink is normally run last on the printing machine because it is more difficult to erase every trace of this colour between jobs. But, the other ink colours are usually laid down on the machine in accordance with the preference of the minder.

The finisher takes the paper from stock and gives it to the minder, together with the job sheet. The finisher then takes the plates from the file and makes sure that everything else that is needed for the job is given to the machine minder. Once the job has been printed, the finisher then carries out the next process, which would be collating it, folding it, gluing it, making it into sets, perforating it or numbering it, before it is actually trimmed down to its finished size. Once the job has been completed, the finisher cuts the job to the size requested by the client.

If a client does not wish to have a standard size paper for the finished job, this can prove very expensive. A non-standard sheet is called a *bastard size* as a print job cannot be fitted exactly to it and there is paper left over. One classic example of this is a four-page folder with a pocket in it. Only one of these folders can be fitted onto a SI2 sheet. There is a tremendous amount of wastage on the sheet because so much paper is needed for the flap. Thus one way of keeping paper costs down to a minimum is by using standard sizes.

Machines and sizes

The type and size of the machine used to print the job also matters. If, for example, an A5 job is printed on an A2 press, it would only work out cheaper on an extensive run. A short run would be more expensive because of the cost of the machine time and the set up and wash up costs, as well as the job planning. To run the job on an A2 would mean that the A5 sheet would be eight up (see Figure 3:2, below). Planning an eight up job takes twice as long as planning four up on an A3 sheet.

Figure 3:2 Two ways of planning an A2 print job

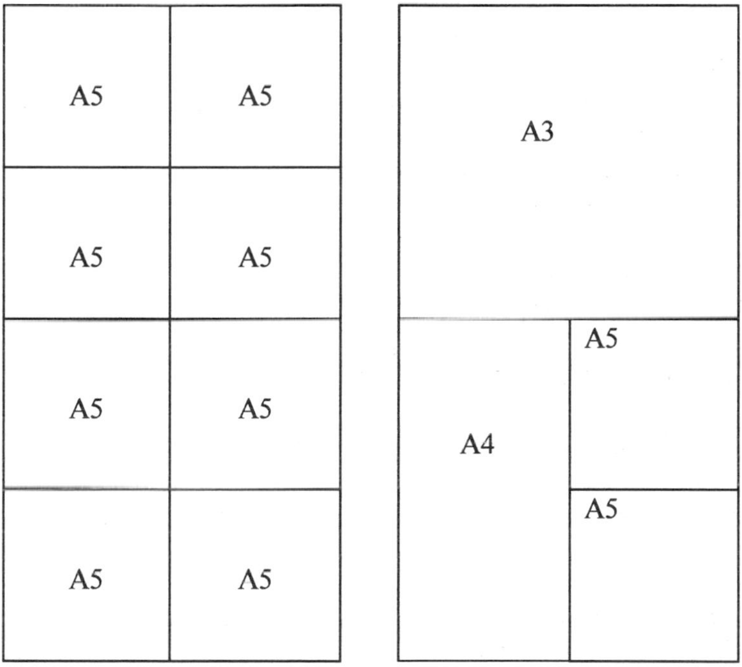

A5	A5
A5	A5
A5	A5
A5	A5

A3

A4

A5

A5

In many cases the A2 machine runs slower than the A3, therefore, an A2 job would take up more machine time than an A3 job. The running of the A2 may be quicker in some cases because, for every sheet that the A2 produces, the A3 has to produce twice as many sheets. The initial costs of the repro, the plates, the make ready, the wash up and the ink colours are only charged once. It is, therefore, cheaper to have a longer run if you can use all the posters or leaflets than it would be to have four smaller runs each incurring the setting up costs. The more impressions you have, the cheaper per thousand it is. This is because the first thousand has all the running and overhead costs added to it. It will be the same cost per thousand for every other thousand that you *run on*. If you have the choice to produce 200 posters or 500 posters, it would be better if you can produce 500, because the run on costs are minimal as it is only the paper, ink and the run time that are paid for after the initial costs have been met.

In many cases the printer or artist is called on to produce the art work for the client. This is sometimes a thankless job, but it can also give the printer a chance to show the client his expertise in design and art work.

If you were promoting a Country & Western show, the poster could be designed in the form of a 'Wanted' poster and be printed on a parchment type of paper, which would be more fetching than on white. But, you would not promote a soul or rock 'n' roll band with the same idea. So, the origination of the poster is important and the type of music that the origination is reflect has to be matched by the artist's design. What the printer or artist really needs to obtain from the client is some idea of what he really wants. Some clients do not know what they want and they rely on the printer for creative input. Other clients know exactly what they want and either prepare it themselves, which is cheaper, or guide the printer and artist through what they perceive the punter wants to see as advertising for the show. If you, as a promoter, inform the printer of the sort of poster which you would like to have, and the artist follows your specification closely, then you will be happy with the end result. If the artist and printer are given licence to do as they feel fit when originating, designing and printing the poster, you can only be shown the type of paper and the original art work. It is often not until the finished poster comes off the printing press that you know that what the printer or artist has designed is what you really wanted. There are two ways of getting around this problem and they are both extremely expensive:

- You can ask for a supply of wet machine proofs of the job before it is run.

- You can also have a chromalin proof, which is the same quality as a colour photocopy of the job but takes a great deal of setting up by the artist.

Some clients always require wet machine proofs. This is where samples of the job are run on the machine before the total job is run. These are then approved and the job is run off, if the proofs are satisfactory. In this process all the repro, the make readies and the washes have to be done just for a few sheets of the finished product. A wet proof is more accurate because it is exactly what the client will get when the finished product is run off. Some repro companies have got special proofing presses to do that for them, but it depends on time available for the printing of the job.

The importance of printing

What many promoters fail to realise is the importance of the quality of their printed matter. When the printer quotes for a job, that item might cost 5p a sheet but, when it is printed, the promoter will quite happily stick it in an envelope and spend five times that amount to post it. The post gets it to its location, but that is all it does. Whether the person reads it or not depends on the design, artwork, printing and colour. It is at this point that the leaflet starts working. It is very rarely going to be as expensive as the postage, but not all promoters see this as part of the equation. If a leaflet comes through the door and it is photocopied on thin paper, then a common usual reaction is to put it in the bin. If the promoter cannot take the trouble to produce a good leaflet, the punter begins to query what the product or service that he is buying will be like.

In some cases, music promotion, often in a youth cultural arena, is looked upon in a different way. A thin, fast produced, grungy flyer is more likely to attract its market because of its very seediness, but there are standards: the art work has to be sufficiently well produced and in the style of the subculture to enable that group to identify with it. Some rave printers and designers go to great trouble to get the flyer just right because, in some cases, they rely solely on a flyer to promote the show. But, there are the cowboys in the promotion game with no regard for long term satisfaction but an eye for a quick profit, and this can lead to slap dash, cheap promotion and cost cutting to make as much money as possible in a short space of time.

If you spent £500 on a flyer and it went out to 10,000 people, but the flyer was badly produced, then you may attract only 200 people to your event. If you spent £2000 on a beautifully-produced flyer and it went out to 10,000 people, you might have 5000 people turning up to your event. So, you have sold more tickets by producing better literature. At shows, record companies distribute glossy leaflets about CDs as a marketing ploy; they know that, if the leaflet attracts people to the show, then there is a better than even chance that those people will buy the CD. For instance, the hard four-letter word stance of East West Records, with their rock bands like Pantera, shows that they perceive what their audience want. The very sight of 'parent advisory lyrics' on a CD is enough to make most teenagers, if they like the band, buy the product because they are seen to be rebelling.

With the advent of dance music, micro-marketing factors have become very important. For instance, for raves and some dance clubs, high quality, heavyweight-card flyers are produced, which portray beautiful designs but are only available in certain shops or handed out to certain people. The very nature of micro-marketing underlines some sort of exclusivity where those that are in the know or those that are chosen are able to gain the knowledge to gain access to the event. The movement away from blanket and macro-marketing of events by the dance fraternity is a youth cultural development that has its roots in the illegal rave culture of the late 1980's and early 1990's. Its inception came about through secrecy and an underground culture which enabled groups of teenagers to access the forbidden. Although I have never agreed with illegal raves, because of the irresponsibilities of promoters without licenses and their scant regard for health and safety, their exciting and early underground image set a new standard for the promoters of the 21st century. Some of the early rave and underground club flyers are now collectors items, owing to their rarity and beauty.

For some reason printing is the last thing that a promoter considers when starting in business. He will discuss the possibilities of setting himself up, appoint an accountant, get a VAT number and find premises. Only at the last moment will he consider his need for stationery and other printing which, by that time, have become extremely urgent. It would be better for a promoter to consider his image and printing requirements at the very outset, thus developing his portfolio with image and print ideas at the forefront of his negotiations. Thus, printing should be regarded as a major attribute, and should be accorded its proper rank in setting up the business.

Conclusion

The best way of saving money, if you know what you want, is to put an A3 poster, an A4 poster and two A5 leaflets on the same A2 sheet, ensuring that there is no wastage (see Figure 3:2, page 75). For the promoter the biggest waste of time is inexperience. If a promoter leaves a job at the printer and keeps going back to change it, then he is being charged for each alteration. Copy that has been confirmed must be checked carefully. The spelling, details, design and layout are all important and must be checked by more than one person to make sure that they are right. There is nothing worse than receiving a finished job from the printer only to find that it has the wrong day or month on it. In this case the poster has to be printed again, which almost doubles the cost of the printing. Also, planning ahead with posters and leaflets by asking the printer to run them together, saves money. A wise promoter gets all his printing requirements in one operation rather than in two or more different ones. Now that we have dealt with the way in which the promoter obtains his printing, we will look at the way in which a promoter markets an event.

Chapter 4

Marketing the Event

Developing a system

Many people think that marketing means just publicity or advertising. This lack of understanding of the complicated role of marketing has often led to the downfall of a promoter or venue. Although advertising and publicity form part of the marketing machine, other factors can provide more initial impetus in a marketing push than the two mentioned.

To promote music well, an efficient publicity and marketing system is needed. This system must be able to produce clear and precise material at a low cost, and which ensures that the promotion is represented in the best possible manner to its public and target markets. It must also provide each of the marketing tools needed to promote each specific event, whether it is a mailing list or a piece of hype to start the spark needed to initiate a word-of-mouth spread about a concert.

As a promoter, your marketing machine's component parts must be finely tuned so that each event receives the same care and attention as all the other events taking place (yours or other people's). The first step when marketing any event is to produce a marketing plan and action sheet, detailing every move to be made during each stage of the process (see Figure 4:1, page 82). These stages are usually dated so that a time scale can be followed. The promoter can use a universal marketing checklist where each tool is detailed. This checklist also includes the target of the tool, any further activity or information needed and a yes/no column to be dated when the action has taken place. The plan and checklist are exceptionally useful, as anyone looking at them can see what has been accomplished and what is still to be done.

Figure 4:1 The Marketing Plan

(As used for the Ian Botham and Viv Richards show at Shenley Leisure Centre, Milton Keynes, and the Joan Armatrading concert at Woughton Leisure Centre, Milton Keynes, by Chris Kemp. Courtesy of Buckinghamshire County Council.)

AWARENESS			
Prepare internal mail lists	Internal record scrutiny	Send out for new lists	Contact specific periodicals
National press angle	Listings editorial	Programme notes	Internal client contact
Overprint	CEEFAX TELETEXT	Ticket Agents	
STAGE ONE			
Price up and discuss poster sites	Contact agent and record company for record release	Contact press and management company for photos and posters	Contact clubs with interest
Prepare internal research documents	Contact specific periodicals for prices	Contact local press for advertising prices and editorials	Discuss and price up leaflet drops
STAGE TWO			
Discuss budgets for promotion	Isolate budgets	Produce advert procedure	Produce mailing procedure
List contacts	Institute marketing plan		
STAGE THREE			
Produce posters	Send posters out	Place ads in local papers	Place regional ads
Place ads in national papers	Place ads in magazines	Identify and mail target markets	Talk to local press re angle for editorial
Contact specific periodicals for editorial	Contact local radio for programming	Contact local TV for programming	Produce and send leaflets
STAGE FOUR			
Introduce specials	Chase up press	Introduce new ticket concessions	Elicit buzz around the show
Introduce personal radio appearances	Talk to PR people	Invite guests	Contact agent for further advice
STAGE FIVE			
THE EVENT			
STAGE SIX			
THE POST MORTEM			

The first component of your marketing and publicity system is good communication links, both internally and externally. A promotion with good communication links will always have the edge. For example, good communication channels between the promoter and the newspapers may initiate first-class editorial coverage and an advertising campaign. To do this, though, you as the promoter must first put in a lot of time and effort to discover certain vital elements about the media that you are working in. You must find out the copy dates for both editorial and advertising for all the newspapers, both within the venue's catchment area and nationally. Without this information your marketing machine may not even start, let alone succeed. Once these dates have been logged, you can send out press releases and advertisements in time for the copy dates. A full list of newspapers and periodicals must be built up nationally, regionally and locally so that you have as much knowledge of the press network as possible.

As well as these lists, which should include names of contacts, addresses, telephone, mobile, fax numbers and email, you should build up a database of articles printed by papers and periodicals about the concerts at your venue, so that you can draw up and cross reference patterns of editorial entry in each paper and periodical. This will help your targeting for the future. Market research is discussed in Chapter 1, but one factor worth another mention is the simple question asked of each punter at the door, *Where did you find out about this concert?* This can elicit a favourable response for more than one newspaper or periodical. If this question is asked at each concert for a year, then you can build up a picture of the most effective newspapers and periodicals for each genre of music and, thus, target more effectively in the future. It can also inform you which of your marketing tools are the most effective. In the case of newspapers and periodicals, such information can tell the promoter which newspapers and periodicals are worth advertising in/sending editorial to and which are not. In both the short and long term, this could save you a great deal of money.

You must remember that it is pointless sending out a press release two days before a newspaper is due to hit the shelves and then expect it to feature prominently. The press release must be sent at least two days before the *copy deadline* to ensure that it has an even chance of getting in the paper. Most local weekly papers have a ten-day advance copy deadline, because the entertainment pages are often written at least one week prior to publication. Public holiday periods must be carefully planned, as some papers bring out double issues, or they may close for one week and produce the inside pages of two papers in one weekly schedule. Some monthly magazines have a copy date two months before publication, so it is imperative that you contact all papers and magazines that you use or intend to use to ascertain all the deadline dates for both advertising and editorial. It is always a good idea to telephone all the papers and magazines from time to time to check that copy dates have not changed. In the case of editorial and advertising, personal contact with the writer of the page, or the advertising representative designated to your area, is a bonus as the writer and rep can then put a face or voice to the publicity and advertisements arriving and, thus, make a more personal contact. It is useful to invite the press along to each gig, and looking after them with some sort of hospitality, as this endears the press to the venue. It does not cost much to provide this type of public relations (PR) and it is often a great idea to involve the newspaper with special events, giving them exclusives and permission to take photographs in your venue.

It must be remembered here that a promoter may put on seven or more concerts a week every week for most of the year. If this is the case, then the promoter must have a regular press system where press releases, photographs and adverts are sent out regularly every week in advance of the copy deadline, for both advertising and editorial departments.

As a promoter, you will need to obtain or make up press packs for each band or act that you represent. Obtaining press packs is a reasonably easy task for a major band. These packs are usually held by the agent, the press company, the promotion company, the record company or the management company. They consist of a biography, a black and white photograph, a colour transparency, a copy of the latest CD and, sometimes, a logo. But, if you require more of any item, just ask for what you need. At Milton Keynes, I always used:

- one biography, which could be photocopied 40 times (one for each newspaper in my catchment area).

84

- eight black and white photographs, one for each of the eight newspapers that regularly featured photographs for my venue.

- one colour transparency for a local magazine.

- five CDs for prizes in local paper or radio competitions.

It is more difficult to obtain press packs for some indie bands, mainly because they are on tight budgets. You may not receive more than one photograph or two CDs from an independent company. This is because of budgetary constraints. If 50 promoters each want four CDs, this amounts to 200 copies of a CD that may have had a pressing of only 5000. This drastically reduces the company's profit margin. It is a difficult position to be in because, if the company were to send CDs for a competition and it secured a venue sell out, this may mean increased sales of the CD and, therefore, the releasing of four CDs for competitions would have been worthwhile. The sword can cut both ways; there are subsidiary labels of major companies that I work with which refuse to send out CDs for competitions as a point of policy. This often causes newspapers to produce a smaller article on a band, or not to feature the band at all, as they have no product to give away in competitions. This can have a negative effect on the punters as they have less chance of seeing the band or of being made aware of it. This, in turn, reduces the number of punters at a concert and can affect the sales of a CD or single. A few CDs from a subsidiary label to attract more punters to a gig surely is worthwhile as, in addition, it may mean extra sales of the CD.

The band's press coverage is usually split into three parts:

- The press release, usually detailing the latest release and/or tour.

- The history of the band, their high points and their low points, as well as a number of interesting facts and trivia about the members of the band.

- Cuttings relating to the band from various music papers and magazines. Sometimes these are combined together to form an extended biography.

The internet has made the compilation of press packs easier for the promoter. Each band has at least one web site, a few have more than

50, some official and unofficial. There is no longer the excuse that a biography did not arrive; it is simple enough to make one up from available data yourself.

When sending out any marketing or promotion information, you must check many times to make sure that all the information presented is correct and that the biography is up to date. The information must detail the name of the band, the venue, the date, the time, the address, the various ticket prices and a box office number to contact. If any of these are missed off or given incorrectly, not only are you giving the punter false information, but also you are putting up barriers to punters turning up for the concert. I cannot stress how important correct information is. If the venue is new or obscure, then a small map showing the site of the venue is important.

There has been a trend in recent years to produce arty publicity shots. Although these look good, their basic problem is that they do not reproduce well in newspapers and local papers will not print them. Also, local papers are loath to print anything controversial. In 1994 I tried to get a local paper to print a picture of Chumbawamba in front of a cross but they refused, saying that it was too controversial for their readers. This was a shame as the picture was clear, well photographed and very presentable. Colour transparencies have also become quite arty. Only recently I received a picture of Urban Species with the lower half of the band completely obscured by shadow. The picture was in portrait (upright) format which meant that, if the paper enlarged the picture to go on the front page, then two of the band members would have been cut out.

The use of CDs as sweeteners for the press as well as for promotions is usual practice as writers like to receive new CDs from bands. This may also encourage a writer to keep your venue in the limelight.

You must send in editorial matter regularly every week. It is pointless sending editorial too far in advance as often it becomes lost in the massive amount of publicity that papers receive every week. It is also futile to send in copy too late as it will definitely not go in the paper as it has already gone to print. All press releases must be sent in at the right time every week so that there is a constant flow of information to the entertainment or music desk and, as a result, the venue or promoter is constantly in the mind of the person producing the entertainments page. This increases the profiles of the venue and the promoter as the writers and editors are constantly aware of programmes of activities on offer. Many promoters have failed because they have not kept their press information going out to the newspapers and magazines consistently, week in week out. It is vital to do this sometimes depressing job to keep the venue in the limelight. If my venue does not appear in more than six papers a week, I want to know why and I follow up press releases with telephone calls asking if they have been received. This not only keeps the editor on his toes, but also he knows that you care. If a press release is late, but not too late, you can fax it, and with the confirmation slip you know that it arrived.

After a while it becomes apparent which newspapers constantly support you, which papers sometimes support you, and which papers never support you. You can then trim your target lists accordingly.

The psychology of advertising is a fascinating area. The placement, size, colour, attractiveness and position of your advertisement are all important. But, even more important than any of these is the dialogue between you as the promoter and your advertising contacts. From the development of this dialogue, deals on the costs of advertisements can always be negotiated. It is even possible to place your advertisements through an agency at very reduced rates. This depends on the volume of the advertisements, because it may cost you more to place them through an agency if this is done infrequently.

Once you have made contact with the various national, regional and local newspapers, magazines and periodicals, you can decide how you are going to advertise. Are you going to place just one advertisement in the media or are you going to place a series of advertisements? This all depends on the band that you are promoting, the size of the audience that you want to attract, the amount of money that you have to spend and where you are most likely to target your audience.

If the band that you are promoting is mainstream, capable of attracting between 2000 to 3000 people, then a larger, more elaborate and more expensive campaign should be mounted. If you are trying to attract an audience of 200 to a new indie band, then you need a different perspective. For the purpose of this book, we will concentrate on a club venue holding 500 people that regularly attracts top new bands on the indie and metal circuit.

The amount of money that you have to spend on the promotion of a band will rely on several factors:

- The amount that you have budgeted for the band.

- The genre of the band.

- The number of punters that you expect to get through the door.

- Whether you feel that both national and local advertising are necessary.

At this point it is helpful to know what national advertisements are being placed by the record or management company, which it would be foolish to duplicate. This can be discovered easily by telephoning the company responsible for the advertisements and finding out if any are being placed, and if your tour date is included in them. If you have budgeted carefully for an event, then it is silly to spend over that amount. But, perhaps you can shift budgetary amounts around from one place to another if you feel that advertising in newspapers will be more effective than, say, posters. If you were expecting 100 punters to the show and then the band's CD races up the charts, you may want to spend a little more money to make sure that people know that your venue is featured on their tour. The knowledge of genre is important because it will enable you to track down magazines and periodicals which specialise in appropriately.

If, as an example, you promote a very popular middle-scale heavy metal band for which you hope to achieve a capacity audience, you may advertise in magazines of that genre, such as *Kerrang*, *Metal Hammer*, and *Terrorizer*. As a promoter I always used *Kerrang* because my market research told me that 85 per cent of my audience found out about concerts at my venue through that magazine.

To cut down costs, my advertisement featured all the bands appearing at my venue for the coming month. This increased the appeal of the venue and decreased the costs of each individual promotion. It is interesting to note here that, if punters receive a list of events in advance or are able to view an advert showing the 15 concerts promoted in the month, they are more likely to re-visit the venue as they feel that it has a reputation for the kind of music or that the promoter is catering for their needs. This loyalty is important for the promoter to note. I used to insert adverts two weeks prior to the date of the first concert listed in the advertisement. Occasionally the record company also ran adverts and these appeared either at the same time or before my own. If they did appear at the same time, some people felt that this was unnecessary duplication, but at times this stresses that an event is happening and, if one of the adverts is missed, the other could be seen in the same magazine. With every advertisement sent to a magazine, a story line and a listing accompanied it, so that the gig went into three parts of the paper: an advert in the ads section, a news item in the small news section and a line entry in the gig guide. It is also pertinent to talk to the features editor to find out whether the band you are promoting is heavily featured in any of the issues before your concert date. If this is so, an advert in that issue would be advantageous.

The cost of adverts vary in the national press. Regular advertisers receive large discounts, and it is often an advantage to have a regular spot as people, being creatures of habit, tend to look in the same place for particular adverts. Once you have momentum, do not stop as this tends to lose people and it will take a while to pick up speed again. Advertisements are costed in column centimetres and it is easy to get an idea of the size of a magazine's columns by buying a copy and looking in its ads section. This will also give you some idea of the style and attractiveness and, thus, the sort of advert you would like to place. With a magazine like *Kerrang*, the staff have a lot of expertise and it is often best to let them produce your advert and send a proof to you to view. People working on magazines can produce a better advert than the average promoter could ever hope to achieve, because they have been working in that medium for a long period of time and have lots of experience. They will usually have the band's logo to hand to reproduce on your advert. Some promoters, though, like to produce their own adverts and do a very good job. There is nothing more satisfying than seeing your own handiwork in print on an adverts page in a national magazine. Conversely, there is nothing more soul-destroying than looking for your home-produced advert and failing because it does not stand out on the page.

If you are putting on a show on a tour for which a major promoter, such as SFX or SJM, is promoting the rest of the dates, you will usually be asked if you want to buy in on the advertising. This means that you will pay a contribution to the company to appear on the tour adverts for the show. This is often a good ploy because it looks very professional and it gives you an identity with a major concert promoter.

Advertising in the local press often costs more than the national press or magazines, but it is sometimes more effective. Success in the local press is often difficult to quantify or qualify. In Milton Keynes, the local press comprises four different papers. From market research, paper one and three were read by people wishing to see a wide range of art and entertainment, but not a great deal by the youth concert attender. Papers two and four had a cult music page and were read avidly by the youth of the city, so it was better to advertise for indie and rock bands in paper two. Paper two also struggled for readership which meant that, for the same price of an eighth of a page advert in papers one and three, I could have a half page in paper two. But, paper one had a magazine featuring a weekly television pull-out. If I advertised in the pull-out, I was almost guaranteed a week's grace in the magazine rack with a chance of more people seeing my advert. All these factors had to be weighed up when deciding where to place my advertisement.

Size and position are also important and I have always felt that placing an advertisement on the right hand page (recto), away from the bottom corner where people place their fingers to turn the page, is about the best place. As the old adage goes, *big is beautiful*, and has far more impact than a small advert. Having said that, good design and layout of a smaller advert can make it stand out on a page more than larger ones. Logos, details, colour and how striking the advert is all go a long way to attracting clients to your venue. Any special offers must appear reasonably large on an advert as this is another attractive point. A venue offering tickets for one gig at a low price, if you also buy for another gig, is an enticing proposition to punters. Local and national newspapers offer discounts for placing a series of adverts, and it is a good idea to extend your advert to other papers in the same group in different areas, usually at a small marginal extra cost for much wider coverage.

Awareness is a key factor in promotion. Are all the places that should be aware of your promotion informed about it? To be able to answer this question the promoter should be aware of his target audience and audience size. If you do not know the size of the market, do not enter it. Once the target audience has been identified by market research, you can start to generate a ticket purchasing response. But, getting good ticket sales is more complicated than it first appears. Whether you consider what you are selling as a service or a product, the same steps apply:

- The genre of music must be established. This is important because each musical genre will be marketed differently

- Punters must be able to identify with their own specific genre. And so, the genre being targeted by the promoter must be clearly apparent.

- A promoter may put on a club night for a specific genre of music. In this case the punter will be exposed to the spefici genre and will identify the genre with this night, creating loyalty with repeat visits to the club.

- A promoter may use a covert system of identification, such as colour or design coding of different genres, so that uninitiated customers can follow their musical style through the colour or design of a logo or poster.

The concerts of such a genre may take place on a certain night of the week as a regular club event. The identification of genre also creates a target audience. For example, if you were to put on the band Paw, by classing them as grunge, you could extend the boundaries of their genre to include other styles of music from bands such as Therapy, Pearl Jam, Nirvana and Soundgarden. You would be able to target a wider audience through the genre, rather than just the band itself. With the cross categorisation by record companies of the indie and rock bands into sub-genres such as grunge, they have broadened the areas of musical taste which will, in turn, expand target audiences from cross-over genres, creating a larger audience base and generating potentially higher ticket sales.

This knowledge of genre is also important for other reasons. Punters may read a press release or other promotion about the band relating to their genre. They may be bombarded by constant reminders on posters and flyers that the band are playing at a local venue or club. This constant bombardment of images elevates the status of the band in the eyes of the punters, creating interest and awareness. In some cases it is just hype, but in other cases a band which gets rave reviews in newspapers can elevate its status in punters' minds so that they want see the band play and/or to buy the CD.

From market research carried out at concerts in Milton Keynes, the audience could be split into several distinct areas. This is shown in Figure 1:7, page 20.

- The first group are those *fans of the band* who come specifically to see the band play.

- The second group are those *genre-specific* fans who also come to see other bands within the genre.

- The third group are those who *attend anything at the venue* because they like music and are interested in the total experience.

- The fourth group are the *opportunists* who have never heard of the band but are curious to see what they are like.

- The fifth group are the *clubbers*, the friends and the drinkers who come because of the atmosphere or for other reasons extraneous to the band.

People attend for one or more of these reasons and the figure of each of the five categories attending changes from gig to gig.

Those punters who receive the total experience or who enjoy a concert greatly will pass on positive information to others about the venue or the band. This word-of-mouth pathway is very powerful and is one of the major marketing tools that builds a venue's reputation. It is difficult to get a venue described in print, so word of mouth up and down the country has increased attendances at many venues. But, this information can also work negatively. If a punter or group of punters

destroy the good reputation of a venue than it is to get a good reputation back again.

**Figure 4:2 Parts of the marketing machine
interrelating on a promotion**

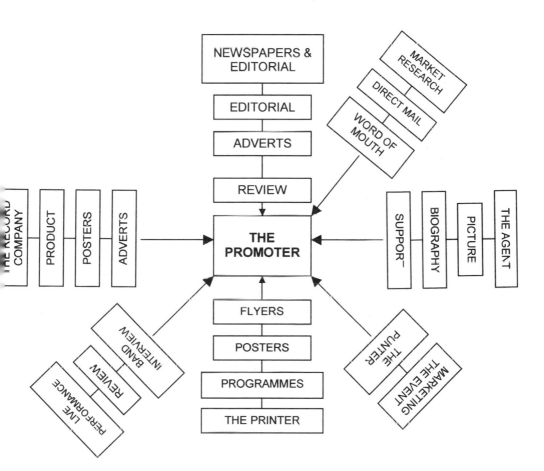

Two of the venues which created a big buzz in recent years are Rock City in Nottingham and Wulfrun Hall in Wolverhampton, both of which increased audiences by good management and the diversification of bands and genres. Word of mouth encourages others with a passing interest or an interest in that kind of music to attend a

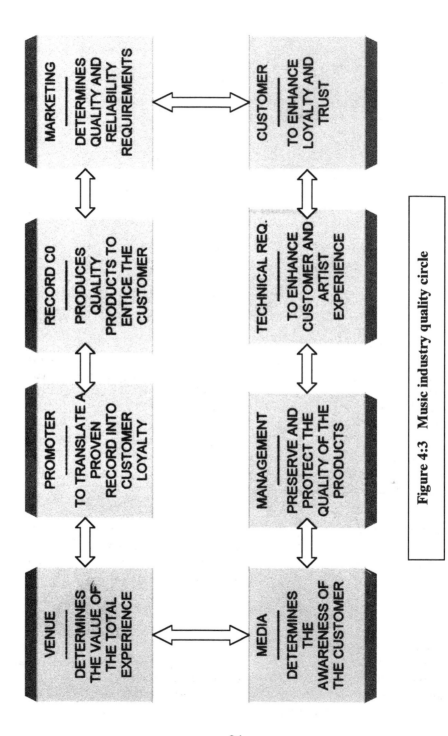

Figure 4:3   Music industry quality circle

concert or buy a record. I have bought music and attended concerts often on strong recommendations from other people. I have also booked bands on the strength of a clever agent's patter some of which have disappointed, but others have sold out. How the punter perceives quality within the industry is shown in Figure 4:3, page 94.

Competition for the punter's pound is another factor that determines ticket purchase for a concert. There is both active and passive competition for this.

Active competition includes other promotions taking place in the area as well as other styles and genres that might appeal to the punters whom you are trying to reach. The concert venue itself may militate against repeat visits. If the atmosphere is wrong, then the punter may not return. Cinema, theatre, discos, clubs, raves, the 'match' and other active pastimes may engage someone's interest more than the the desire to go to your venue on that night.

Passive competition is a little more confusing. A passive product or service is less easy to define. The increase in armchair-theatre technology has increased passive factors. A warm house with television and video at your fingertips, dial-a-pizza and other luxuries have increased the pulling power of the home. Watching a video with friends, staying in to watch the 'match' and spending time with the family have all become direct competition to going out in any form, whether it is to the pub or to watch a band at a venue. A new breed of entertainment, the home computer, has meant that children prefer to play games in front of a screen rather than play sport or make their own entertainment. The number of hours that children spend playing computer games is very high and has changed the face of leisure activities. There may be a change in direction when children and adults become bored with computers and virtual reality. The question is whether they will begin to crave once again the adventure of outdoor sports or entertainment in the form of music, art and dance.

Both macro- and micro-environmental factors can affect these decisions, which are out of our control. The weather can change an evening out to an evening in, when only dedicated fans will brave the elements to see a band. At my venue, I could always expect a lower audience on a wet night, unless the band were really famous. Another interesting fact is that the bar takings on a warm night were less because punters arrived later after going to a pub, perhaps with a garden or an interesting feature, before arriving at the venue.

Political and economic factors can also influence the way in which a promotion is viewed by the punter. A change in local or national government policy can alter someone's spending power. In a case like this, extras, such as attending a concert and eating out, are early casualties. Putting your prices up, say for tickets or beer, must be done carefully as too many small increases or one large increase can severely hamper customer loyalty and even, in some cases, change that loyalty to other venues.

Technological factors often effect the decision to visit a club or a gig. The use of video machines, big screen entertainment, virtual reality and other exciting innovations can attract people to the venue. New digital recognition cards for members are also a bonus and these are discussed later in this chapter.

To many punters the visit to the club is of paramount importance and they expect a total experience. If the club is marketed as a total experience, then it is up to you to fulfil this promise and to keep your customers. In the fluid world of music things change very quickly and you must make sure that you are moving with the times. To have a total experience and to keep the punter interested is quite easy and very financially rewarding, if done properly. Cut-price drinks at certain times of the night, quick cheap food, exciting bands, an excellent disco, friendly security, efficient staff and accessible merchandising all need to be carefully monitored. To create maximum impact and maximum profit as well as a caring, inventive service is an art. Once attained, it is even harder to keep the level high and not be complacent. Owing to competition, the punter expects a high standard. If this is not met, then the club will lose custom and even lose all its customers to another club or venue.

The difference between the night club or pub and the club venue is that the club venue has major bands which can outweigh other factors that draw people to other clubs. Many rock and indie clubs now stagger a night's entertainment to present a band until 10 p.m. and then a disco from 11 p.m. This offers the best of both worlds. But the clubs, in some cases, subsidise the band nights. This ploy can double profits but can also double the price of alcohol or soft drinks and the price of the ticket, lowering enjoyment of the evening.

Figure 4:4 The 'Marketing Machine'

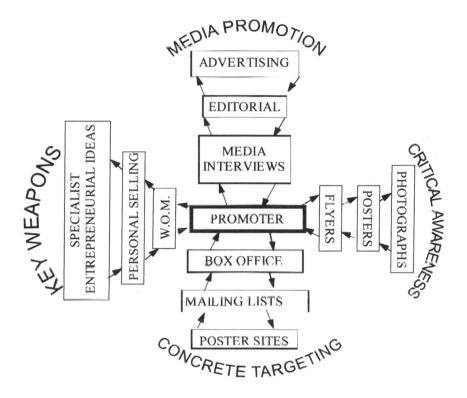

Note: W.O.M. = Word of Mouth

Once the target audience have been identified, they need to be made aware of the product or service. This can be done in many ways, one of which is the choice of communication channels. These can be personal, non-personal or both. A key factor in personal communication channels is word of mouth, a fierce and formidable weapon used to cement a band's reputation and standing in the world of music. Non-personal communication uses various media selected for their effectiveness. If you have knowledge, you have power. Once

97

the knowledge has been gathered, the promoter can put the marketing machine into gear. We have already looked at the press and now will look at other components of the marketing strategy. The timing of all marketing is crucial: if your campaign is too late, then you lose custom; if your campaign is too early, people lose interest. Timing is vitally important.

Earlier in this chapter we showed how the individual facets of the marketing strategy interrelate with the promoter (Figure 4:2, page 93). Figure 4:4, page 97 illustrates the concept of the marketing machine, showing four main areas:

- Critical awareness
- Key weapons
- Concrete targeting
- Media promotions.

We have dealt already in this chapter with media promotions in newspapers and periodicals/magazines. We now turn to concrete targeting with the use of the *mailing list*. Mailing lists can be assembled from market research at the venue. This can be done in many ways, but two of the most common are:

- Everyone entering the venue for a concert is logged against that particular genre of music. They are also logged against other genres that they show an interest in. The promoter or his representative questions punters as they arrive at the venue and notes down their answers on a pre-printed form.

- There is some form of membership, either free or paid for, whereby punters feel that they belong to part of a group. Today record companies and large promotion agents use this to good advantage. Reply-paid slips are given to each person attending a concert, inviting them to become a member of the band's fan club at no cost. These names and addresses are then used to mail awareness cards telling the punter of a forthcoming tour or CD, thus increasing sales of tickets and product to a core target audience. For music clubs, the membership idea generates a core of interested attenders who, if you give member discount, will come to almost any event.

From mailing lists and market research you can find out a number of important facts.

- Where do people come from? See Figure 1:3, page eight. From such information you can build up a map of the venue's catchment area for each type of genre.

- How far will people travel for local, regional or national bands? This information can save money from the marketing budget as you identify target areas, saving costs. Lists can be built up for press, poster sites, radio stations, other venues, music and record shops as well as ticket purchasers. Once the lists have been compiled and are in use, they must be monitored to see if they are cost effective; it may be that they are a waste of time and you are just throwing money away by sending them out. If you regularly repeat your programme of events, then you will be able to build up mailing lists for each. This will mean that, even before the tickets for an event go on sale, you could sell out by targeting the previous audiences for similar events.

Posters and leaflets are another valuable marketing tool. Both of these tools appear in the critical awareness sector of Figure 4:4, page 97, and are specifically used for awareness campaigns. Posters come in various sizes, shapes and colours, and these attributes can mean all the difference between success and failure, as shown in Chapter 3. If you are having posters or leaflets printed, you must make sure:

- You have the right number. Too many posters means that you waste money. Too few means that you will have either to pay extra for a reprint or will not have enough for your outlets.

- You have outlets for the posters and leaflets and are not going to waste them.

A key factor in marketing is public relations (PR). A good PR person can engage willing and able people to distribute and display leaflets and posters. It is no good constantly sending leaflets and posters to venues, shops, theatres and libraries if these are not being used to the best advantage. A telephone call or courtesy visit to these places can often ensure that posters and leaflets are regularly changed, distributed or displayed. This is because the exhibitors can put a face to the promoter, or they realise that the promoter is mobile and may at any time turn up to see if the posters are up or that the leaflets are out. You can motivate distributors and exhibitors by hidden benefits. You could include a pair of tickets a month for events that you are promoting, or you could give each successful distributor or exhibitor a pass which will admit them to any of your concerts free of charge. This would encourage them to continue giving out and displaying your leaflets and posters. To keep enthusiasm high, you may decide to hold a PR party every three months to which you invite press, radio and distribution and display contacts.

Figure 4:5 Jeff Waters from Annihilator
during a gig at the Woughton Centre. This gig sold the majority of its tickets through the National Advertising Campaign. © *Chris Kemp - photograph*

The promoter's PR and charm often pay off when dealing with difficult situations or when approaching record companies or agents. Tact and diplomacy are always advised, no matter how harassed or short of time you are. Remember the person at the end of the telephone is going to do you a favour. If you treat them well and efficiently, they will pack the jiffy bag with CDs, photographs and biographies. If you are sharp or nasty to them, they may just forget about it.

Fly posting is a different matter. In most cities and towns throughout Britain, fly posting is illegal. Many companies still do this lucrative and often dangerous activity. Gangs of rival fly posters are at war in many cities and some people have been badly mutilated or even shot. A small promoter does not have much choice in the matter. If the record company is handling the fly posting, it will happen anyway and large posters will appear all over the area. If it is left up to the venue, then it becomes more difficult and is very time consuming. The promoter may pay for a group of people to fly post for him. The only problem with this is that most local councils will prosecute the venue holding the gig if the posters are dedicated. There was a case in the mid 1990's when Norwich City Council fined Polydor for a number of fly posters around the city. It is more difficult to prosecute if the flyers and posters list all the venues at which a band is appearing. The fines for fly posting vary, but they are usually quite high. For instance, in Milton Keynes the fine is £1000 per flyer or poster. Sometimes councils are more lenient and they will either charge you for the time and effort of taking the flyers down, or will expect you to remove them at once to avoid the fine. I have often put the fly posters up with sticky tape. Although this does make it easier for rival gangs to tear them down it also makes the life of the street cleaner much easier.

If you consider the case against fly posting, you can see the councils' point of view. They are trying to provide a clean, attractive environment for people to live in and posters do spoil it, hence the hefty fines incurred. But, if you look again from the promoter's side, a prime city-centre posting site may greatly increase the numbers of punters and, thus, mean the difference between failure and success.

Word of mouth, rumour, competitions and discos all go hand in hand. Word of mouth is one of the most potent forms of spread for information about venues and artists – but how are rumours and information harnessed? Such things are part of the total experience at a disco or club night. At club night discos, the DJ is omnipotent. The word she spreads and the music she plays is readily assimilated by the audience, and transferred to others very quickly. This means is the best way to get information to such a captive audience. One of the ways to increase this audience at your venue easily is by holding competitions with music prizes. The prizes must be of a good standard or, as has been seen at many clubs, no one will enter the competition. The frequent use of freebies as prizes, ensures that punters keep coming back to the club. Once the punters are there, then the DJ can announce forthcoming events and elicit a quick response to new events.

When I promoted Iron Maiden, under the guise of the Holy Smokers, in Milton Keynes, a letter was sent to selected club members stating that it was a members-only gig with the date of ticket release on the letter. On the day of release all tickets were sold within 25 minutes. The disco, DJ and club night are an essential part of any evening, but punters' attraction to these rather than to bands is puzzling. As well as clubs, the armchair theatre is another alternative for the punter. As Paul Willis (1990) states,

> *Television has become a pervasive part of the cultural and symbolic life of young people. Surveys of young people's spare time show that, along with listening to the radio and playing records and tapes, watching television is the universal leisure activity ... going out doesn't necessarily mean no television. Pubs, for example, often have sets behind the bar, sometimes tuned to one of the new satellite-delivered stations like the rock music channel MTV.*

As music is listened to more and more, but live music becomes less and less important to our youth, we must compete with what has largely replaced it, TV , the game culture, lip sync, the bedroom studio and the DJ. If we look at recent writings, which suggest that the average youngster between the ages of eight and 16 spends 22 hours a week playing on computer and virtual reality games, then where is our future audience going to come from? Take a quick look at music and interest in it in society today. The advent of the computer game, the exciting rave and dance cultures, ambient music and its popular experiences, such as Megadog, as well as the state of the CD, art and entertainment industries at the moment, make the future for the promoter in rock, indie and pop look bleak. So why do we continue? I feel that one of the main reasons is that the cyclical motion of peaks and troughs in the music industry, which has such a history of constant flux and change, makes worry futile. Something is bound to happen that will again change people's perception of the live gig. Already the record companies and game wizards have begun to experiment with interactive CD (CDi) where the buyer can view a whole concert, take part in it, or even change passages of musical tracks himself. While the legal implications of this are mind boggling, the idea looks promising. Another idea that is developing, both in Europe and Japan, is the virtual artist. The virtual artist does not really exist but is totally manufactured. The personality, music, visual representation and publicity have been created by a company who feel that it is no longer important to have a live artist when everything can be created artificially.

The use of clubs as both feeders and alternatives to gigs gives the promoter a finger on the pulse of all that is going on in the industry. One element of the musical genres of the late 1990's which has enabled the promoter of live music to expand his audience concerns the way that punters dress. The uniform, once so important in each genre of music, has become less and less important. In both dance music and new punk, as well as indie and grunge, punters wear everyday clothes and not stylised uniforms suggesting one genre or another. This allows for inclusiveness, which does not limit central membership to the genre. Not only does this increase generic membership, but it enables anyone to be part of the genre. This expands audiences for events. You do not have to wear special clothes and you do not have to live an alternative lifestyle. All you have to have is an open mind and a love of music.

A spin-off from clubs is the membership scheme. Launching such a scheme in the club can, if couched in the right way, increase attendances at gigs. If you offer discounts to club members for live shows, it increases membership take up. If you charge a small administration fee for the membership card, this can cover the costs of setting up a scheme and a database, which will make the possibilities endless.

If the venue buys a software system to deal with memberships, then the software can be used in a number of ways. A membership card can be issued to all those entering the club and attending concerts. If the card includes a bar code and the cost of the card is, say, £3 for the year, then this is not out of the reach of most people. Each time a member enters the club, their bar code is scanned into the machine. The promoter can then build up a profile of the punters for clubs and various genres of music. You can pinpoint regular attenders and those who like a mixture of music, those who only come when one genre of band is on, those who only attend the club and those who only attend the gigs. You then have ready-made target mailing lists which can be selected in category order. All of these types of mailing list are useful because they stop blanket mailing, and targeted mailing reduces costs, in the long run making the difference between a loss and a profit.

There are many uses of *specials* in the music marketing business. Specials are areas that are unique that others have not thought to explore. Some specials, such as television, are too expensive for most promoters as the cost of an advertisement is extremely high. Radio, again, is a good medium and it is used in a very similar way to newspapers. One problem with radio is that, with the advent of new commercial stations, promoters are often turned down, even if willing to pay, because the type of advert does not fit in with policy. On many occasions, when I have dealt with radio, joint promotions have been turned down because the music does not figure in the top 40 and the radio station does not play it. The damage that this may do to their image far outweighs the amount of money that the joint promotion may cost. Some radio stations will continually back venues in their areas, proudly presenting their programme of events, and sending DJs along to introduce the bands. Other radio stations will either interview bands or ask record companies if they can record a portion of the concert to go out on the air at a later date. Giving radio stations the PR that you have extended to the newspapers is very easy; you just include them in all PR work.

The use of public transport to show your posters, including sides of buses or posters inside trains and buses is another part of your marketing strategy. Again you must look at how cost effective this is. If your posters contain a month's worth of gigs and the cost can be spread over that month, then it may be worthwhile to do this. Also, if the venue is on a bus route, Adshels (a type of bus shelter) or other means of paid poster advertising may be worthwhile. Giving out leaflets outside other venues is also advantageous as like-minded individuals gather there. Only do this on the day the band is playing and if the band is similar in genre or is playing at your venue later in the tour. It is pointless to blanket a venue or club with flyers that list bands which are a completely different the genre or have no association with the genres that the punters listen to. This will waste untold amounts of money, not only in staff costs and staff time but also in the preparation of the flyers and posters.

Another part of marketing strategy is *bumping up* the venue profile. Literature about the venue, including bands that have played there, comments from fans, and cuttings from various newspapers and magazines, should always be photocopied and kept. Send these cuttings to the local papers whenever you can. For example, on the tenth-year anniversary of a venue, the local paper may do a short piece with a photograph of you or the venue; this is all good publicity. It is also worth letting a local photographer into the venue free, in return for photographs of gigs, as these also become useful. Papers often print action-packed stories with pictures from an event. All publicity is good publicity – if there is a story in it, send it to the papers.

It is always a good idea to look after the national press, as they tend to write more favourably of a venue that gives good hospitality. A prime example of this was a boxing match at my venue in 1992 where Joe Bugner's son was having his first professional fight. We let the press run special telephone lines through the walls into the hall to transfer film of the fight to their respective press offices. We also created dark rooms, press rooms and various other areas especially for them. The press enjoyed it and thanked us for our hospitality. Bands often go back to venues that have either treated or promoted them well to record live CDs. This happened on several occasions at my venue with Radio One and bands like Jagged Edge and Thousand Yard Stare.

The use of record shops to push bands and venues is a good choice. The record shop can also be used for other promotional activities – signings, a ticket outlet, a place to sell the band through posters, flyers and word of mouth. You can benefit from this flexibility and the fact that the most popular record shop is the place where punters congregate on a Saturday to hear music, to buy tickets and to meet friends. Find out the most popular record shops and use them to your own advantage. Knowing the proprietor of the record shop also has hidden advantages. One of these is that, when an agent offers you a band, you can check with record shops in your catchment area how the band is selling. Another useful idea is to establish contact with the record label and to look at the style and amount of publicity bands usually receive from that label. As you do this, you are adding to the knowledge needed for your publicity and marketing strategy. This knowledge is invaluable and the more you have the better position you are in to promote.

Figure 4:6   A member of Joan Armatrading's Band (bassist)
on stage at the Woughton Centre, Milton Keynes. This gig sold
out well in advance because of a joint promotion with Chiltern
Radio Network. © *Chris Kemp – photograph.*

By selling tickets in various agencies around your catchment area, you can pinpoint the best place to have other agencies. For example, if agent A is outselling agents B, C and D by four times, then perhaps another agency near to A would be an advantage. It also helps with the allocation of tickets so that the ticket books for reconciliation can be kept clear and you know how many tickets to give to each agent or ticket office.

Another advantage of knowing the owner of the record shop is that you can use the shop for a signing. The signing is a great vehicle for PR. Many tickets for events are sold on the day because members of a band are signing copies of their new CD. People will often turn out in large numbers to get CDs signed. Remember, if there is a queue outside a shop, it draws people out of curiosity. Once you have them in the shop, you have the chance to promote the gig and to sell tickets to them. The signing has a double advantage, to both the shop owner and the promoter. Sometimes the owner will have a signing by a band that is not appearing on stage. This still has a spin off because the shop then has a captive audience to which you can sell your product. Always use the shop to full advantage with large colourful posters and notices telling the customers that tickets are sold in the shop for your gigs. You can even offer discounts for bulk buying, etc.

Producing an entrepreneurial spirit

You need to have fresh ideas for as many of your marketing campaigns as possible. If you, as the promoter or marketing manager, produce the same promotional tools for each event, both the public and the promoters or marketers become tired more quickly. You need to keep abreast of new fashions, products and people in order to produce new and exciting ideas. Always involve your staff in think-tanks as some of the most unlikely people come up with the best and most original ideas. One of the greatest examples of the past ten years came from the marketing manager of the Brixton Academy. In conversation with this astute and talented man, I was impressed by his enthusiasm for his job, and I will always remember my meeting with him for this reason. A new club was to start at the Academy and a new angle was needed to promote it. The idea was to print thousands of flyers on tissue paper with the name of the club on them. These flyers were then wrapped around lemons bought in the markets of London. A team of people then gave the lemons to people they thought were likely to come to the club. It was such a successful campaign that many people were turned away from the doors.

There are individuals around who are natural marketers, but most people entering the profession will need training of some sort. Without training, the individual is vulnerable when things begin to go wrong. Training is in two forms:

- Training courses, where the participant learns new ideas and shares ideas with others, thus gaining new marketing techniques and hearing others evaluate theirs.

- Hands-on, where an experienced professional works with the trainee on the job, helping them to increase their knowledge of both tried and tested methods and of new systems and ideas.

A combination of these two processes seems to be the best for most people.

There are many ways to monitor success in marketing – and this is not always by your ticket sales. Many of the promotions you put on will fail and others will be complete successes without marketing. As Kotler states, *'the aim of marketing is to make selling superfluous'*. (Kotler, 1972) A number of venues around the country have managed to do this. They have been so successful with their marketing campaigns that every event sells out and they do not really have to market anymore. But, they still do as they feel that they cannot afford to become complacent. It is an art to gauge the right amount of marketing and when to use new marketing techniques. It takes years of trial and error and, because of the very nature of the business, a dead certainty is often the exact opposite. This sends the marketers into a panic wondering what went wrong, where it when wrong and why it went wrong. There are no hard and fast rules for marketing only that you need to do as much marketing as possible as cost effectively as possible. There are key areas for the marketing entrepreneur to be aware of. They include:

- How much the record company is marketing the product.

- How much the management company, promotion company and the press are behind the band.

Once you have established these, you can set out your own campaign. To be able to target effectively, you must have an exciting package to send out to your prospective market which will encourage them to come to you to try the product or service that you are providing.

Whoever is in charge of your marketing must be made to feel part of the team and must be given responsibility. They must be able to gain as much first-hand knowledge of the acts as possible so that they have a chance to come up with ideas that might best suit each act. For example, acquiring a CD for the marketer may increase their feel of the music and, thus, their perceptions of the type of targets and markets likely to be interested in such artists. From this they can produce a plan of action.

Radio promotion

In 1989 James Delanoy joined Chiltern Radio from Local Government. James had organised events but had not become directly involved in music. Initially he set up links with Cambridge Corn Exchange and Chiltern Radio began publicising their events. The first national promoter with which Chiltern Radio had dealings was MCP; their first two shows were Ian McCulloch and The Primitives. Chiltern's biggest coup was to be part of the Milton Keynes Bowl promotions. Their first big show at the Bowl was Bon Jovi in 1989.

Chiltern Radio offer the promoter a marketing service. As a general rule, before Chiltern Radio will get involved, the band must be a play-listed artist. There have been some exceptions, such as Nigel Kennedy, where the popularity of the artist has been the key criterion for the radio station to market the artist. Although Chiltern Radio do not play classical music, they felt that their audience would be interested in Nigel.

Chiltern Radio operate with set advertising rates. A promoter has an advertising budget for each venue and it would be impossible for him to obtain good coverage for his show at commercial advertising rates. Chiltern Radio offer a considerable increase in air time at a reduced fee in return for tickets to give away to listeners. This is because of the inherent benefits to both the promoter and the radio station.

The radio station represents the show to its listeners and the listeners associate the show with the radio station. Chiltern get a banner at the event, a DJ from the network compères the show and the radio station is credited on all the publicity. It is a good profile-raising exercise. James knows this because, when the shows go wrong, the first place people complain is to the radio station. Fortunately, there is not usually a problem, but there are a couple of classic examples where things have gone wrong for Chiltern Radio on the new network station in Bristol.

- Salt 'n' Pepa wanted to get a similar identity for this station in the West Country as Chiltern had in the four counties of Bedfordshire, Buckinghamshire, Cambridgeshire and Northamptonshire. The band were to play on *Top of the Pops* that night and then to get a helicopter to the show in Bristol. The band did not make it and the show had to be cancelled.

- Colour Me Badd was also promoted by this station. The band appeared for 25 minutes and did not appear back on the stage.

The problem with these two shows was that the audience blamed the radio station and not the promoter, and this gave Chiltern Radio a bad identity. The switchboards were jammed with complaints and the new station did not get off to a very good start. On 99 per cent of occasions, the concept of the profile and the identity attached to it is worthwhile for Chiltern. On the occasions that it does not work, it can be a very bitter experience.

Chiltern Radio can make quite a lot of money out of the shows it advertises. The company has done research in Cambridge and Kettering. The credit card booking numbers for the Cambridge Corn Exchange and the Kettering Arena show that the majority of the audience are from the Chiltern Radio broadcast area. The deal on Simply Red was to give the promoter, MCP, a week's free coverage for 50 pairs of tickets to give away to listeners. The two shows sold out within a week. It worked well. The radio station ran a campaign which stated, *You haven't got your Simply Red tickets yet? Chiltern Radio has. Tune in on Saturday.*

This sort of hard marketing has an effect. The station had hundreds of people telephoning to ask if it was giving away Simply Red tickets.

There was an increase in listenership because Chiltern Radio had something that everyone wanted.

Chiltern Radio also handles comedy. There are not as many new bands coming through as in the late eighties so the radio station has had to diversify a little. The Gold stations deal with the likes of Freddie and the Dreamers and Gerry and the Pacemakers. Chiltern Radio receives a lot of offers to co-promote bands on the Gold stations.

New ideas in commonsense

Marketing is really commonsense, but there are still many promoters who fail to use it. They still take on bands purely on an agent's word, without consulting people with marketing knowledge or other agencies. Sometimes there are advantages in taking on an agent's lesser bands. For instance, you may be given the chance to also promote some of the agent's major bands. It is pointless to continually promote bands that lose money; in the long run this will damage both your pocket and your reputation. It also damages the credibility of the agent. The promoter needs a clear head. It is not always a good plan to go by what different people say. It is your money, your reputation and your decision, so use commonsense and make your decision carefully.

It can be seen that marketing strategy and its components are vitally important. The permutations used in your particular strategy must be finely honed until they give you the best possible results. This is time consuming, but important to stick at the task until it is finished. Once the system is running efficiently, you will wonder how you managed without it.

The section on radio promotion is printed with the kind permission of James Delanoy now an independent promotions manager.

Conclusion

It can be seen that marketing is the key element in attracting punters to a concert. Marketing is not just about advertising, but also includes PR, media development and new initiatives. Although marketing is important in attracting punters to a show, an event cannot take place without a venue. The next chapter reviews venue management.

Chapter 5

Venue Management

Introduction

Good venue management is vital to the success of the promotion for both the internal and external customer. The choice of venue is often determined by the way it is managed or even by the personality of the manager. The relationship between the promoter and the venue is sometimes tenuous, and only exists because of the mutual benefit to them both. In other cases, this symbiotic relationship has been brought about through many years of friendship between the promoter and the venue manager. There are also cases where the promoter *is* the venue manager, and has full control over both management and promotion. Here the promoter/venue manager can offer packages to agents that a promoter buying into a venue cannot match. An example of this is the inclusion of special hospitality arrangements, where in-house catering within the complex restaurant will be offered, rather than buying in outside caterers. The costs of catering could be swallowed up in the restaurant budget, rather than the promotions budget.

A badly-managed venue often leads to problems at the event; these are varied, and range from poor venue preparation, to staff shortages. Although these are not the responsibility of the promoter, such problems can cause a strain on the event and make for a worrying evening for the promoter. Good management practice always makes the promoter confident in the management structure and usually leads to re-booking of the venue. The promoter is the first line of contact with an artist and their entourage. If the venue manager makes mistakes or fails to prepare for the event properly, this reflects badly on the promoter, because of the relationship between the promoter and the artist. The artist and their entourage are not bothered about whose

113

fault it is, they want the problem to be solved immediately, so that they can proceed with setting up, and the 'get in' without undue worry.

Size and style of the venue

The style of a venue is very important as artists always like to work in a 'music space'. Many venues today are sports centres, or dingy pubs which, although having some positive points, may have many more negative ones which include poor acoustics, cold rooms, corporate management, lack of interest, poor marketing, lack of hospitality and poor controls. The artist and their entourage like to feel 'at home' in a venue, so that they can give a great performance in the space provided. I have seen artists retire to their crew bus from a sports hall with glum looks and weary heads. A venue that is serious about live music has no excuses for not trying to overcome problems. Poor acoustics are sometimes unavoidable. In a sports hall, although curtain tracking and curtains may be expensive, the longevity of a promoter's' live' programme could depend upon it. £5000 spent could be a great investment for the future. An artist entering a sports hall, and seeing that the venue has provided a covering to combat poor acoustics will feel much more at ease; more so than with a venue that puts profit first, before service to both the internal and external customers. One major acoustic problem which occurs in such halls is, either all the walls are brick or metal, or all the walls are curtained. A fully brick or metal-walled building has problems with the reflection of the sound waves from hard surfaces, causing the sound to 'bounce' around the room and making it difficult for the audience to hear anything clearly. The problem with a fully curtained auditorium is that it absorbs sound. This is especially hard for vocalists as they have to push their vocal chords to the limit to create the right sounds. This causes voice strain or laryngitis which can cause tours to be cancelled. The best possible auditorium for a concert is one which is acoustically baffled, where there are equal amounts of reflection and absorption, so that a good sound can be created.

There is no excuse for cold rooms; the majority of venues have heating which should be used to provide a comfortable temperature. The major problems with cold rooms are:

114

- The artists feel cold, and this can affect their performance as well as their impression of the venue. It is possible that on the next tour they will refuse to return.

- The musical instruments, and even voices go out of tune. Guitars tuned in a cold room will immediately go out of tune when played on a warm stage. The manager who says he does not know how to work the heating should not be managing the venue, as all areas of the venue's functionality should be under his jurisdiction.

Corporate management can have different objectives, and make a gig difficult to promote and produce. Many leisure centres and venues have such a system, run from a County Hall or Council Office, and the staff on site may have no control over certain external factors. For instance, if the artist's tour manager complains about the size of the P.A., the room in which the concert will take place, or even about the lack of hospitality, the venue manager will quite often not be the person responsible for changes that may have occurred; it may be someone twenty miles away at home who has to be contacted to change the decision. This causes problems, especially at weekends when Council Offices are closed. It is one of the reasons why new contracts between agents and promoters state that someone able to make 'executive' decisions must be on site at all times.

Lack of interest and lack of marketing go hand in hand. A venue which pays only 'lip service' to music usually relies on the promoter to do all the marketing for the event, but seems to reap the benefits. It is difficult to change this sort of management, and it is usually best to steer clear of these venues, even if it means a drop in capacity.

There is no excuse for not providing the artist's rider. If the promoter takes them down to the 'bare bones' they will see that it costs very little to provide everything. It is often better to supply everything on most riders[1], than to have a disgruntled artist and tour manager causing problems for the rest of the gig. Other items put on the list for effect

---

[1] A rider is an addendum to a contract stipulating hospitality, lighting and sound requirements.

can often be ignored and, if you think that an artist is going over the top with a rider, then contact the agent or the tour manager, and he will advise you accordingly.

The tour manager will always be in the best position to check through a rider. Recently, with the artist Dream Theatre, I found the rider I had been sent was excessive. On contacting the tour manager I found that the rider sent was one for an American tour the year before and the rider had changed. It is always best for the promoter to fax any changes to the rider directly to the agent, and then to let him deal with it. Always keep transmissions and their confirmation slips, as they can prove that a fax was definitely sent on the date at the time given. Looking at the rider, it often seems a great deal to provide but, when you cost it out, it is not so much at all. The amount of work needed to provide the artist with a good meal and drinks is not as much as it would first appear. The trouble that can be caused by skimping on the rider is really not worth it.

The promoter sometimes pays the venue manager to provide the hospitality through the venue's in-house catering. A price per head is negotiated and the venue manager offers a series of menus with varying prices. The promoter chooses a menu and sends it to the artist. If the menu is accepted, the deal will be struck with the venue manager. It is often better for the promoter to use in-house catering as it lifts a big burden off his shoulders. I can remember three nightmare years when my assistant Jayne and I prepared all the food for the artists in either the school kitchen, or in the staff room microwave!. This caused us much grief as we also had to serve it out, and to take the abuse if it was not up to standard. It was cheap to do, but exhausting and caused many problems with artists. Providing a better service through the venue caterers was a blessing. I will never forget the day when Jayne and I had spent five hours preparing food for an American band, but they refused to eat it and insisted on us paying for them to eat out. The show was nearly cancelled but, in the end, I had to agree to their demands. The crew ate the left-over food, so it was not wasted.

The atmosphere of the venue is important. Many larger-named artists remember well the small venues that they enjoyed playing in their early days and request to play the venue as a warm up later in their career. The best venues always create some kind of ambience which is conducive to drinking, conversation and music, mixing these three liberally. They are venues that people attend because they feel that they 'belong', not only to the venue, but also to the group of people with whom they are sharing the experience. These venues are always well attended and a great many people go, not just for the artist, but also for those intangible factors that enhance the total experience. If you can create an extended living room in a venue, people will be comfortable and inclined to return.

Choice of venue

Access to a venue matters greatly, not only for the punter but also for the artist and tour crew. It is not only its location, but also its site aspects that are important.

A venue needs easy access for the artist and crew; the nearer the loading bay is to the truck parking, the easier the 'get in' is. The 'get in' area for the equipment should, if possible, be on the ground floor, without stairs. The access should be close to a quiet area where the vans and trucks can be parked with reasonable ease, and, most importantly, an area which is safe and secure. Ramps should be supplied if the access is from the floor to the stage. In Derby Playhouse, the access is straight onto a ground level; the hydraulic stage is then elevated, once the P.A. and lighting towers have been rigged. In some venues lifts are installed if the concert room is on an upper floor. The more difficult the 'get in', the more crew should be employed by the venue management. Some artists will refuse to play venues with stairs and prefer those with an easy, level 'get in'.

It is the venue manager's job, in conjunction with the promoter, to make sure that the building is ready to receive the artist. The venue manager, and the promoter should enter into a dialogue as soon as the contract is signed, detailing what the artist requires. Early dialogue can relieve all sorts of concerns on either side, and it should never be left to the last minute to tell an artist that certain requirements cannot be provided.

The artist may require anything, from two days before the show to 30 minutes before doors open, for set up.

Access by road, rail, and air in some cases, is very important for the artist, their entourage and the punters. You will need easy access and parking facilities for HGV 'Tractor' units and their 40 tonne trailers and also for double decker tour buses.

A venue with bus and train 'links' with cities that stop running before the end of the concert, puts barriers up between the audience and the venue. It is the promoter's 'mission' to breakdown as many of these barriers as possible, thus increasing the size of the audience.

The more 'barriers' that the venue introduces between itself and its audience, the smaller the audience it will attract. There are two types of 'barriers'– active and passive. *Active* barriers are those that are consciously put up against those people wanting to attend the gig. *Passive* barriers are those that subconsciously affect attendance at a concert. These active and passive barriers are split into several areas: physical, sociological, and psychological. Physical barriers include the ticket price, parking, transport, facilities for the disabled, site access, age access and clothing discrimination.

Socio-psychological barriers include the banning of certain groups of people, over emphasis on discrimination against drugs and under-age drinking, as well as confiscating fashion accessories. The attitude of unprofessional door supervisors / security stewards who hound groups of people because of their 'tendencies', has caused many punters to stay at home rather than to frequent many of the more "paranoid" venues. Passive barriers include other technological factors, such as television and radio, leisure activities, and the increase in the use of the armchair theatre. Such competition to the 'live' venue has led to a decrease in live music audiences over the last ten years.

Of interest to anyone travelling to a concert by car is the ease of parking and access to the venue. At some venues parking is very limited and even non-existent. If punters have to walk a long distance to a venue, they may think twice about attending again. Those punters with cars who travel to venues far and wide are usually in the 25-40 year old age bracket and they have the most 'disposable' income. To put up barriers to these people is not in the interest of the venue management or the promoter as it will cut down the concert's income considerably.

People with disabilities also need access. The promoter who caters for them at all his concerts, not only offers a full service to his audience, but is seen by the authorities to have an effective equal opportunities policy. Any venue manager looking at facilities for people with disabilities should invite them to the venue to give their recommendations/observations on the infrastructure and arrangements and their suitability. The Pitz in Milton Keynes had a member of the public with a disability on the management team. I spent many hours with this person discussing alterations to the facility to make it more user friendly for people in wheelchairs, and for those who were deaf and/or blind. The recommendations, and developments from these meetings, included automatic doors, secure plywood sheets in all the door mat wells, greater access to the lift facilities in the building, a hearing induction loop, and Braille cards on doors and walls. It paid dividends as the number of people with disabilities, especially those in wheelchairs, attending concerts increased. But, there is no point in having facilities for people with disabilities at a venue if you do not inform them that the facilities are there. All information about the club had a logo showing that we catered for people with disabilities.

The prestige of the venue often affects whether an artist will choose to play it. The promoter must look at the overall potential of the venue to exploit it as much as possible. In the 1970s, and 1980s the Marquee Club in London was the place where all artists wanted to play, it had such a great reputation and 'anyone who was anyone', played there. In the 1990's the emphasis changed slightly with venues like Camden Underworld, Brixton Academy, and Nottingham Rock City becoming some of the best venues in the country. In the 21st century, venues like the Astoria 1 and 2, The Forum, and Ilford Island moved to the forefront of a developing music scene. This change has been brought about by ceaseless work from the promoters of these clubs, raising the reputation of the venues through constant 'limelight' and marketing.

One of the main ingredients in this success is the 'atmosphere' created at the venues. They are laid back, non- violent, and very well run.

Another factor often important in the choosing of a venue concerns what other facilities are available. In an interview, Nick Peel from MPI (Miracle Prestige International) stated that a lot of American artists liked to play the Pitz in Milton Keynes because the venue has pool tables, a swimming pool and game consoles. Rather than getting bored, kicking their heels around the venue and on their bus, they were able to come inside and enjoy themselves. Another venue I know has a bowling alley, which again helps to relieve the boredom of waiting for the show. Good dressing rooms and food facilities are important. The word that artists use for bad facilities is a *toilet*: *"you should have seen the toilet we played last night"* refers to the state of the venue and its facilities. If you manage or promote at a *toilet* then you will not get good artists for long because they will stipulate that they will not play there again. A coat of paint, a few comfortable chairs and a television do not cost much, but make the world of difference If the artists are treated well, then they do not defecate in the showers after a gig, nor do they fill the piano up with food – as I found on two occasions when my 'service' was not what it should have been!.

A promoter may choose one venue over another because of staff commitment. When working with David Walker-Collins at the Roadmender in Northampton, I entered the venue to start preparations for the gig and found that he had already organised everything; I spent the rest of the day kicking my heels. This type of service is very pleasant when received, and it makes the promoter want to use the venue again because it makes life so much easier.

The management, and administration of the venue is also important. You need to be able to trust the management, and their word, at all times. If a promoter does not have faith in the venue manager's word, the relationship between them is tenuous.

The cost of the venue is another consideration when choosing where to promote a concert. This cost varies considerably from venue to venue as it is related to the service provided. Some venues charge for every single item that is required, whilst others charge an overall fee for the use of the whole venue and all its facilities. There is, of course, room for negotiation, and the best negotiating tool is the bar profit. The promoter does not see any of the bar profit, and, if the venue manager is charging an exorbitant price for the venue and is also taking the bar profit, then it would be wise to threaten to pull out. The venue manager will know that he cannot afford to let this happen.

The cost of the venue is a concern that is central to the everyday running of the promoter's business. Looking from another angle, the charge made to the promoter by the venue manager also affects how the venue's budgets work. If the venue cost is too expensive it has two consequences:

- Punters suffer because the ticket price has to be increased to cover the overheads, fixed costs, and promoter's profit.

- It makes the promoter think twice about promoting further acts at the venue.

The venue manager tries to make hiring the venue economically viable. The actual costs of the venue include staff time, administration, electricity, gas, and the number of rooms hired. There are other costs, such as a contribution towards publicity, crew or an electrician. If the cost of the package is more than the hire fee, then the deal will not be viable to the venue manager. But, the venue manager can call on other extraneous income that is not available to the promoter. Bar takings, cloakroom income, food and vending are all spin offs. It may be that the venue manager feels that the promotion is sufficiently large to offer a cut-price deal to the promoter for the following reasons.

- Having the artist at the venue will increase the venue's reputation, and the promoter may put more of this type of artist into the venue.

- If the venue opens on that night and the manager has to pay the staff anyway, he may lose more money by not having an event or by having a sub-standard event.

- The extra profit from food, ticket commission and bar takings may far outweigh the loss on the deal with the promoter.

For these three reasons the promotion may go ahead. In some pubs and clubs the hire of the venue is free if a certain size of audience is guaranteed; but, in others, support artists are still asked to contribute to the P.A. and publicity to play at the venue.

The calculation of the venue hire fee can be complicated. It is sometimes calculated on the following basis; a percentage per head, an *ad hoc* calculation, a carefully costed and worked out sum, or even the total running costs for the evening, plus 25 per cent, after the promoter's costs are covered. Whichever way it is calculated, it has to be settled between the venue manager and the promoter. Compromises are often made, even after the gig, because it is usually in the interests of the two parties concerned to stay on a sound footing. It may be that a low hire fee is charged but a high percentage is guaranteed to the venue for tickets sold from their box office. This is a good ploy as it makes the venue try harder to sell the tickets for the gig; the more sold by the box office, the higher the income the venue will accrue.

Negotiating the finer details

In many cases, the agreement between a venue and a promoter is done by a handshake, and no agreement is committed to paper other than fax confirmations stating that there is an agreement. In other cases, a long legal document has to be drawn up detailing the actions of both the lessor and the lessee, or the licenser and the licensee.

The basic clauses in both agreements are the same. They detail the licence period and the designated hours of the period to be used. Once these have been decided, the hire charge of the premises, if any, is stipulated. The exact style of the event has to be noted, for example, live music, mime, comedy, theatre, dance, and the facilities to be used are also stated.

The Indoor Public Entertainments licence standard conditions and any special ones, e.g., lasers, indoor pyrotechnics, should be referred to, and the implications considered carefully. They are designed to protect the health, safety, and welfare of both the artist(s) and the punter. Any breach of these may have a very serious outcome for the venue, and the management team, particularly the named licensee(s). A successful prosecution by the local authority could result, not only in a substantial fine/ imprisonment, but also the revocation of the licence, ending in a closed-down venue and catastrophic P.R.

There then appears both a licenser and a licensee undertaking, which detail such concepts as:

not to do any matter or thing which would or might constitute a breach of any statutory requirement affecting the Premises or which would or might vitiate in whole or in part any insurance effected in respect of the premises from time to time.

Excerpt from the rider for Annihilator, a Canadian thrash metal artist.

The basic requirements of these undertakings are that neither the promoter nor the venue manager will abuse their position. A number of general points are then stated, usually including a 'get out' clause for the licensee if the events are not going very well, which indirectly is usually a 'get out' clause for the licenser.

I must stress here that, in my opinion, it is always best to get everything down in writing and signed by both parties. If anything does go wrong and an injury or death were caused through negligence, if nothing has been committed to paper, the blame for the incident may be shifted from one party to another.

Once the agreement has been drawn up, or the word-of-mouth contract, shaken upon; then the finer details of the venue are discussed. You, as the promoter, need to make sure that you have written down everything that the venue will provide and everything that you will provide. Once this is typed and signed, you are covered for any eventuality at the venue. There is nothing worse on the day of an event than arriving at the venue to find that there is no crew or security as the venue manager thought that you were providing them and vice versa. Rushing around at the last minute is not only stressful but a waste of valuable time and energy.

Many of the details in the contract should be given to the venue manager so that she has an itinerary of how the day will proceed and how much she and her staff are involved. Staff time, and administration are crucial to the venue manager and, if your event is taking place in a multi-purpose building, the staff may be required to do more than one job at a time, for instance, setting up five-a-side football or badminton courts as well as working at the venue. The promoter must always be aware of the pressure on venue staff.

Stage and box-office management

From the moment that a concert is confirmed, the wheels of the box office machine have to swing into motion. Tickets have to be designed, ordered, and manifest forms provided. Tills have to be programmed and each box office in the promoter's network has to be primed with the exact details of the event. Communications here must be clear and precise. It is usually best to hold a box office briefing to make sure that all staff are aware of the system being used for the concert.

Firstly, the details are passed on to the staff. The till code book is updated and the ticket books have the till codes for the various price permutations written on the cover. The tickets are normally numbered. The ticket books should be checked for any mistakes in details, or numbers, that the numbers run concurrently, and that all the books are for the same concert. All staff should be primed on credit card bookings and a limit made on the send-out date for those credit card bookings made close to the date of the show. Tickets for bookings made after that date will have to be picked up on the night of the event. A file should be set up for credit card bookers who wish to pick up their tickets on the night and a file made ready for ticket returns. It is usually stipulated that anyone wishing to return their tickets cannot have them re-sold by the box office until all the other tickets for that show have been sold. A record of each credit card ticket sold should be kept in a file at hand in case tickets are lost in the post.

When tickets are sent out to ticket agents, a record of the tickets and their numbers should be kept. This record should be signed, and dated, by both the giver and the receiver. If this is not done, there is no record of the transaction taking place and the receiver could keep all monies taken from the ticket sales as the box office manager would have no evidence that the tickets were ever given to the ticket agent. It is permissible at times for the ticket agent to issue a voucher which details the amount paid and the tickets purchased. The details are relayed to the venue, or main box office, and the tickets bought are taken off sale and kept until the voucher is presented on the night of the concert. Many box offices are computerised, some have a Tickets.Com system which prints tickets as they are sold. If the seats are numbered and the punter has a specific seat, then the computer, once it has sold such a seat, erases it from the computer selling programme. Although the Tickets.Com system is not fault free, it has many advantages over a manual box office system and is clean and efficient. Its secondary advantage is that, if the venues linked with one box office are all on the same system, the box office can sell tickets on its own computer for all the venues on that system. Another advantage of this network is that, if a promoter's ticket outlets are on the same system as the venue, the reconciliation on the night of a concert can be a lot quicker and easier.

Stage management has always been a 'grey' area in promotion and venue management The stage manager of a concert means different things to different people. From the tour manager's viewpoint, the stage manager is the person who is responsible for the technical side of the stage, which entails ensuring that all the technicians and crew set up and produce the equipment exactly to the proficient technical specifications laid down by the artist. From the venue manager's point of view, the stage manager is the person who organises the show, gets the artist(s) on and off stage at the right time and who deals with any problems of the venue. To the promoter, the stage manager is the person who masterminds the show, ensures the safety of the crowd, ensures that the security and crew are in the right place at the right time and liaises with the tour manager on any problems which might occur before, during or after the performance. There are still many promoters who feel that their job is over once they have counted the money and the artist is on stage. After show care matters, and those managers and promoters who have experienced equipment and belongings going missing will know how important it is.

Good stage management results from good planning because, unless someone is stipulated as stage manager before the event, the job of control becomes very difficult. It is a good idea for the venue manager to nominate someone as stage manager. This person may be the tour manager, a representative of the venue manager, or the promoter or his representative. Once the stage manager has been appointed, and a point of contact made, all enquiries appertaining to stage management can be dealt with by that one person. The liaison is then between the stage manager, technicians, tour manager, crew, artist's manager, venue manager, and the promoter. As everything is channelled through one person, the whole idea of stage management becomes easier. If only one person is telling the artist that they need to go on stage, this improves relationships between all parties, and stops any individual arguments, and/or misinformed orders. The stage manager is then the sole user of signals and the sole controller of the event through others' commands.

Conclusion

There are many aspects to the management of a venue, but the most important is the safety of the audience and the performers. The next chapter deals with health and safety issues.

Chapter 6

Health and Safety

Licenses and insurance

The safety aspects of promoting concerts, particularly in the UK now, are the single most important factor for a wide variety of reasons, financial, legal and ethical. Everyone involved in the business should have regard for the rules, regulations, and 'Best Practice' manuals which cover these areas in great detail. Licenses and insurance are given only a brief mention here, but are included because of their importance.

Without the relevant licenses and insurances, a show should not take place, for legal reasons. A building, or outside area, i.e., 'the premises' needs a Public Entertainments Licence (PEL) before a public gig can be staged. An application for a PEL has to be sent to the local authority, with copies to the Area Commander of Police and the Chief Fire Officer. Safety Certificates for the electrical /gas installations, and drapes/scrims will be required. Visits may be undertaken by local authority and emergency services staff, depending on whether it is a new application or a renewal. Other influencing factors will be opening hours, audience size / profile, special effects and any relevant 'history'. The Local Authority Officer, and the Fire Officer are concerned with the safety of the building and its occupants. They will focus on a safe means of escape in an emergency evacuation, the size/number of fire doors and the adequacy / maintenance of the fire fighting appliances. The standard of the public sanitary accommodation is becoming increasingly important as the public's expectations increase – refer to BS 6465 Part 1 Code of Practice for the scale of provision, selection and installation of sanitary appliances.

Providing there are no adverse observations / objections from the authorities or local residents, then the licence should be granted, although there may be local practices / protocols to consider beforehand. Information on these can be obtained by 'networking' with the relevant 'movers and shakers', i.e., Licensing Officers of the Local Authority and the Police as well as with the Fire Safety Officer.

Figure 6:1 A fire point backstage at the Metallica Concert, Milton Keynes Bowl © *Chris Kemp, photograph*

Fire Safety is a complex subject, i.e., the size and number of the fire doors will ultimately determine how many people will be allowed into the building. Each properly-constructed, single fire door exit width (525mm) will accommodate 40 people per minute; the evacuation time of the building will vary, depending on its design, construction and use, two to three minutes. The minimum width of a single fire exit door should not be less than 750mm, and, ideally, should be two exit widths, 1050mm. But, a single, large door-opening can only comprise four exit widths (maximum) for evacuation calculation purposes; any width in excess of this will be ignored, as it is for revolving doors and turnstiles. Please note that 900mm should be allowed for wheelchair access/egress. If a fire occurs, it will in all probability affect one of the exits, making it unusable. Therefore, the Fire Safety Officer will stipulate that in each calculation the largest single entrance/exit is ignored. Fire safety is also used to determine the occupant capacity of the licensed area(s). Each person is allowed 0.5 sq.m. of floor space within the auditorium: standing–seating, or 1.0 sq.m. tables/chairs. A deduction of ten per cent of the gross floor area will also be made for stages and other structures: P.A. lighting rigs that are floor mounted. If they take up more than this allowance, then the occupant capacity will be reduced accordingly by the licensing authority.

Sanitary accommodation (internal) is expected to meet the latest edition of the Building Regulations / British Standards (BS) 6465. Part 1. For outdoor events, the 'Pop Code'-1999 provides guidance, although there may be local requirements, so ask for advice first! Normally, the calculations are on a 50/50 split between male and female but, for a young female audience, it could go to 10 / 90 ratio.

If the building and/or services are in need of urgent repair, then the PEL will not be granted. Further inspections of the premises may be made after repairs have been carried out or the correct standards attained. If a licence is not applied for 28 days in advance of an event, it is possible that it will not be granted because there is not sufficient time for all the parties involved to view the venue and make their observation / objections known to the local authority.

The food storage/preparation/display facilities, along with bar serverics, have to comply with ever-changing Food Safety legislation. Further, the venue has to meet the expanding Health, and Safety laws 'as far as is reasonably practicable' at all times.

The Fire Officer's routine, and 'during performance' (DP) inspections, are important; they will check all relevant factors, both internally, and externally, and particularly access for their appliances (fire engines!) The Licensing Authority will be advised of any shortcomings in writing, which may be referred to at the Council's Licensing Committee; and they do not treat these representations lightly – be warned! Seek advice and draw up checklists in order to ensure that you comply with <u>all</u> the licence conditions.

Further stipulations on the licence may include very specific requirements regarding Door Supervisors, a very emotive issue at some venues, due to the use of, and dealing in, illegal substances.

In respect of crowd control methods:

> At each standing audience event, a suitably designed barrier should be erected between the crowd and the artist to provide for the safety of both and also an emergency evacuation. I instituted a barrier policy at a venue after an incident during a Gang Green concert where a 'stage diver' slipped and broke his legs on the edge of the stage.

Figure 6:2 The barrier in use at the Metallica concert, Milton Keynes Bowl   © Chris Kemp, photograph

Noise control is a major part of licensing; if the venue is in a residential area, the licence application may be refused, unless adequate sound compressor/ limiter devices and graphic equalisers are installed, tested, 'locked off' and monitored by competent sound engineers – to the satisfaction of the Council acoustics expert. The 'bottom end' bass frequencies of 64-250Hz are the real problem as their long wavelength may result in complaints from, literally, miles away, particularly during certain climatic conditions, e.g., a 'temperature inversion'.

**Figure 6:3 The Milton Keynes Environmental Health Unit
noise control system in use at the Metallica Concert**
© *Chris Kemp, photograph*

Issues, such as public nuisance in the locality and vandalism, may be taken into account when the venue's PEL comes up for renewal.

The Council's Licensing Committee is required to act in a quasi-judicial manner, but the 'rules of natural justice' must be strictly adhered to at all times. Council Officers, Environmental Health, Fire Safety and Police Officers may all be present and give evidence or expert advice. The licensee may be asked to give an explanation of part or the whole of the application .A licence will usually be granted for up to one year (maximum) and may be varied throughout its duration, e.g., times/dates/ conditions. It can also be transferred to another person(s), subject to satisfactory police checks being completed.

Everyone at a gig or an event should remember that compliance with health and safety legislation is vitally important in ensuring the safety of all those involved. The development of the Pop Code (Second edition-1999), along with detailed advice and 'Best Practice' guidance from the NOEA, BEDA and the PSA, has put the U.K. at the 'cutting edge' in respect of indoor and outdoor concert safety worldwide. New measures are instituted regularly by progressive local authorities, e.g., Milton Keynes Council – All Night Dance Music Events – and leading promoters, e.g., SFX, Mean Fiddler – undertaking detailed risk assessments/action plans to make sure that venues are safe for the audience, the artist and those who work within their confines.

Four very important introductions over the past five years have made venues safer.

- A residual current device (RCD) has to be installed (preferably hard-wired) in the power circuits at the venue. The RCD stops the possibility of electrocution of those working on stage and within electrical areas. Its basic function is to trip out any electrical sources when the flow of the electricity is interrupted or surges. This prevents an artist being electrocuted by a power surge, perhaps caused by an over-zealous fan throwing a pint of beer over the player's instrument. As the surge is felt, the RCD cuts out the electricity, stopping injury or death to the player. Unfortunately, they cannot be used in three-phase supply.

132

- The 'C' form plug is another device which has made the life of the electrician and the PA / lighting technician much easier and safer. Many years ago a band would turn up with three bare wires and then tail them into a junction box in the wall. This was always extremely hazardous as, sometimes, the 'electrician' was never sure whether the electricity was turned off, or whether someone might come and turn the electricity on whilst he was still working with the system! The 'C' form plug comes in two parts. The female component is part of the junction box and is the connection to the three- or single-phase power supply. The band then turn up with a male 'C' form plug which connects to the female 'C' form plug in the junction box, connecting the PA and lighting to the venue power. The artist may also turn up with just wires. The venue can supply, for hire, a male 'C' form plug which the artist's electrician can feed the wires into. She can then fit the male 'C' form plug into the female 'C' form plug to connect the power supply. This innovation saves worry about unsafe electrical practices at the venue, because it keeps the electricity on a safe, external footing. Electricity is the most dangerous hazard in the venue. You can't smell it, you can't see it, you can't hear it but, if you touch it, it can kill you outright! The legal requirements for 'fall and arrest' equipment can be found in the PSA manual.

- Over the past ten years the standard of the door supervisors/security stewards in venues has changed with many relying on large nationally-recognised security companies. These companies provide professionally trained staff for all security needs.

- But, due to lower profit margins in smaller night clubs and other venues, they tend to recruit and train their own staff. The problem with this is three fold. If low wages are paid, the standard of staff is often poor. Secondly, most people's idea of a door supervisor / security steward is a big man who is heavy handed and who acts as a 'bouncer', i.e., someone who is there to cause trouble at the door with the attending audience. Thirdly, when local security are used, their familiarity with the local punters may be counter-productive. They can refuse people from the town that they or their friends do not like and they can let in known troublemakers or drug dealers which is bad for the club's image and reputation.

**Figure 6:4   Professional stewards on duty at
a Milton Keynes Bowl concert**
© *Chris Kemp, photograph*

- Over the past few years, a number of Door Supervisor registration / training schemes have been started by both local authorities, concerned venues and private training companies or educational establishments. These schemes have two objectives; firstly, to give staff the correct professional training to equip them with the skills to be doormen /women. Secondly, to help staff to present a more professional face for security to the general public and punter alike. One of the biggest benefits of such a scheme is that it makes the punter feel more at ease when entering the venue, due to the 'greeter' role and an enhanced customer care focus. These schemes, for example, Milton Keynes Clubwatch (part of Thames Valley Doorsafe, and now recognised nationally as an example of

'Best Practice', Home Office 1999), have enabled a wide range of individuals with differing abilities and skill levels to be trained to be good doorstaff. They should be the management's 'eyes and ears'. It has also meant that everyone wishing to be on the door has had to go through a personal development programme. This createds more of a consistent standard, as the majority of the staff on the venue's doors, and working within the unit (management team included) have the same training and are interchangeable. Unfortunately, a national registration scheme is not favoured by the Government (Home Office) at present, despite pleas from every aspect of the music and leisure industry!

Adequate public liability insurance (PLI) is vital for both venues and promoters. Many venues will not allow promoters to their venues without their own PLI. Some local authorities stipulate in their license conditions that adequate PLI cover must be provided (£5 million) as the main use of PLI is in the unfortunate occurrence of a very serious injury or death. If the promoter has done everything within his power to check all eventualities, by undertaking risk assessments, and has made sure that all the licensing conditions have been complied with, they will probably be able to rely on their PLI, if a claim is made.

If though, the promoter has knowingly evaded responsibility, i.e., allowing reckless 'stage diving' from the stage, without putting precautions in place to keep the audience well away from it or, perhaps, letting fifty more punters into the auditorium than the licence permits, then they will be held criminally liable. Here public liability insurance is useless. Public liability insurance cover can range from £2 million up to £50 million, depending on the frequency and type of event promoted.

There are many pitfalls when dealing with health and safety, and the promoter needs to be well aware of as many as possible. Below are listed a number of serious problems that are encountered by both promoters and venue managers on a regular basis:

- Safety chains on par cans[1] are not attached to the lighting bars or safety chains from the gel frames[2] are missing. This can cause one

---

[1] Par cans are the lamps that are generally used to light concerts. The par 64 is the standard light used.

of two incidents. Firstly, the G clamp[3] holding the par can might slip or shear, causing the lamp to fall into the audience. Secondly, either the gel frame safety chain is missing or the lamp is upside down and the gel frame can fall out into the audience. Both of these instances can cause injury or even death.

Figure 6:5   Par cans safely chained to a lighting bar
© Chris Kemp, photograph

- Oil from smoke machines or beer and water on the stage can cause members of the band to slip or fall and injure themselves. The same accident can be caused by trailing wires[4] on the stage.

- A punter may get behind the front-of-stage security staff and dive off the speakers into the audience. The general audience reaction is to move away from the area, causing the hapless punter to hit the floor, with potentially serious injury.

---

[2] The gel frame is the double sheet of metal used for housing the gel which is the coloured filter used to cast colour onto the stage.
[3] The G clamp is a piece of metal shaped in a G which is used to clamp the light onto the lighting bar.
[4] Trailing wires are often caused by snagged leads from microphones or instruments as well as wires from the PA system.

Figure 6:6 Looking back from the barrier at a large, outdoor concert *© Chris Kemp, photograph*

- Members of the audience can be too drunk to stand, or become a danger to themselves and others. This is often spotted by security staff or a bar manager; the solution is to isolate them quickly and then deal with them appropriately.

- PA and lighting systems can be too close to exits and entrances. These must be checked early on in the set up as most tour managers will resist taking down the PA / lighting once it is up. But, such an installation can reduce the audience capacity of an event.[5]

- Over-zealous guest lists can be a shock to you as a promoter later on in the evening, especially if you have stated that the band can only have 20 guests and, when the list arrives, you see that it has 100 names on it. If the show is 'sold out', the guest list will take the capacity well over the limit. The tour manager will have to cut the list accordingly. If an incident occurs, and it is discovered that the venue is 80 people over its capacity and that this was known by the tour manager and the promoter, they can be held criminally liable.

- A barrier which is not secured properly under the stage, if the engineers specification requires it to be, is a big problem. Barriers are very heavy and some crew think that this very fact makes them safe. ('A' frame or 'Mojo' barrier systems are designed to be self supporting, and to 'flex' under high imposed load conditions. For example, at the Metallica concert in Wembley Arena the barrier did not move from the chalk line on the smooth concrete floor!) But, an unsecured barrier is a death trap. If it falls over, many tonnes of metal can bear down on the audience.

- Equipment in reach of the audience. The main problem here is with the cabling from the stage to the sound and lighting desks.

  This cabling should:

---

[5] A PA system which encroaches on the audience must be measured and a concommitant number of punters must be reduced from the overall door numbers.

a) be flown[6] above the desk , or

b) go under the floor[7], or

c) go around the walls, and above the doors, or

d) as a last resort, go under rubber matting 'gaffer' taped to the floor from the board to the stage.

The rubber conduit must be well taped so that punters do not trip over it. In reality, permutations of a)–d) may have to be implemented.

- The emergency lighting system and fire fighting equipment must be checked before each concert. The reason for this is twofold. Firstly, if the emergency lighting uses a 'trickle feed' battery, it may need servicing to enable it to work at its full capacity, and this can run down at any time. Secondly, at some rowdy events, punters may either let off fire extinguishers or fiddle with fire-prevention equipment. This must be checked before each gig because, if a fire were to occur and a fire extinguisher was empty, it could result in loss of life or the destruction of the venue.

- Liquid Petroleum Gas bottles (LPG) contain a very, very dangerous commodity. These are used by caterers for temporary cooking equipment. Most PEL's will have stipulations regarding LPG bottles and these must be strictly adhered to (keep them in the open air). The licensee/promoter should make caterers aware of the LPG requirements on entry to the venue.

- Members of the security staff on outside doors at sell-out concerts often let punters in for money over and above the occupant capacity. Ensure that you can trust your staff at all times, change the supervisory staff on the team frequently.

- Toilets are often an area for 'play' at teenage concerts. Beware of punters stuffing newspapers down the toilet, or putting tissues in

---

[6] Flown, means that the cable is taken above the audience and suspended from the roof and taken down the back wall of the stage to the equipment.

[7] Some venues are provided with a conduit which carries the wiring from the desk to the stage.

the sinks and turning both the taps on. Both of these cause the facilities to overflow. Make sure that you have the cleaners checking these regularly, or have toilet attendants.

- Staff working on the barrier should use steel-toe-capped safety footwear and steel reinforced (finger) gloves when erecting / dismantling the barrier.

- The different types of fire extinguisher should be checked before the beginning of each event. Specific extinguishers are used in dealing with specific fires, e.g., if an electrical fire occurs, there are two types of extinguisher that can be used. One is dry powder, which can put out electrical fires without harming the user of the extinguisher. But, powder does not penetrate the spaces within the equipment and secondary fires could erupt later. If a CO2 [8] extinguisher is used on electrical equipment, it starves the fire of oxygen and penetrates into the heart of the equipment. Without oxygen, the fire cannot re-ignite. A water or foam extinguisher should never be used on electrical equipment as such use could cause electrocution for the user. Water and foam should not be used on burning oil as this will only spread the fire by carrying the oil to other areas of the venue. If a person is on fire, it is best to roll them in a fire blanket to stop oxygen feeding the flames.

These are just a few of the many hazards that a promoter or venue manager has to deal with when working at an event.

One of the key areas in health and safety is event planning and the resultant risk assessments. Assessing risk is necessary when working with people in potentially dangerous situations. The assessment of risk comes under three headings – severity, likelihood and risk class. Each of the headings is further split into categories.

Severity is split into:
- Equipment damage
- No injury
- Trivial injury

---

[8] Carbon dioxide

- Minor injury
- Major injury
- Fatal injury

Likelihood is split into:
- Impossible
- Remote
- Possible
- Probable
- Likely

The risk class is split into:
- High
- Moderate
- Minor
- Acceptable

The promoter or venue manager will fill in a risk assessment form for every event. A sample form is available on the PSA website on *http://www.psa.org.uk*. The idea of the risk assessment is to make sure that the promoter and venue manager are aware of risks being taken when planning an event. Different music genres can have different hazards associated with them. The promoter and venue manager need to get a feeling for the number of people at risk at an event, both internally and externally. They need to ascertain what action is required to reduce the risks as much as possible and they need to have an action plan ready. Risk assessment is vital as it makes for careful event planning. If the event goes badly wrong, and there is an internal or external enquiry, the risk assessment form may prove how prepared or unprepared the event managers were. This can help to lift the blame from someone.

Review and evaluation enable promoters and venue managers to change and develop their processes. For concert promotion, which changes constantly, ongoing modifications are useful. New musical genres change audience perceptions and attitudes and a system like the risk assessment process is important for the industry as a whole.

When the PEL has been granted, there are other things integral to venue promotion that should be considered before an event takes place. The PRS (Performing Rights Society) licence and the PPL (Phonographic Performance Licence) are needed, not only for the safeguarding of copyright, but also because they are instrumental for paying royalties to the artist. A Phonographic Performance Licence is needed anywhere where recorded music is played. At the end of each performance, the tour manager asks the promoter to sign the PRS form to ensure that the royalties for the music are paid. The PRS fee for a performance is usually three per cent of gross takings.

For someone opening a venue for the first time, a liquor licence is needed. There are two ways of going about this:

• Employ a bar manager who will apply for a Justices On-Licence, enabling him to be the licensee of the premises.

• Employ an outside publican to operate the bar. He can use his own licence, with an application for an extension to another premises, to sell alcohol on the venue's behalf.

The Licensing Act 1964 is the relevant legislation.

When the liquor licence is applied for, the Police, Fire and Local Authority will be sent a copy of the application in case there are any objections to the venue selling alcohol to members of the public. The condition of the premises, and the 'fitness' of the licensee, will also be considered by the Licensing Bench (Magistrates Court). Objections usually come from other publicans in the area. If there are no objections, the licence is usually granted. An extension in hours to the venue may be more difficult. If the venue serves food, 'a substantial meal', and has a PEL, then it may be quite easy to get a Special Hours Certificate (Sec.77) permitting the sale of alcohol until the terminal hour of the PEL, maximum 0200hrs the following day.

The critical point about venue management is the relationship between the promoter, and the venue manager. It is symbiotic and needs to be nurtured carefully. The venue manager and the promoter need to be on good terms and in the business for reasons of longevity and not purely for short-term profit. This relationship has many benefits and this mutually beneficial theme is an area that keeps venue managers and promoters working together for many years.

**Figure 6:7   Stage set up for a gig at the Pitz
in the Woughton Centre, Milton Keynes**

Hospitality

Hospitality can be viewed from several different angles, the first is
from the artist's perspective. When an artist is on the road for a period
of weeks, or even months, the only real providers of comfort are the
hotel and the venue. On a shoestring tour, it may be just the venue
that is providing the hospitality. It is reasonable to expect that the
venue will provide food and drink of an acceptable standard. The
refusal by promoters to do this causes many problems.

Conclusion

It has become increasingly difficult to obtain cheap public liability
insurance (PLI) to cover venues, especially with so many

unscrupulous and 'cowboy' promoters holding events with little, or no experience, and without the correct licences. Local authority venues have PLI of, usually, £5 million; outdoor and higher-risk events will perhaps need more cover. Ten years ago, several major insurance companies did their own PLI for all promotions, but now premiums have rocketed and they are out of the reach of most small promoters. PLI of over £1 million is needed for most venues. If an accident happens, and the venue is not covered, the manager will face heavy fines and even a jail sentence. Each time that a promoter hires a venue, the venue manager must ask for proof of their PLI. More and more insurance companies are doing PLI for events but, those who take out the insurance, must make sure that they are truthful in all aspects as the slightest lie in the insurance application will mean that their claim will not be honoured.

There is a difference between criminal and civil liability. If the promoter or venue manager does everything possible, i.e., exercises 'Due Diligence' before, during, and after an event and, for some unforeseen reason, a problem gets out of his control and a punter is injured, then it may only be the civil liability that is questioned – their 'Duty of Care'. But, if the defence of 'Due Diligence' cannot be claimed, then the promoter and/or venue manager may be found liable in the criminal/ civil courts if they did not bother about the safety of the audience or performers. If a death occurs, the promoter or venue manager may be liable for prosecution under the Health and Safety at Work Act 1974. It is vitally important that anyone dealing with the health and safety issues reads all the relevant HSE-Guidance Notes, e.g., The Pop Code, and the PSA handbook. Both the HSE and the PSA have websites for information.

Chapter 7

Staffing, Crew and Security

There are many small promoters who take full responsibility for every aspect of a promotion. In contrast, in a venue where the venue manager is also the promoter, and in the larger promotion companies, other members of staff share the load of the promoter. These backup staff are part of the organisational structure and without them a promotion will not work efficiently. At the individual level, a promoter has a many-faceted role. For example, he has to be the finance officer, the administrator, the front of house manager, the marketing officer and the press officer all rolled into one. The individual promoter does have to use some staff, security and crew and these must be paid to set up the event correctly and legally. Without such staff, the promoter would not be able to function efficiently. This chapter examines the staff levels needed to ensure that a promotion runs as smoothly as possible.

Choosing staff and crew

Choosing staff to work with you, as a promoter and at the venue, can be a problem. Several important questions have to be answered.

- Who can you trust?

- Who will work hard?

- How much are they worth?

- Are they dedicated? This question outranks the previous three.

The question of honesty always arises. The difference between a genuine mistake and embezzlement is often quite difficult to spot. Where people are working with money, a system must always be set up to make sure that it cannot go missing. Once such a system is in place, the promoter's life becomes easier as responsibility lies with other members of staff. One way to develop staff is to give them responsibility so that they feel valued.

Staff working in different parts of the promotions business need different attributes. For instance, someone working as a crew member needs to be strong and agile, to be able to make split-second decisions and to work quickly. At a formal interview, a keen crew member may respond well but, in the field, may be totally unsuitable for the job. One way to choose crew members is to hold auditions where several crewing scenarios are played out. These role-plays are supervised by a PA technician and his crew as well as the promoter or venue manager. The suitable candidates can then be hired for future work, and a pool of staff built up.

There are a number of problems with crew members. On the one hand, problems may be caused by the promoter, for example, low pay, poor conditions, poor equipment and lack of perks can all contribute to low morale and dissatisfied staff. On the other hand, crew members can be unreliable; they can turn up late, drink or take drugs when working and be insubordinate. You need a code of conduct, a job specification and the requirements of the crew member clearly stated so that they understand their roles and responsibilies. This code of conduct is a two-way process and the promoter should not abuse the crew in any way, such as expecting them to work 14-hour shifts without a break. All crew members should be provided with food and drink and given plenty of breaks during their shift. If a member of the crew causes a problem by not adhering to the code, he is given a warning and, if the behaviour continues, he should be dismissed.

Drinking and taking drugs by crew members should incur instant dismissal as all faculties are needed for the strenuous task of erecting and dismantling the heavy and expensive PA, backline and lighting gear. One crew member under the influence can put all the crew in jeopardy. Here it is essential that the promoter has knowledge of the Health and Safety at Work Act 1974 and relevant employment legislation.

The reasons why a crew member wants to work in the industry are relatively simple. Working in the music business has a lot of plus factors. A member of the crew is able to mix with artists and to identify with them because he is working on an event where he is in close proximity to the artist. Some crew members find this romantic, others just like to get their CDs and photographs signed, which increases their standing amongst their peers. The motivation, when talking to crew members, is one of challenge and satisfaction. Let us be clear, being a member of the crew is a thankless task, with little reward for many hours of toil and hard work, interspersed with hours of sitting around waiting.

It takes a special person to give up time to do this job, but good crew members are dedicated and will turn up whatever the weather and regardless of the time they have been out until the night before. One type of person who relishes this work and can empathise with artists is someone local who is themselves a band member. From the experience of crewing, they can talk to and gain knowledge from technicians in sound, lighting, and instrumentation. Crew members can usually be trusted because they are dedicated to the promotion and to the job. Many of the crew members I have used are now working at venues in managerial roles and promotional capacities, others are touring with bands all over the world.

There are times when a venue becomes reliant on its crew who have covered for the venue technician or barrier crew in cases of sickness. This relationship has a lot more positive than negative aspects as it exposes crew members to different experiences, which they would not normally encounter. The benefits of working as a member of a team are invaluable and friendships made during crewing are often kept for life. The main job of the crew member is to erect and dismantle the stage, the front of house and on-stage sound systems, the lighting rig and the band backlines. Without the crew, the show could not be held. The crew also erects and dismantles the barrier and, by these tasks, is indirectly responsible for the safety of the punters in the venue. Most crew members are well versed in safety procedures, including the lashing of high speaker stacks to the stage and the chaining of lights to gantries. They are also aware of the catastrophic effect that an unsupported barrier can have if it falls into the crowd. They spend a lot of time testing the barrier, the PA and lighting systems for safety. A crew is a closely-knit unit and works under the guidance of the director of the band crew or the tour manager. These people work the crew hard and play on weaknesses; so it is prudent to train your crew well and to make them aware of the problems they will face when dealing with band personnel. If there is a weak link in the crew, the promoter can be sure that the tour manager will let him know and insist that he replaces that person. Do not use just any 'old body' on the crew, as this is a specialised job. Many promoters think that they can get away with a minimum, inexperienced crew for the job. This is not so. If you think carefully, three of the prime factors that a show relies on are safety, sound and lighting. The audience do not notice what the promoter or the crew have been doing, or the hundreds of hours of work that have gone into the preparation and promotion of the show. All they are worried about is being safe and seeing a good show with perfect sound and great lighting. The crew, although not responsible for the sound and lighting, are responsible for their correct set up and for some of the safety aspects of the night. So, the crew are vitally important to the overall production of the show, and this should not be treated lightly. The crew members are as important as any other member of the show team. If you, as a promoter, choose your crew carefully and look after them, you will keep them for a long time and will build up a relationship that will pay dividends. When you call them in at short notice or expect them to work long hours on back-to-back shows, they will respond with good will.

I have found that in this business there is no substitute for loyalty. The crew should be carefully rigged out. In my latest specification from the Environmental Health Department, all crew must be dressed in T-shirts with six-inch letters on the front displaying the word CREW. They must be provided with hard hats, gloves, ear plugs and Toetectors (shoes with steel toe caps) to ensure that they comply with the Health and Safety at Work Act 1974. One of the major problems with crew members is that they do not like to wear the safety clothing provided. They can choose not to wear these safety items, at their own risk. I have provided them with the regulation clothes and that is where my duty ends. The only item that I can insist that they wear is the uniform shirt which is as much for the safety of others as it is for theirs and, although they grumble about this, I do not get much dissent. I did have a serious injury to one of my crew working with Iron Maiden. When the driver opened the back of the lorry, a sink unit belonging to the catering staff fell out onto the legs of a crew member, tearing his ligaments and tendons. Five years later he is still awaiting an operation to repair the damage. What this shows is:

- That no safety clothing could have prevented the accident.

- That you never know what to expect.

The crew have to be vigilant at all times to avoid accidents. I have always told crew members that, if anything is too heavy to lift by themselves, they must always wait for others to arrive before lifting it, even if it means incurring the wrath of band's crew members or the tour manager. It is better to be safe than to pull or tear something and to be off work for a long period of time. Crew members are often asked to double up as barrier staff. This can be tiring and the promoter must make sure that staff have adequate rest and time to relax before a gig. Often crew members are interested in lighting and sound and, if training courses are available, it is prudent to send them. If the promoter is short of a lighting or sound technician, he can use a crew member who has had training in this discipline. This also increases the strength of the relationship between the crew, the venue and the promoter.

Whilst interviewing two members of the Noise Factory crew in Northampton, who I will call Bill and Tim, they related the reasons why they crewed. The main reason was to supplement their dole money and to acquire contacts and networking opportunities. They enjoy crewing to a degree, but they never watch the shows as they do not like many of the bands. In their opinion it only takes one song to weigh up a band, the sound quality and the lights. To them it is just one of those things that you do. Both Bill and Tim prefer working on club nights because it is far more creative, they can make stupid decorations and have fun, which is far better than tour mangers *"whingeing about the smallest things"*. Another factor seems to be that crewing is so much better than working in an office.

The major bugbear about crewing to Bill and Tim is the way that they are treated by band personnel. *We are treated worse than scum and the band do not take into consideration anything that we have done,* said Bill. The attitudes of people in the music business seem to leave a lot to be desired. If the gear coming into the club is really bad, but the band and crew are fun, it makes for more enjoyable working. If someone says *thank you,* it seems to mean such a lot to the crew. I hasten to add this bad behaviour does not happen very often. Out of all the genres of music that Bill and Tim have worked with at the venue, the rock band crews have been the worst, especially the American rock bands with exploded egos. Some of the indie bands have been the best to work with, those who are easy going and have a beer with the crew after the lorry has been loaded.

One of the big drawbacks with crewing is that there is little or no social life and crew members can become very insular. Working with people who try to stitch each other up day in and day out and working with rude, insulting people takes its toll on a crew member's sensitivity.

The easiest part is getting out of the venue and reloading the truck. *It is so much quicker than the get in and, if the band have been horrible, the quicker that we get them out the better,* said Tim. Over the past five years the workload has increased immensely. At first the crew only had to sort out the backline for the band, but now they are expected to set up the backline, the front of house, the monitor system, the barrier and the backdrop. Bill states, *it's a weird life because you live in the night.*

If the promoter does not want the hassle of providing his own crew, it is possible to hire an event company. At many events I have found it impossible and impractical to ask my crew to set up some of the bands I have booked. So, I have used firms like Stage Miracles, who agree a price for a number of crew. They turn up on the day and erect and dismantle the equipment. It really does lighten the load. There is no chasing lazy crew or having to get more crew in because existing crew are not adequate. These are the professionals; bands respect this and work well alongside them. It does cost more to employ a crewing company, but the positive side to this is the total reliability of the hired crew. If a difficult tour manager approaches you, as a promoter, on the morning of a gig and asks, *Where are the crew?* and you state that Stage Miracles or another professional crew will be arriving at 10 a.m., you can guarantee that you will not have any bother for the rest of the day. Crew firms are a first-class alternative to house crew. To train and bring crew up to an acceptable standard to work on gigs is very difficult. Band members expect a certain type of service and, if they do not get it, the crew are the first to suffer. When we held a big gig in the large hall, it was often more sensible to employ an agency crew for several reasons.

Firstly, the tour manager with a larger artist tends to expect more, and the tentative enquiries they make about the crew, the times of start, etc. are always pitched to find out if a local crew has been employed. If it is a local crew, their attitude tends to be antagonistic. In my experience, when dealing with local crew, because of the amount that they are paid and with early morning starts for the bigger events, there are always problems with absenteeism and unreliability. Secondly, when a professional crew are assigned, I know that they will be there on time, whatever the weather. This method may cost more in the long run but it is a cleaner and tidier way for the promoter to work and it prevents the pressure tour managers put on the promoter when local crew wander off, refuse to lift, or do not really know what they are doing.

In spite of this the merits of local crew are many. The comradeship, the building of a team and letting young people work within the industry close to bands, has benefits. It is a great talking point for them at the club or pub. When they visit other venues they often get into concerts free, either through the band or through friends that they have made on the circuit when working at other venues. To gain good service from crews, they must be well looked after, valued and, above all, trusted. Without these three factors the crew will eventually revolt and the venue will need to recruit new crew members. To feed and clothe the crew for heavy work is inexpensive, although making sure that they adhere to the stringent health and safety laws is quite difficult. Compromise is the key and assurances that they will be well looked after, if they abide by the rules and regulations. You should also offer them the perk of free entrance to events when they are not working.

Legal requirements

There are many legal requirements when you employ crew. All the crew should be contracted to work by the promoter and venue manager. This means that they are covered by insurance in case of any damage or injury. If the PA falls on them and they are injured, they can claim on the insurance. All crew members must be over the age of 16 but, at this age, they are only able to work restricted hours. Crew members aged 18 years and over can work normal crew hours. It is advisable to use more mature staff for this type of work, as the way that some bands and road crew treat the house crew is appalling and it may upset some of the younger members. All crew members should be given contracts and the details of these thoroughly explained to them. If an accident happens to a member of crew on the premises and he is not properly covered by insurance and had been issued with a contract, the promoter is liable for damages.

Sensible security

It is hard for a promoter to find sensible security personnel in his own time, to train them properly and then to explain how to balance the lighter aspects of their work with the heavier. In six years at a venue I had to change the security staff three times. Some security personnel are inherently violent, some lazy and some fail to take the job seriously. I found the security I had used between 1990 and 1993 to be first class, house trained and very user friendly. I have also had experience of firms like StarGuard and Showsec who give a first-class service. A relatively new service is available where security guards are trained centrally to bring them up to a certain standard and qualification. Night clubs and venues alike join in the scheme and only employ the security personnel trained on this scheme. Such organisations, including Club Watch, do raise standards but there are still many poor security guards. A large amount of publicity has been given to this practice; it has brought clubs a higher profile and a better image. Mick Upton, the director of Showsec, has spent over two years developing an NVQ for security guards, so that they have some sort of security qualification before taking up a post in a club or venue. Other practitioners within the industry are now developing a wide range of NVQs.

A major problem with security is familiarity and how to deal with it. Familiarity with a venue can only be good but familiarity with punters sometimes works adversely. The more that security staff feel that they can get away with slack and sloppy marshalling, the more they will try it on. Often, when using hand-selected crew or unprofessional security firms, I have sacked staff for acts of misconduct. I have then had to go through the security selection process all over again, employing a new and more professional crew. On one occasion with a Thrash band called Exodus, a member of the security manhandled a female photographer and threw her bodily into the audience. Because the security staff were not familiar with Thrash culture, they could not handle the concept of crowd surfing and I had to employ another firm who could deal with it because they had been trained properly and briefed before each event. Employing hand-picked security is difficult and some smaller promoters have failed when using this method. Unprofessional security personnel bring friends and chat with punters during the concert, causing problems. If a security member is not 'on his or her toes' during the evening and something happens, it may be too late to avert a disaster.

When you employ security of high calibre that you can trust, the event has a different complexion. At one such concert where I employed almost exclusively West Indian security personnel, a member of the public drew a machete on me at the front door. Within two seconds, just before the machete was completely out of the assailant's coat, a security person had apprehended him, taken the weapon and deposited him face down on the carpet in an arm lock. This type of approach worked well. Good security staff can exchange light repartee with punters yet have an efficient and effective way of dealing with trouble. On another occasion a punter threatened to attack me at a Thunder gig but, before he had laid a finger on me, he was on the floor disarmed and waiting to be dealt with by security. Five seconds before I had not been aware of any security staff nearby.

153

Security staff must be reliable. If they are contracted from a reliable firm you, as a promoter, can be sure that they will turn up at the venue on the right night, at the right time. If you hand-pick security and do not carry out the proper documented procedures, you do not have the same sort of confidence. If you use a reputable security firm, you can be assured that the right number and type of security staff will turn up.

At the beginning of each event the head of security should meet with the venue manager, tour manager and promoter. The reasons for this are threefold:

- To establish contact among staff.

- To explain the strategy to security staff for the night.

- To go over any special considerations for the night.

Good security staff carry walkie-talkies or use headsets so that they can call reinforcements if there is any trouble. The headsets are important so that the head of security can contact his staff at any time and direct them to areas of concern. It is also policy to provide female members of security to deal with female problems. It is politic to have these staff on standby for trouble in women's toilets, to check women's bags and to carry out searches on women, if these are required.

Up until now crewing and security staff have usually been men, but more and more women are taking up the job. This is good for trade as it makes women in the audience feel more at ease, as they have someone to call on if in danger. Security staff are employed for the safety of the punters. If there is a fire, a flood or a blackout, then the security staff are trained in methods of escape and first aid. They are also aware of all the exits, entrances and any problems within the venue. If a fire starts, then it is their job to help people to escape from the building. Many punters see the security person as an imposition, someone there to spoil their fun. This is not so. Security staff enhance the punters' enjoyment of the show by being there to keep them safe and reassured. It is true that the security staff are also there to keep the artist from harm and to stop people injuring themselves at the concert. A good security guard will be able to tell the difference between a member of the public who is there to enjoy himself and one who is there to cause trouble. If he has any doubts, a quick word with the culprit often stops potential trouble. Most people who attend concerts do so because they like music; it is only a small minority who are there to be disruptive and it is quite often the presence of drink or drugs that make these people aggressive. Security guards have to be proactive rather than reactive; they need to spend time watching people in the venue. If the bar manager has a problem with a character whom he thinks has had too much to drink and who is becoming violent, he contacts the head of security and a watch will be put on the offender. If the problem continues, the offender is warned. If he persists, he will be asked to leave; if he refuses, he will be escorted from the building. It is also the security guard's job to make sure that anyone in difficulty from heat or noise is looked after. If a punter faints or is injured, then it is the security guard who goes into the crowd to pull the person out. If he has fainted he will usually be given a seat outside. If he is injured, the security guard will ask for an ambulance to be called, for a member of St John's Ambulance Brigade, or for the designated, trained person in the building. Often a security guard will be trained so that he will administer first aid to the casualty himself. If the person is injured, an accident report must be completed by the venue manager detailing the casualty's name, address, time of incident and other details. The parents, partner or next of kin of the punter will be contacted and informed.

Many venues today are drug free but it is, of course, impossible to impose this as the norm. Drugs, such as Ecstacy, are more often than not being taken before entering the venue. This makes the job of security harder as the drugs are already in the boady of the punter before entry. From years of watching punters in venues, it becomes easy to spot those on drugs and those who have drunk too much. Telltale signs are the eyes, mannerisms and general behaviour.

After many instances of drug abuse in my venue, I went to the Drug Squad to ask for advice on hard drugs. It is a difficult problem. If a promoter wishes to search punters, it is an invasion of their privacy and the promoter must provide security staff with mesh or steel tipped gloves in case of concealed hypodermics. The advice from the Drug

Squad was that, if the problem was not overwhelming it probably would not need to be controlled; those few people usually found within the venue were recreational users and, thus, self-regulating.

If we caught people abusing drugs, we could hold them until the Drug Squad got there, but the contact stated that it is not a good idea to try to detain an addict as their behaviour is very erratic and could end in injury to the apprehender. Their only advice was to put up posters stating that anyone found using drugs would be ejected from the premises, thus distancing those punters not using drugs from those that were. The security staff were satisfied with this but other, than actively searching corners and toilets, security staff are not going to spot drug users and their time can be better spent looking after the punters in the building.

The positioning of the security staff is important, for both positive and negative reasons. From the positive viewpoint, punters like to know that security staff are there but prefer them to be unobtrusive. Putting security staff in front of the stage often antagonises the crowd and gives the anti-security lobby reasons to barrack them. One of the most awful moments of my career was when I had to step into the pit during a concert by Napalm Death. An injury had occurred the previous week at a concert and the venue had banned stage diving. As a result I was asked to increase the security patrol in the pit to stop people getting up onto the stage and diving. The band started and the crowd went wild. I had already been on stage, amid a salvo of boos and spitting, to try to calm the audience and to tell them why no diving was allowed. A struggle ensued. I had a line of security, crew and staff in the pit. We were being attacked by the audience from the front and abused by the band from the back and, in the end, we had to abandon our attempts to stop people diving and just let the mêlée continue. Luckily, no one was injured. But, stage diving now has to be recognised as a normal event. It had always been my policy to allow a safe environment for stage diving. On this occasion I had been advised by senior management to stop the practice. This incident proved that trying to stop these antics was more dangerous than allowing it to continue. After this concert, I tried to make stage diving as safe and user friendly as possible with the security staff assisting those who wished to dive, so that as little injury as possible was caused to surrounding punters.

The security staff's nightmare bands were Acid Reign and Lawnmower Deth. Their antics on and off the stage caused havoc. The basic problem was that the band made the crowd act the way they wanted. When Pete from Lawnmower Deth shouted, *"everyone on the floor with your legs up in the air"*, what he did not realise was that, as the crowd went down, there was no longer a forward pressure on the barrier and those at the front pulled the barrier with them. The stays began to warp and it was only by the quick thinking of the forward security staff that 50 punters were not crushed by the barrier. Another little action by these two bands was to get the whole crowd running in a big circle around the hall in time to the music. This caused chaos and anyone falling was trampled by those behind. I directed the security to go into the crowd and slow the circle down, so that as few as possible of the punters were hurt. It worked, but the staff, the security and the crew were exhausted by the end of the night.

As with the crew firms, the use of a professional security firm does cut down the work and anxiety but puts up costs for the event.

Backroom staff who deal with the tickets, finance and administration of the operation should be carefully chosen. It is often easier to use the venue's staff as they are already employed to do this. This does not usually incur any cost, but it may result in the promoter having to pay a percentage of the ticket money to the venue as a cover charge for administrating the event.

Where there is a box office at a venue, the box office manager is responsible for selling tickets for each event and for the sale of tickets for other people under any franchise arrangements. The box office manager is responsible for the ordering of tickets and for the distribution of those tickets to the various agencies working on behalf of the venue. Correct information entering and leaving the box office is imperative. For instance, if a show is cancelled or a date is changed and their tickets are still valid, then the box office must be informed so that the staff can make arrangements to refund or to tell punters who have already bought tickets that the date has been changed. They will also need to be reassured that the tickets they have bought are still valid for the rescheduled date. Ticket agencies also have to be informed of these changes. Each box office must be sent posters and leaflets for each event that they are selling tickets for, as well as up-to-date promotional material. It is also the box office manager's task to keep the ticket reconciliations up to date and to supply agents, record companies and the promoter with tickets and up to date figures of ticket sales. The box office manager also has to keep track of the tickets for each show that he is selling for other agencies and box offices. For each show that the office sells, they take a percentage or a booking fee as their income.

Thus an agent selling for outdoor shows or large venues, like Wembley or the NEC, can make a lot of money over the year on a commission basis. Credit card sales of tickets through telephone bookings are also an income earner as a fee is charged for the administration of this process and this fee is then levied as income for the box office. Therefore, not only does the box office make an income from ticket sales, but also through the use of credit card facilities. The credit card controller must ensure that all staff know how the slips are processed correctly and must be aware when stocks are low so that new stocks can be ordered before the slips run out. The box office, because of its financial ties, is linked very closely with the finance office and the accounts manager.

Although the promoter of a small company usually deals with the finances, the bigger venues and promotion companies have their own staff to deal with these procedures. These managers are concerned with the raising of invoices for all purchases made by the promoter, the credit control of the venue or company and the drawing of money to pay bands and artists. Money for the artist is related directly to box office takings. If pre-sales for a show are good, there will usually, in a solvent company, be money to draw against. In a smaller company, this money must cover the expenses, or the company will become overdrawn. It is the financial manager who makes sure that enough money is available to cover all eventualities. Waiting for cheques to clear, producing budget statements and producing five-year plan projections are quite easy on paper but, when it comes to putting budgets into practice in an area based mainly on chance, problems occur. Often, when a promoter works at a venue, he does not receive the money owing to him until at least 14 days after an event and, in some cases, up to 60 days. For this the promoter needs a contingency plan, which covers the money needed over the period after the event until the cheque from the venue clears. This can cause cash flow problems. If the money is paid on the night, then the financial controller can tell the promoter that he will be paid in cash after the gig and after the box office has deducted its share. This net amount is then paid to the promoter and the income, minus the expenses, is the profit.

Although there are many other staff roles in promoting, only those which directly affect the promoter or the venue manager have been covered here. Other positions, such as that of stage manager, are described in other chapters.

Conclusion

Staffing, crew and security are integral to an event. When people work on a promotion, they cost money and it is essential for the promoter to get value for money from his/her staff. This only happens where staff are well-trained, trustworthy and competent. Good staff are the backbone of the industry.

Chapter 8

Getting the Promotion as Perfect as Possible

There is really no such thing as the perfect promotion, although many promoters will tell you that there is. Each promoter has his or her story of the best promotion; it may be the one that made the most money, the one that gave the most satisfaction or it may just have been the audience's reaction on a particular night. Owing to the nature of music promotion, there are many things that can go wrong or right. Unexpected things happen which make promotion a difficult, if not at times impossible, task.

Successful promoting

The key to any successful promotion is to leave nothing to chance and to make sure everything has been planned well in advance. All paperwork and negotiations should be completed before the show and everyone should know what their roles are for the day. Each eventuality should be checked and any small considerations that are niggling in the promoter's mind should be sorted out. If the risk assessment has been carried out, the promoter and the venue manager will have some idea of what to expect on the night.

Every promotion should have a promotional plan which details three main areas of action.

- All aspects of artist, show management and administration.

- Marketing and publicity.

- Staffing and security.

The first step is to look at the financial implications of booking a band and a venue. A budget must be drawn up, detailing each area of the event to check if it is economically viable. The promoter is offered a band and a provisional date, or set of dates. An offer is then put in for the band, with those dates on which the promoter can promote the show. Whilst the process of considering offers and routing is carried out by the agent, the promoter looks at venues for the band. When the promoter has found a venue, a provisional booking is made for one or several dates to cover the movement of the band through the routing process. When the band is confirmed, the promoter confirms the venue. All details of the contract are checked over the telephone with the agent and the ticket price and fee are settled. When these have all been done, they are very difficult to change, so the promoter must make sure that he has what he thinks is the best possible deal. Once the hard copy of the contract and rider have been received by the promoter and any changes are made, the contract is signed and both returned by post and faxed to the agent. Proof of postage and the fax transmission slip are filed. The promoter checks the details for the concert that will appear on the tickets and all promotional material and then arranges for the tickets to be printed.

Whilst this is going on, the promoter contacts the agent, record company or management company for tools to promote the band. The promoter needs to procure as much marketing material as possible to make sure that the show is a success. Awareness is a key factor for this. If the band, as is usually the case, are touring on the back of a CD, then that is a pivot on which to base the promotion. The record company can provide samples of the CD to use in competitions and as sweeteners for the press and other promotional agencies, so that they will give the best possible coverage. Any publicity is good publicity – especially if there is a scandal line or a strange photograph. The promoter needs to procure black and white photographs, a biography and, if he is able to get a colour spread in any of the local newspapers, a colour transparency.

You need to prepare mailing lists of newspapers and magazines in the venue's locality to send compiled press packs. These include details of the show, a biography of the artist/s, a black and white photograph of the band, press cuttings from national papers and magazines about the progress of the band, and some sort of product to elicit either a fair response to the mailout or a review of the CD. To do this properly, the promoter also looks at public awareness of the band. A record company often ties in posters and leaflets with a tour, but the promoter needs to ask the record company early for these as many companies do not send them out until near or on the date of the show. If the promoter cannot get any posters from the record company, he will have to produce his own. These need to be done well before the show to make sure that they are sent out to poster sites, pubs and clubs in the area. Leaflets have always been important as these can be given out at a number of shows before the show that is being promoted, as well as being sent directly to people on mailing lists. The word of mouth and PR (public relations) systems have to be set up, where the promoter informs a number of key people to spread the word of an event; these may be record shops or club DJs. Advertisements in selected national, regional and local newspapers and radio stations need to hit the target audience with maximum effect. Unless the band are internationally renowned, there is no point in advertising too far in advance of the show or too late for punters to buy tickets or to get out of other arrangements. The prime time for targeting must be decided on. As soon as these promotional activities are done and the tickets arrive, the show goes on sale. It is imperative that the promoter always checks that the details of the show are correct on the tickets before they go on sale.

Although the major features of the promotion are finalised before the deal is struck, many minor details may be discussed nearer to the date, as long as they do not have a bearing on its financial viability; these need to be agreed early.

After the show goes on sale, the minutiae of the venue booked are discussed, including what the promoter requires from the venue and what he has to provide. If the venue has its own lighting and sound, the technician needs all the details from the technical rider. The band technician or the technician used by the promoter needs to know the details of tail in (how the power system is connected) and what equipment is being brought in. The get in time, length of hire, cleaning arrangements, catering arrangements, merchandising areas, box office arrangements and staff included in the hire all have to be agreed and contained in the contract between the venue and the promoter so that each of them knows exactly what is going on. This must be clearly set out and contracted so that no ambiguities arise. The promoter should, by this time, have received a contract from the agent which he signs. If the contract differs from the original conversation that he had with the agent or there are any problems with it, he must always reply in writing with the proposed changes to the contract, and keep a copy. In the real world of club promoting nine out of ten contracts are never exchanged, therefore, the promoter should always take a copy of the contract and have it on file for when the band arrive. If there are any problems, then he has the copy of the contract to show the tour manager. Changes to the contract made by the band are often faxed to the promoter on the day of the concert or never arrive at all. With some American bands, different contracts may have been sent to the band and to the promoter and, when viewed together, the contracts do not resemble each other at all.

The staff and the crew must then be booked with a clear indication of what time they must arrive, how long they will be required and how much they will be paid. Once these parameters have been set and each detail has been checked, the promoter is as ready as he can be for the show. If any area does not go according to plan, it must be reviewed. For example, low ticket sales would be reviewed by the promoter, the agent and the venue management to see what can be done to improve them.

Final arrangements

Two days before the show all last minute arrangements should be checked. Staff should be confirmed and advised when and where they will be working on the day of the gig. All security staff and the crew should be checked. The promoter must make sure that the ticket numbers are accurately checked and that the number of security staff and crew booked is enough to avoid any confrontation with the tour manager the next day. Although these details may have been reviewed well in advance, if they are checked again two days before the show, it allows time for extra staff to be called in or for the security to be increased, if the show is selling far better than expected. It also gives the promoter the chance to cancel staff if the promotion is not selling well.

A *get in time* will have been arranged and the crew should be brought in at least half an hour in advance of this time in case any last minute adjustments to the stage or buildings are needed.

On the day

The day of the show starts very slowly with the arrival of the PA (public address system) and lighting. PA and lighting companies provide specialist crews to sort out their stock, but they will expect the local crew, or the crew brought in for the occasion, to do the donkey work in getting the sound and lighting materials erected. The main bulk of the day will be spent erecting the gear and fine-tuning it ready for the arrival of the band. The crew of the sound and lighting companies usually expect to eat, and to be provided with breakfast is a bonus for them and makes them feel that they are valued by the promoter. Therefore, it may be politic to feed all the crew. An electrician must be on stand-by at the venue to *tail in*. Tailing in is where the electrician connects the cables from the sound and lighting equipment to the mains. In a venue with one three-phase and one single-phase system, the sound will be run off the single-phase and the lighting will be run off the three-phase system. All equipment must be switched off before tailing in and the electrician will make sure that the mains supply to the input box is also switched off. The input wall boxes have residual current devices (RCDs) in case there is a sudden electrical surge. Often in venues female C form plugs are used. If the sound and lighting companies are notified in good time, they may turn up with male C form plugs on their cables. This saves time and effort as the technicians do not then have to tail in but can just plug their male C form plugs into the female C form sockets. Once the systems are set up and tailed in, the technicians fine-tune the equipment. The lighting company gel and focus the lights and the lighting designer sets up his lighting sequences and patterns for the evening. The sound engineer checks both the front of house and the on-stage monitor mix, making sure that the sound is perfect for the evening show. Each microphone is tested and each speaker cabinet and effect is tested to make sure that it performs to the highest standard. Remember that this will be tested in a hall without an audience and that modifications will need to be made during the performance.

During the get-in or setting up period, the tour manager consults the promoter on several points. One is food and drink. The promoter must make sure that the rider[1] is met and that the specified time for food is adhered to on his side. The promoter should make sure that the money for the band will be ready. If payment is by cheque, it should always be shown to the tour manager early to allow an authorised person to change the name of the payee, if needed.

Provided that everything has been thoroughly checked, the promoter's life is usually quite easy on the day, but there are always unexpected things that happen. An example of this took place when I was promoting Magnum in a small venue holding 500. The band were warming up for their world tour. The production was so large that, when the third lighting tress was put up, it came three metres over the front of the stage. The tour manager wanted to increase the size of the stage, but this was impossible as it would have cut down the audience to 400 people and 500 tickets had already been sold. I had to negotiate the taking down of the third tress and its replacement back onto the pantechnicon. It was a difficult decision to make and everyone was furious – the tour manager because it compromised his lighting show, the crew because they had to dismantle it and the technicians because they had to re-patch the whole system to run only two tresses. It was impossible to do the show without taking the tress down. In the end my decision as the promoter was final, whatever consequences and sacrifices resulted.

A bugbear at many shows is the insistence by bands that they do not need a barrier, even though licensing agreements stipulate that a barrier has to be in place between the stage and the audience for safety

---

[1] The rider is the sound, lighting and other requirements, including food, stipulated as an addendum to the contract.

reasons. Before we bought a barrier, many people were crushed against the front of the stage and one lad broke his thigh trying to dive from the stage into a mobbed crowd. The promoter must be ready for anything. 'Sold out' signs must be prepared and runners employed in case the show sells out and people need to be diverted away from the venue, to stop crowds massing outside and starting trouble.

The genre of band often dictates the type of night that will be experienced. For instance, if a promoter puts on a Punk, a Rockabilly or a New Wave band, he knows that the audience will be extra rowdy and that he needs to prime the security staff how to deal with trouble if it occurs and how to tell what is trouble and what is playful barging and pogoing.

The band usually travel separately from the crew. When they arrive, they will require part of the rider; this should already be in the dressing rooms as organised with the tour manager in advance of their arrival. The band will want to relax because, contrary to popular belief, there is nothing glamorous about club touring. It is hard work and it is tiring and, for someone not used to it, completely draining. This is especially so for someone on a tour that has not been well routed and planned. This could mean an eighteen-hour drive from one city to another in a coach or mini bus. The band could be cooped up every day like this, playing a show, travelling between venues, sleeping, and then playing again. To help the band relax, it is worth asking the venue manager if the band can use any extraneous facilities that are available. My venue had good facilities. Word quickly spread about this and bands used to put the venue as one of its first choices to play because relaxation and fun were some of the top priorities when touring.

The band may be tired and irritable so it is best to make them feel at home and to keep punters well away from the back stage and hospitality areas when the band first arrive at the venue. During the afternoon, the main band will play a sound check to make sure that the sound and lighting are at the right levels for their performance. The main band's equipment is always set up first and, once in place, it is unlikely that they will allow it to be moved; so, the support band's backline has to wait until after the main band's sound check before it can be set up and tested properly. There have been occasions where, because of the length of the main band's sound check, the support band has had little or no sound check and this sometimes causes the promoter a lot of problems. The support band may be getting only a small amount of money for playing the gig, but they are an integral part of the show. This is not only because they extend the entertainment time, but also because these support bands may one day be doing their own headline tour and the promoter may want to book them. If he does want to book them again, the band may tell their agent that he has treated them badly in the past and will play only for a vastly inflated sum, or not at all. Even if a promoter has a tight budget, a few sandwiches and a few six packs of beer will make the support band feel well looked after. Some bands choose their own support and stipulate right at the beginning in the contract that the support band must be fed and watered. The contract must be adhered to, unless the promoter has re-negotiated the deal. Some egotistical artists, who worry about support acts putting on a better show than theirs, deliberately allow as little time as possible for the support to set up, hoping that they will fail to do so properly.

The merchandising crew arrive in the afternoon. The record company may send a crew member in advance to prepare screens with pictures and empty CD cases to put in the venue foyer to create awareness of the band. The merchandising crew require a well-lit space where punters will be able to buy. The best space is usually one of three places:

• An area that the punters will pass going in and out of the venue.

• An area within the hall itself.

• An area facing the bar so that punters going in and out of the bar will be lured into buying merchandise.

Merchandising is important as the items sold appeal to those people wishing to be identified with the band. This identification makes people buy merchandise and, thus, be recognised as supporting or being part of the generic subculture. The merchandiser may expect the promoter to supply staff to sell the merchandise. Even if this has not been agreed in advance, the promoter can usually find someone to do the selling, as merchandise managers offer good rates of pay. Merchandisers usually state that no other competing goods can be sold on the premises. I have had to deal with pirate merchandisers who were expelled from outside the venue. In another instance one group, who had a franchise to sell merchandise, were trying to steal boxes of T-shirts from a rival group of merchandisers by forcing their van open with a jemmy. Eventually, the police were called and the incident was quickly sorted out.

After the sound check, the band will usually eat. Many bands have members who are vegetarians as well as meat eaters. Some band members may be vegans or have special dietary requirements. These requirements must always be met as proper feeding of band and crew members is essential.

Opening the event

In the early evening, as the security arrive and the barrier crew arrive at the venue, a meeting should be held by the promoter to introduce the head of security to the crew, the tour manager and the venue manager. At this meeting a plan of action is discussed, where all representatives talk through the plan for the evening – where security will be placed, where barrier crew will take up positions, who is in charge of the security operation – and any faults or problems seen at previous gigs are considered. When everything has been planned and prepared for the show, the security staff and crew have a break before doors open. The tour manager and promoter then do a box office reconciliation to see how many tickets have been sold in advance. These are logged and all the tickets now are for door sales which may vary in price. The tour manager discusses with the promoter and venue manager a *door time*, and what times the bands will go on stage, come off stage, and the break between the bands. A list of these times is compiled. One copy is posted on the bands' doors, one on the entrance doors, one in the ticket office, one given to the head of security, one given to the barrier crew and one each to the promoter, venue manager and tour manager. Before the doors open, the tour manager makes sure that the technicians are happy with the technical aspects and that no further adjustments need to be made. The venue manager checks that his staff and building are all in order and the promoter double checks that all fire and safety equipment is in place and working, before any punters arc let into the halls. Once each member is happy that everything is up to standard, the doors are opened.

A strong contributor to the success of many promoters is their PR on the door and around the venue in general. Many punters coming to the venue want to share ideas, transport difficulties and other problems which they have experienced when either finding out about the concert or getting to it. The presence of the promoter on the door for much of the night can be a rewarding experience as he can learn things about the gig that he did not know and thus reassess his planning capabilities. Another thing that the promoter or his designated representative can do is to take everyone's name and address to be put on a mailing list. This gives the promoter a mailing base to use for other shows within the same or similar genres. The promoter can also gauge, as can the members of security on the door, the type and mood of the audience, which can be relayed back to other members of staff so that they are as aware as possible of the type of response that the audience will give. But, staff should not make judgments on the way that people dress or on their personal habits, because these factors do not give any pointers to the way that an audience will behave. Spotting steel-toe-capped boots, studded belts and knuckle-dusters does not mean that these people are trouble makers because this is usually ritual dress – they wear it because it is their way of showing their allegiance to a band or their allegiance to a style or subculture. As Ted Polhemus (1994) states in *Street Style*, when referring to heavy metal:

> *An extraordinary collection of musical sub-styles have gathered under its umbrella: Satanic/Black Metal (e.g., Black Sabbath, W.A.S.P.), Glam Metal/Sleaze (e.g., Motley Crue, Hanoi Rocks), Thrash Metal (e.g., Metallica, Sepultura) and Death Metal (e.g., Slayer, Paradise Lost), all attracting their own devoted followers. At the same time, different styles of dress have emerged which are appropriate to each musical specialisation. Perhaps, most importantly, the spandex jeans, leather, snakeskin, leopard prints and profusion of metal accessories associated with glam rock and sleaze metal have provided a much-needed antidote to the at-times-almost-ubiquitous badged-denim look.*

I have in the past known staff who look on Travellers as trouble makers, but, like most other people, they are just there to enjoy themselves and, when talking to them, staff have found them to have very strong opinions on most matters and have been surprised to find that they are well behaved. I always tried to teach my staff never to judge anyone by their appearance. To new staff it is a culture shock dealing with people showing allegiance to specific musical genres. It is not something that has touched their everyday lives and it comes outside their comfort zone. The immediate feeling is one of threat and the defences go up. Gradually this feeling is dispelled. Violence at musical events is very rare and it is usually started through drink or a member of staff misjudging a situation.

When punters are in the building, all staff, including the tour manager, must know where the promoter is. The promoter is the pivot of the show, he is the contact amongst all parties; if anyone wants anything, they go to the promoter. If not enough beer has been left in the dressing room, it is the promoter's fault and he must be found to rectify the problem. Instances, such as lack of toilet paper, cold showers, people in the wrong areas, and lack of guest passes, are all brought to the promoter's attention and he has to find the relevant party to sort everything out. As the night goes on and the pace becomes fast and furious, with demands being made on all sides, the promoter stays calm and rides the storm. The better the relationship the promoter has with the tour manager, the better the night will be. Always remember that you, as a promoter, will be keeping one eye on ticket sales as you are dealing with problems, hoping that you will make the break-even figure that takes you into profit. As you become more experienced, you will find that, because of the tightly knit agencies, the tour managers will often be the same for several bands that you deal with. I had personal favourites, such as Steve Whaite. I knew that when he walked through the door with a band, I would have no problems and everything would be taken care of at the beginning of the night and that I would not see him again until I paid him at the end of the show. The more times you deal with a tour manager, the more he understands your style and the more you understand the way that he works; thus, life at shows becomes a lot easier.

When most of the punters are in and drinking, the promoter may circulate to find out if people are enjoying themselves. If flyers are given out at the door for the promoter's other shows at the venue, he must make sure that the tickets are on sale as there is bound to be a hard core of punters who buy tickets for other shows as soon as they are advertised. If advance tickets are cheaper, many people tend to buy them. Often at shows there are two types of leaflets:

- A leaflet detailing the other shows that the band are doing on tour to try to get punters to go to more than one show.

- A Freepost leaflet for more information on the band or for joining the band's fan club. As these are pre-paid, it encourages fans to send them back, thus immediately securing a fan base to put on computer for mailing and commercial purposes.

At the stated time, the support band takes the stage. All staff members must be in place before they go on. A problem in the crowd or with the equipment is as likely to happen when the support are playing as it is when the headline band are on stage. The promoter should never relax controls and should treat the support band with the same enthusiasm as the headline band. When the support have finished, they come off stage and the crew and their technical staff remove their kit from the stage and load it onto the waiting van. The headline band's equipment is then put together ready for their set. When the band go on stage and start, the promoter and tour manager can sort out the final details of the deal. The promoter often does not get to see the main act as he is sorting out the fees (or fees and percentage) for the main band. Once this is done, the promoter is then free to continue with his duties for the rest of the night. At the end of the concert, the band often request a room where they can meet the management or record company as well as friends and relatives. Whilst this is going on, the crew are taking down the main band's backline. They then take down their PA and lighting and load it back onto the van. The promoter cannot leave the building until everything has been cleared away. Time is of the essence because, if things are not cleared away by a certain time, the promoter will incur financial penalties from the venue manager. If any of the venue staff have to stay behind to clear up or to put the venue back in working order after the time that the promoter has been allotted, this may incur further costs. A little food and drink for the bands and the crew at the end of the night always goes down well as crewing is not the easiest of jobs and a promoter who does not look after his crew deos not keep them very long. After each event, the promoter should hold a post mortem with the parties concerned to go over any difficulties or plus points of the gig. This is always helpful when planning another concert.

Conclusion

Although a promotion can never be totally perfect, it is possible to get close to perfection. Two key elements, essential to any promotion, are sound financial planning and good administration. The next chapter concentrates on these two areas.

Chapter 9

Finance and Administration

The economics of promotion

The inherent skill of promotion is to maximise the profit margin whilst still maintaining a quality service to both the internal and external customers. This skill taxes the commercial awareness and competence of the promoter. A promoter inept in the skills of economic survival will soon lose credibility and fade into obscurity.

A promoter must be aware of his own financial position. Once that is clarified, he can set financial parameters within which he must keep in order to continue a viable business. This is known as financial *risk assessment*. These parameters can be set up as budget headings and must be part of any planning for promotion of acts or artists. Some promoters have other businesses which support their promotion activities. These should also have set parameters, and the promoter should keep an account of any money passing from one area of business to another. This is difficult in multi-faceted businesses, but it is important to keep correct financial records at all times, not only for personal and economic reasons but also for tax and VAT purposes, when financial accountability must be proved.

Keeping accounts is difficult because the promoter is never engaged in a single promotion at any one time. He usually has a flow of different promotions throughout a one- or two-year planning cycle. To balance these, predictions made on past performance and present economic standing are useful but cannot be relied upon because the music business is fluid and ever changing.

Making ends meet

A promoter must be a great bargainer. Remember, all agents work within a sliding scale of fees, which has been developed to encompass venue size and overall costs. If a promoter has a good relationship with his agent and managers, negotiations take place until an agreement on price has been reached. For instance, if a band specifically ask to play a venue because they are always treated well when they visit, then the lowering of the fixed guaranteed fee may be possible or, if all the other gigs on a tour are 1500 capacity, but the promoter's venue holds 800, a price differential is usually possible.

Some unscrupulous agents charge a high fee for bands when it is blatantly obvious that the concert is unlikely to break even, never mind make a profit. These agents are well known, and the trick is always to offer them a low guarantee and a high percentage and to hope that this is accepted. Offering such a deal means that the onus on the promoter is slightly alleviated, giving him more financial leeway to market the gig more effectively. To make ends meet can also mean cutting down on various unwanted aspects of the promotion, but this must be done without endangering the quality of the event or the integrity of the promoter. A small decrease in public address (PA) size may not seem to affect the overall sound, but it may anger the band manager who has specifically asked for a specific size to increase the quality of the sound, rather than to boost the decibels.

One of the corners that can readily be cut is in advertising. 500 posters and 1000 leaflets look great when they arrive but, if the promoter uses only 100 posters and 500 leaflets, he has miscalculated. The cost could have been cut by perhaps £100 had the marketing and promotion been more carefully planned. It may be better to spend just a little bit more on catering, thus ensuring the happiness of the band and their crew, rather than skimping on the catering and suffering an unhappy and uncomfortable night with whinges from the whole entourage, including managers and technicians. If the band and the manager are happy, then most of the promoter's problems are solved.

Cutting corners on technical requirements is not recommended, but cutting staff surplus to requirements can save money without sacrificing quality. Promoters promise to give regular concert attendees, who show an interest in helping with the crewing of events, a chance to show their worth. They may reward their patience with paid employment for a series of future concerts. But, when the concerts begin to lose money, and the promoter does not want to go back on his word, he feels obliged to keep the crew members on. The best way to cope is not to make rash promises and to ensure that staffing arrangements are not over-adequate for the task. If a contract states that the promoter is required to provide four crew, then he must provide four crew. Any extra people will raise costs. Negotiation does not only happen between the promoter and the agent. Many negotiations take place – between the promoter and the venue, the promoter and the PA company, and on the price and quantity of posters and leaflets between the promoter and the printer.

Making ends meet is hard; it is not always practicable to get ticket money to the venue on time, because of constraints on the promoter. Cash flow problems often hit promoters and force banks to foreclose on overdrafts and loans, rendering the promoter bankrupt. The importance of financial planning and budgetary control is discussed later in this chapter.

Ticket reconciliation

At the end of each gig a ticket reconciliation is almost always demanded by the tour manager for one or more of many reasons. A manifest shows:

- How many tickets were sold.

- At what price they were sold.

- How many were sold in advance.

- How many were sold on the door.

- Income from concessions.

- An approximate final figure of the promoter's gross and net takings.

- The band's percentage, where a fee/percentage deal has been struck.

Ticket reconciliation is an integral part of the evening's proceedings and often causes friction between the tour manager and the promoter. This is usually a result of box office inefficiency, which can be caused by a number of reasons, but means that the promoter cannot give the tour manager an accurate reconciliation of ticket sales. The promoter must remember that he is contractually bound to present the tour manager with a ticket manifest at the end of the performance. Failure to do so can result in prosecution. The tour manager may also call for a count of attendees and may even put a member of his staff with a counter on the door. This usually happens when the tour manager questions the honesty and integrity of the promoter.

The manifest must give the numbers of all tickets sold in advance and at the door, and a signed letter from each ticket agent with the stubs of the tickets sold at the agencies. Only then can all the tickets be accounted for. It often states in the contract that, if a full reconciliation is not available at the end of the night, the tour manager can request 100 per cent of all money taken from the tickets sold on the night. The promoter must remember that the tour manager is managing the band's money. Hotel and food costs for the band must come out of this money as well as other costs, such as transport and petrol.

Any tickets sold over the venue's capacity cause other problems. If capacity is breached and the tour manager and agent have been forewarned, they may ask for a percentage of the extra money. If the promoter has not warned them, then all the money from over sales may be confiscated by the tour manager. If the tour manager is a stickler for regulations, the promoter may even be reported to the Environmental Health Department and the venue's entertainment licence could be revoked. Conversely, any tickets not accounted for at the end of the night will be charged at full price to the promotion.

As a promoter, it is always advisable to plan the type and configuration of your manifest. Even the way your tickets are printed influences the way in which your manifest is presented. Four-part tickets are an efficient way to present a ticket manifest. Such tickets furnish the promoter with enough surplus sections to enable him to produce evidence of ticket sales to the venue manager, the tour manager, the auditors and any other interested parties. This will provide proof of where, how, for how much and by which ticket agent each ticket was sold. Special preparations should be made well in advance for picking tickets up, and the promoter should make sure that the ticket agent has a specially-produced form on which to prepare a manifest. This saves both time and energy, as the promoter, by producing this form, has delegated the job of preparing the ticket outlet manifest to the ticket agents themselves. A special delivery point for tickets could also be set up as the promoter will be busy all day. It may be possible to delegate the responsibility to one of his trusted staff. This sort of trust makes staff feel both wanted and a part of a team.

Ticket outlets

Ticket outlets must be chosen carefully. Their choice always relies on four factors:

- Distance from the venue.

- Frequency of punter visit.

- Accessibility.

- Catchment area.

If a venue promotes only local acts, it is not viable to have a ticket outlet outside a radius of 20 miles (32 km) as the venue's catchment area may cover only three to four miles (4.8 to 6.4 km).

It is not a good idea to sell tickets in a record shop that has few customers, or in an outlet not easily accessible to the type of people that you are trying to attract to the venue or the concert.

A lot of time and effort has to be spent on the siting of ticket outlets. They may be record shops, clothes shops, other venues or ticket offices.

An ideal situation for a ticket outlet for a nationally-renowned club venue is within a major youth-oriented facility with easy access and in reach of all target audiences from the venue's catchment area. It could be sited in a large town or city close to the venue. If the venue has three or four cities or towns close to it, then a ticket outlet in each may be advisable. It would be futile to have a ticket outlet just for the sake of it, it will be costly in the long run in both money and time. Remember that a promoter's time is valuable.

When appointing a ticket agency, it is advisable to hold an informal meeting which can be used as a vehicle to discuss the parameters of the promoter's ticket sales. It can also be used to familiarise the outlet with the manifest procedures and those pertinent to ticket collection. It is an informal meeting where the promoter and the outlet can discuss marketing strategies and ticket paperwork. At the meeting, the promoter can ensure that the ticket outlet signs, in triplicate, a contract or statement of intent to sell for each set of tickets. One copy is kept by the promoter, one copy by the ticket agent and a spare copy kept is on file as proof of the transaction. If a court case ensues and the promoter cannot prove that the outlet was given a series of tickets, no reimbursement will be made. The promoter must also stipulate the way in which he wishes to receive payment for sold tickets, for example, by cheque at the end of each month, and should keep the same system for the duration of time that he uses this ticket agency.

Fees and percentages

When negotiating a contract, there are several ways of deciding on the deal. Figure 9:1, page 182, shows four of the ways in which a deal can be fixed.

- A *straight fee* (Figure 9:1a, page 182). The promoter pays the agent a set fee plus VAT for the band with no percentage or other costs on top.

- An *overhead deal* (Figure 9:1b, page 182). The promoter's overheads are paid off first and the rest of the profits are split in favour of the band. This does not happen often but, when a band knows that a venue is struggling, it may do this to help the promoter. The band members know that, if the gig is promoted properly, they stand to make a good profit.

- A *straight fee plus a percentage* (Figure 9:1c, page 183). A set of costs is sent to the agent and a break-even figure is quoted. The agent usually costs in a slight profit in the promoter's favour. The percentage of the excess money is then worked out which, if the guarantee (set fee) is small, is largely in favour of the band. For example 70/30, 80/20 or even 90/10.

- A *straight percentage* (Figure 9:1d, page 183). This usually only happens when the agent is sure of a huge sell out and that the company will make a great deal of money from the promotion. For the promoter, if the band is carrying production, then his costs are minimised and any ticket money taken by the venue has a percentage profit for him when his overheads have been cleared.

This method is in the promoter's favour only for two reasons.

- o If the promotion loses, because the overheads are small, so too are the losses.

- o If the promotion sells out, although the profits are nowhere near as large as they would have been if a straight fee or a fee and percentage had been paid to the artist, the risk is still minimised.

Other deals can be worked out in the following way:

- o A straight hire to another promoter or promotions company (not shown in Figure 9:1). This would only happen if the promoter is also the manager of a venue. This can be lucrative for the promoter relying on a set amount of money coming through each week to pay his overheads. The three largest income earners for promoters who manage venues are outside promotions, clubs and classes. Outside promoters hire the venue for a fee, clubs pay a fee and a percentage of ticket sales, and classes usually pay a straight hire fee at an hourly rate.

- An either/or system (not shown in Figure 9:1) where a fee or a box office percentage is taken, whichever the greater.

Figure 9:1 Four ways in which a deal can be fixed

The graphs assume that the promoter's expenses
amount to £600 in total.

Figure 9:1a

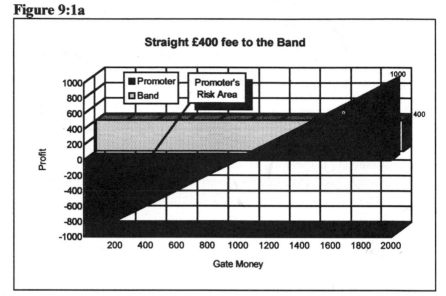

Figure 9:1b

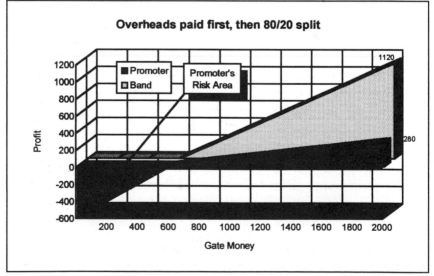

Figure 9:1c

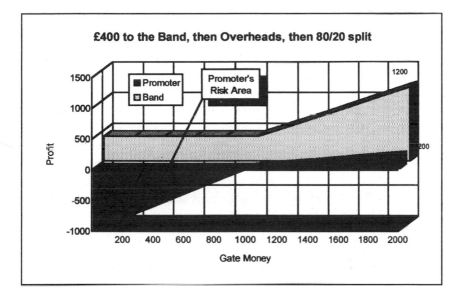

Figure 9:1d

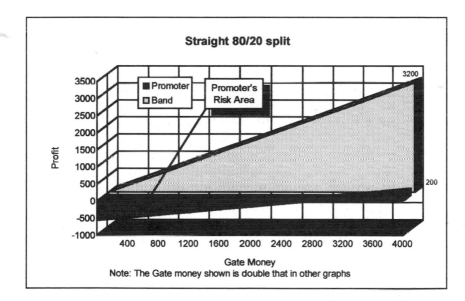

Whichever deal you strike, it must be the best for you. The most usual deal is the guarantee plus the percentage (Figure 9:1c, page 183). But, with such agreements the you must read the small print in the contract carefully and understand the full implications of such a deal. One of the commonest mistakes that a promoter makes is the reading of the type of payment in the contract. Cash or cheque should be clearly stated and, where the wrong style of payment is noted, you must send a letter to the agent with the proposed change and reasons for it. One of the most difficult parts of the contract to interpret is the percentage deal. Watch out for clauses stating net payments rather than gross, and clauses stating *or whichever is the greater*. In the latter case, a misreading of the clause can be very costly leaving a promoter unable to cover his own costs even if the concert is a sell out. Also beware of the VAT trap, because, for most promoters, all tickets sold are liable for 17.5% VAT. If a promoter forgets this in a calculation, he will find that, when the ticket manifest is calculated, he will be 17.5% down on the income he expected.

Administrative Documentation

Administrative documentation is very important to a promoter. The more efficient and effective the documentation, the easier the job seems to be. If there is no administrative documentation you can be sure that there is something wrong.

The contract

For a specimen contract refer to Figure 9:2, pages 188-9. Many contracts are verbose while some may contain only two pages. American contracts are full of *when*s and *wherefore*s and sometimes ask for the most demanding requirements. If you, as a promoter, receive an American contract, the secret is not to panic; telephone the agent and discuss what the band really needs. The contract comes in two parts: the contractual obligation and the rider. The two parts form a whole and you must sign both to complete a deal. If the rider is ignored, then the band will refuse to perform. I have received many strange contracts from bands asking for accessories, such as a dozen multi-coloured condoms, and three pairs of cotton Y-fronts. Because a contract is a legally binding document, once it is signed, any changes that the recipient wants to make to the document must be made in writing within a certain time-frame stated in the rider. In many cases a contract does not arrive until after this date, so a faxed message to the agent usually suffices. There may be times when you do not want to comply with the contract and a compromise will have to be reached.

A contract always starts with an agreement number which should be quoted on any subsequent query, for ease. It is then dated so that any clause regarding to the date can be verified. The promoter's name and the band's name are stated. The promoter is known as the *contractor* and the band as the *artist*.

The terms of the engagement are then set out. This usually contains the name of the venue at which the band will be appearing and what their payment will be. This, and other details, will be verified further on in the contract.

A series of clauses are then drawn up. These clauses include the length of time that the band will play for, from what time access to the venue will be needed, the sound check time, the time that the doors open, the on-stage times of all bands, the support act and payment, the curfew time, the ticket price, the method of payment, and the fact that the rider is an integral part of the contract. This information will already have been discussed between the promoter and the agent at an earlier date. In the promotion process negotiation between the promoter and the agent takes a great deal of time.

The next part of the contract contains a table that details the venue, its address, its telephone number, its fax number and its capacity.

A section is then left for special terms which often relate to parts of the rider; members of the band often ask the promoter to take special care with these needs.

At the bottom of the contract there is a space for signing and agreeing terms. Once both parties have signed the contract, it is legally binding.

The rider is a completely different document, complicated by legal jargon and containing archaic clauses that, in real life, can never be adhered to. The rider has several parts: a technical specification, a hospitality specification and a venue specification. The technical specification states the size of the public address system (PA) required, the type of microphones, the number of channels in the desk, any specials, such as gates and compressors, that the technician requires, the lighting specification, etc. It is often impossible to fulfil all of these specifications, but a compromise can usually be met. The safest and most economical way to deal with the technical rider is to give the band's technicians the telephone number of the sound and lighting company and to let them talk between themselves. If the promoter lets the band and entourage turn up on the day to find that their technical specifications have not been met, there will be serious problems. If a rider cannot be adhered to, then the promoter or the technician should inform the agent or the tour manager immediately. Problems can always be sorted out in advance but, on the day, it may be impossible. Dialogue and good communication can make even the most awkward technician, who has not slept for a week, happy.

The hospitality section of the rider varies in Britain, Europe and America. If a promoter thinks he has been sent an unreasonable rider, he should talk to the agent and find out if the rider has changed. The best person to talk to about changes to the rider is the tour manager. Hospitality is an essential part; the band must be fed and watered well, and a spread of food, good beer and a relaxing setting is always appreciated. If the band members stay on the bus all the time, the promoter will know that he has not satisfied their needs in the venue. There is often a last paragraph in the rider which reads something like,

> *The above list of items has been carefully thought out and specifically requested. Your meeting these requirements accurately is greatly appreciated. If you have any problems or questions regarding the above please contact ...*

Specific and to the point. If the band members do not ask for much, give them what they ask for.

The final section of the rider deals with the nitty-gritty of the deal, including how payment is to be made, with what taxes deducted and what insurances the promoter must have. If the band are from outside the UK, then the promoter may have to obtain work permits and pay other taxes for them to be able to play in this country. It is usually the agent who has to apply for these permits, but it is not unknown for the promoter to be left with the job. All venues and promoters must have public liability insurance (PLI) and all the correct licences for the concert to go ahead. In some cases, the band and the manager will ask to see the PLI document(s) just to make sure that the promoter and the venue are covered in case of any mishap.

Within the rider, are several paragraphs common to all riders. These pertain to discrimination of any sort where, if this is seen to occur by the band or the manager, the band will refuse to play. This may include age, race and sex discrimination by the venue manager or the promoter and their staff. The rider also contains a caveat explaining *force majeure*, whereby if an earthquake, flood, royal demise or failure of transportation occurs, the contract will be counted null and void. Security expectations are also tabled. This includes the amount of security needed and the time that they are expected. The rider may also stipulate rulings on cameras, videos, recording equipment and weapons, all of which, with the exception of cameras, are banned at venues throughout this country, Europe and most worldwide tour destinations. Often a clause is included in the contract stating that the band have a right to stipulate a support act and also sole rights to distribute merchandising. The rider will also stipulate the number of dressing rooms that the band expect, the number of complimentary tickets required, the stage size, the number of stage hands to be used as crew and the size of billing on posters and other advertising for the show that the headlining band requires.

On the club circuit at first glance, the contract and rider look daunting but, when the promoter takes time to read the whole document, nothing is impossible. It is the larger halls and stadiums which have to deal with the really impossible riders. As a promoter, remember that, if the demands of the contract and the rider are not large, it is better to meet them than to have an evening filled with grief from an unhappy band and entourage.

Figure 9:2   A specimen contract

THE TALENT COMPANY

An Agreement made the _____ day
of (month) _____ year _____

Between_____
_____
_____
Telephone_____telex/fax _____

(hereinafter referred to as the '**Promoter**') of the one part **and**

_____
_____

(hereinafter referred to as the '**Manager**') of the other part

It is hereby agreed that the Promoter engages the Artist specified in the Schedule hereto and the Manager agrees to provide the services of the Artist to appear on the date(s) and at the venue(s) and for the fees(s) specified in the schedule hereto and on the terms and conditions contained in the Schedule the Additional Clauses and the Artist's Rider (if any)

Schedule

Artist _____
_____

Date(s)_____
_____

Venue(s) _____
_____
_____

FINANCE & ADMINISTRATION

Telephone _____

Telex/fax _____

Fee(s) _____

_____

Payable by_____

to _____ on _____

The price of admission to be not less than _____

The official capacity of the venue is _____ persons

therefore the potential gross receipts are _____

The artist shall play for a minimum of _____ minutes

Earliest arrival time: _____
Soundcheck: _____
Doors open: _____

Opening artists on stage: _____
Artists on stage:_____
curfew: _____

NET RECEIPTS   = GROSS RECEIPTS **LESS** VAT,
                 LESS AGREED PROMOTION/PRODUCTION COSTS

THE ATTACHED ADDITIONAL CLAUSES AND ARTIST RIDER ARE
PART OF THIS CONTRACT

SIGN BELOW AND INITIAL ALL PAGES

SIGNED BY_____
for and on behalf of the Promoter

In the presence of _____

189

The FEU

Artists and bands working or resident abroad, including the Channel Islands and other tax havens, have to complete an FEU 4 form. How bands get such documentation is discussed in Chapter 2. The form states how much the band can earn for each specific gig on a tour. Any foreign band without FEU (Foreign Entertainment Unit) clearance must have 30 per cent of their payment deducted for tax. The actual FEU will specify a threshold for the band and, when this is reached, the promoter must withhold tax on any remaining portion of payment. Most bands on club tours tend to fall below the threshold FEU tax which makes their life a lot easier.

Budgetary control

In any budget there are two main elements, income and expenditure.

Expenditure has three components:

- Product costs, including the cost of the bands.
- Service costs, including the cost of the PA and lighting systems.
- Marketing and promotion costs.

These three components are integral to the presentation of the show. Without the artist, the venue and technical elements and promotional tools, the promotion cannot go ahead. The service costs include the cost of the venue, staffing, security and crew, ticket administration and any other elements of administration. Marketing and promotion costs include all the tools and services employed for the show.

Income also has three components:

- Box office income, from the audience paying for the show.
- Income from programme sales, T-shirts, vending and other merchandising.
- Subsidy income, which mainly applies to publicly-funded venues or promotions, is derived from private or public bodies and from bar income.

Therefore, we can use the following equation:

$$(D+E+F) - (A+B+C) = \text{Gross profit/loss}$$

where   A = Product costs   D = Box office income
             B = Service costs   E = Related income
             C = Promotional costs   F = Subsidy income

This is the basic equation to calculate the profit and loss of a concert. In reality it is much more complicated, but this calculation gives a basis for financial management of an event.

The budget is a key factor in all aspects of the promoter's business. You need to plan ahead and not to leave the slightest thing to chance. To repeat, a promotion rarely goes smoothly on the night. If you, as a promoter, are prepared for the worst, with all your financial hatches tightly battened down, you should be able to ride the storm. You will not need to panic buy last minute items not included in the budget. Panic buying is the biggest headache for any promoter. Once it starts it is impossible to stop, as the promoter is guided by the optimism factor of *It's okay, we will sell enough tickets to cover it.* But, panic buying can turn a healthy profit into a deficit.

The budget is a financial description of your promotions. Each event should be carefully budgeted. An overall running total must be kept so that you, as a promoter, know where you stand at any time. Changes are inevitable – all promoters have had to re-negotiate the fee or to change their plans drastically. All changes should be able to be accommodated in your budget.

There are two types of budget:

- The flexible budget, which on many occasions is not finalised until the doors open.
- The inflexible budget, which is finalised weeks before the concert and is difficult to change.

The very nature of music promotion makes an inflexible budget very difficult to operate. This can cause major problems, especially with

American bands, where diets and other facets of the promotion can change from minute to minute. The flexible approach to a promotional budget is usually more appropriate than the inflexible one. Owing to the nature of the flexible budget, it is wise to finalise as many areas as possible so that you can plan as much of the budget as you can in advance. This cuts some of the flexibility, but it makes the budget easier to control. The level of contingency can then be calculated and a rough idea of the likely profit or loss estimated. This method allows flexibility with some control and means that changes to the budget are minimised. If the flexible budget is finalised a week before a production, but contingencies are built in to cover foreseeable problems, this is probably the best compromise.

The nature of promotion and its unpredictability means that as many predictable elements as possible need to be set early in the promotion process. Most of the unpredictable elements in the budget come within the projected income bracket. No-one can really forecast how many tickets or T-shirts are likely to be sold, or what the bar profits will be. This is mostly carefully-planned guesswork. No matter how many regression and projection charts are used, the promoter can never really predict how well even the most popular band will sell. Keeping abreast of up to the minute changes in the business does help. It does happen that, just as the promoter thinks that he has picked a certainty, an anomaly will appear and six weeks' hard work will go down the drain. It is one of the pitfalls of being a promoter.

Expenditure is far easier to predict than income, especially if the promoter has his own venue or uses the same venue every week. Venue costs can then be predicted. The only changes that will occur are on those occasions when he needs extra staff, a bigger PA, an increase in publicity or other increases in extraneous costs. Using the same venue a number of times, means that the promoter can assess the audience profile for a wide range of musical disciplines, giving him a better chance of choosing the right band to sell and, thus, being more likely to make a profit. One of the major reasons for getting to grips with costs quickly is that, for an event with a percentage deal, the agent will require a list of all the expenditure forecast for the show. You must prepare a checklist for these costs so that everything possible is included. If a hidden cost is not presented to the agent, and the costing has already been done, the promoter will probably have to bear the extra cost himself.

Bands vary in price. This will depend on several factors. For example, how popular the band is over a period:

- *Transient* popularity, gained over a few months may include a number of top five hits but draws on a short-lived and unsustainable audience. The fee is high for only a short time.

- *Longevity* popularity, where an artist draws a large audience continually. The band is guaranteed to be popular and the fee reflects this.

- *Cult status* where an artist attracts a specific audience from a wide catchment area. The audience is finite, but stable, and the fee is lower.

- If the band tours with its own PA and lights. This increases the cost of the band, but decreases the PA and lighting expenditure.

- If the band has made the big time after they have been booked. Some bands are reasonably priced, and it is the promoter's dream to pick up a band just as it is breaking, when it commands a large following but is relatively cheap. I have managed to do this on a number of occasions including Blur, Belly, The Cranberries, The Qireboys, Terrorvision, The Wildhearts and Eddi Reader. The way a band is priced should reflect their pulling power.

  Beware of overpriced pop bands. This business is fickle and bands move out of vogue very fast. Bands with a proven track record are usually worth paying for as audiences tend to be loyal to them. Bands are expensive and it is not worth taking the risk to promote a band that may not recoup your outlay.

Financial records are essential, not only because the Inland Revenue and VAT offices require precise records, but also for three other reasons:

- To help to make crucial financial decisions. Your records must be up-to-date for this.

- To borrow money. Banks need accurate and up-to-date information

- Future budgeting. A series of records for promotions over a number of years will help with future budgeting. There are records of promoters and managers who just bump their budgetary figures up by five per cent each financial year, without looking at the overall picture in the industry. This is not recommended as some areas of the industry move a lot faster than others.

Each item of business stationery must be labelled clearly with correct headings and the most valuable information to the promoter. Without correct and viable headings, keeping records is futile. All invoices and receipts must have all the relevant details logged. If a VAT receipt has no clearly identifiable VAT number, then it is void. If the receipt does not have the place of purchase or till number, then it also might as well be void.

The ledger contains a record of payments made or agreed. Each year budgets must be monitored. Monitoring is a fail-safe mechanism whereby differences between proposed and actual expenditure are picked up. Differences can then be dealt with efficiently and effectively, putting the final plan or budgets back on the right track.

Final accounts for each event pose a problem; it is difficult to judge when to close them. Accounts must be kept in good order and each month finished off correctly. They can then be audited quickly. All accounting processes should be consistent, and the day-to-day accounting system should be the same as the system used for final accounts. At the end of the accounting process you can derive a profit/loss figure for the year and this tells you whether you have succeeded as a promoter.

It is often useful to collect financial data on a PC. From data input a computer can give a graphical presentation of the promoter's up to date accounts and, from this, a picture of his promotion activities over a period can be shown. Years can be compared, and it may then become easier to understand trends.

Conclusion

The promoter must keep abreast, not only of his own financial and budgetary position, but also the situation of the business as a whole. Each change in the music business directly affects the audiences, the cost of the bands, the costs of the PA, and other extraneous costs connected to the promotion. But, help is available – and from some of the unlikeliest places. For instance, many people have an inherent fear of the tax and VAT men, yet these people can make life much easier for the promoter (and anyone else who is self-employed). The tax and VAT laws are complicated and these people are usually the only help that the promoter can call upon when he is having trouble understanding them. The agent, and many other professionals in the music business, can be called upon for advice, and the promoter must never be afraid or too proud to ask. Do not forget, even if the answer is not very helpful, at least you have asked.

You must keep all financial records in good condition, and produce clear financial records. If the promoter is always on top of his finances, when he is offered a promotion, he will be able to give an immediate answer. A quick answer is always important.

Chapter 10

Managing the Band/Setting up a Tour
by David Walker-Collins

Managing the band

Managing any band is a complex and challenging role, the art of which is difficult to define. Throughout the history of rock and roll music there have been many managers who have become as famous as, if not more so, than the artist they looked after. Colonel Tom Parker (Elvis Presley), Brian Epstein (The Beatles), and Malcolm Mclaren (Sex Pistols) are just three managers who have become household names along with their artists.

The first step in band management is to seek out and find that special talent and spark of magic that you, as a manager, believe in. There are generally two types of manager:

- Those who already have a relationship with the band, be it as a friend or crew member.

- Those who are established and professional.

It is probable that the latter started off being the former.

The main role of the manager is to nurture and care for the career of the band. The relationship between the two parties is an extremely close one and can succeed or fail on the strength of that personal interaction. There must be a high level of regard and personal trust between the two parties if they are to go forward together. Remember that both the manager and the band stand to benefit a great deal financially should the career of the band reach the dizzy peaks of pop stardom.

Once you, as a manager, have found a band that you feel passionately about, you can take the first steps on the road to building your joint careers. Inevitably, this will require some capital investment on your part as well as the sacrifice of a lot of free time. The sorts of tasks in the early days are as follows:

- Watching the band at rehearsals and advising them on their appearance, presentation and overall image. At this early stage it is difficult for many bands to accept criticism and you will find it far more beneficial to offer constructive ideas. Remember, rock musicians have fragile egos!

- When you feel the band is ready, you may decide to invest money in the recording of a demonstration (demo) tape. This needs to be of professional quality as it will be used to sell the band to venues and, possibly, even record companies. This is the first time that you make a financial investment in the band; it will not be the last.

- When the demo is completed, you need to decide on its format. Whilst the cassette tape is the most popular method of presenting a band, if finances allow it is always preferable to produce a CD as this tends to impress potential promoters and record companies. Presentation is extremely important and some money should be spent on high quality artwork to enhance the product.

- You may consider employing a professional photographer to produce publicity photographs of the band. It is important that an image consistent with the music they produce is sustained. It is also extremely useful to keep a scrapbook of press cuttings the band may attract, even if only from small, provincial local newspapers.

- Once the demo has been manufactured, it needs to be mailed to as many people as possible. Lists of venues, record companies, agents etc. can be found in directories such as *The White Book* and *Kemps International Music Book*. These directories are produced annually and are viewed as industry 'bibles'. Although seemingly expensive (at over £30) they are an essential purchase for anyone embarking on a career in management or any other sector of the music industry. The package you send out should ideally include a copy of the tape/CD, a photograph of the band, biographical details of their career to date, and the manager's name and address as a contact.

- A few days after you have spent a fortune on postage you will need to spend another fortune on the telephone. Every person to whom you sent a package will need at least one, and possibly many, follow-up telephone calls. It is the manager's job to badger, press and cajole people into taking notice of his band.

Playing live is a very important aspect of any band's career and one of the manager's functions is to get his bands as many shows as possible. Although it may be very rewarding for a band to play in their home town in front of enthusiastic friends and fans, they need to play to the widest-possible audience in order to gain greater popularity. Managers have to be extraordinarily persistent to persuade promoters to pay out good money for bands to play at their venue. The amounts the manager receives will not come near to covering the actual costs incurred in van hire, petrol, food and accommodation. He will probably need to fund the shortfall himself. One popular method of saving money on accommodation is to tell the band they must sleep in the van! When the manager has a string of dates in place, he must send a further package to every local newspaper and radio station in the area where the band is to play. Getting local journalists to see the band and, with luck, to review them in a positive light helps to create a wider buzz about them and will provide more press cuttings to boost the growing history of the band's career.

After the band have cut their teeth playing shows around the country, it is important for them to play in both the capital of the country and the home of the British music business – London. Playing in the capital is completely different from playing anywhere else in the country. As demand is extremely high, promoters do not have to pay unknown bands sums of money to appear at their venue. In some venues bands are charged to play, even though this practice, known as *pay to play*, is actively discouraged by the Musicians' Union and many sectors of the industry. If the manager does not find his band in a pay to play venue, he may be given tickets to sell for a show in which his band is third or fourth on the bill along with other unknown bands. The audience at such venues are likely to be bewildered European, American and Japanese tourists who, in the long run, are not going to further the band's, or the manager's, career.

If the manager does succeed in procuring one or more London dates at an established venue, for example, The Forum, LA2 or The Brixton Academy, he will again need to blitz record companies, publishers, and agents with information about his band with a view to persuading them to attend the gig. He may then consider it a wise investment to hire a coach and to transport friends and fans of the band from their local town to the gig to be enthusiastic supporters and, thereby, impress record industry people who may be present.

Whilst it is true that London is the home of the music business in Britain, music is a global industry with extremely large markets in Europe, America and Japan. Your band's material may be better suited to one of these markets. There are many British bands whose careers flourish in Europe and Japan but who are virtually unknown in their own country. There are also many examples of bands breaking in America before finding success in their home country, for example, The Cranberries. A good manager needs to decide which markets to concentrate on and, therefore, which record companies are most appropriate to the band's needs. There are many British bands signed to European and American labels whose CDs do not get mainstream releases in this country. They nevertheless have successful careers.

An alternative way of getting the band's songs to a wider audience is to consider the possibility of the manager and the band releasing a CD themselves by starting their own label. More and more bands are following this route in the present musical climate and, as well as securing all money from sales, many bands feel that they also maintain their artistic integrity and independence. Having produced and manufactured an own-label CD, it is sometimes possible to secure a licensing and distribution deal with a major record company or with one of the independent distributors such as Pinnacle, Vital and Rough Trade. If a band issues initial releases on its own label, this shows a degree of belief in themselves and their music and this can impress major record companies, especially if the CD sells well and enters the independent charts now regularly featured in the music press and television programmes, such as *The Chart Show* and *The Beat.*

Should everything go according to plan, then by this stage in the band's development, the manager may well be attracting the attention of record industry A&R (artist and repertoire) staff. These are people employed by record companies to scour the country seeking new talent. They are responsible for signing artists to a record company prior to their rivals doing likewise. In reality the artists have to go to the record companies; that is, they have to perform in London to be spotted. It is a rare occurrence for A&R people to venture out to the provinces, except when a particular genre grows out of a specific town or city. A good example of this is the Manchester scene which erupted in the late 1980s with bands such as Stone Roses, Inspiral Carpets and James. Suddenly, every A&R person in Britain descended on that city looking for a slice of the action. Since that time the industry has retreated back to the capital.

As the band's career develops and the manager's financial investment grows, he may consider it appropriate to formalise his role in their development by having both parties sign a formal contract. Legal advice should be sought in this matter from a solicitor who specialises in contract law. The contract should not be seen as a threat to either party but as an extension and formal recognition of the ongoing relationship between them. Any contract should look after the interests of both the manager and the band. There have been many occasions when a manager, who has started out as a friend of the band, has been pushed aside in favour of a professional manager once the band's career reaches the point where record companies are showing serious interest. Sometimes record companies force a change in management as they would rather deal with people that they already know. They may, of course, also receive some remuneration for placing bands in the hands of specific managers.

Alongside the record deal, the manager will possibly negotiate a publishing contract and an agency agreement for the band to be represented by one of the recognised agents in the business. At this time he should at last begin to see some financial return on his investmcnt. He will probably take on management of all the band's finances and appoint an accountant to oversee their affairs with him. Every relationship between manager and band is different, with some bands more willing to give total financial control to their manager than others, who seek to retain some control themselves. There are no hard and fast rules. It is a matter of balancing practicalities, mutual trust, and personal relationships to form the best arrangement for the manager and the band.

Managing a band is a risky business with potentially high financial rewards and a great deal of personal and professional satisfaction. But, there are pitfalls, such as the loss of the band to a professional manager and the distinct possibility that a band will fall out with each other and split up just at the very moment that they are about to break into the big time. But, if you, as a manager, have weathered all these storms, there are no limits to where you and your band may go.

Setting up a tour

The decision to tour is not made by any one person. It is a combination of many factors which lead the band to go out 'on the road'. Many bands prefer playing live to any other form of expressing their creativity and, consequently, will probably choose to tour constantly. Bands generally tour to support the release of a CD. Therefore, the band's record company has a major say in the setting of tour periods. Once the CD is recorded and pressed, art work prepared, and a release date set, the manager liaises with the record company and the band's agent regarding the release. Ideally, bands tour shortly after the release, but promoters often find themselves with dates set and the CD release postponed. There have been many tours where the CD has been released after the show has been and gone! There seems to be little concern shown by record companies when this happens as there is little contact between them and promoters, except through agents who are unfortunately left to make the explanations. But, tours could not happen without the support of record companies. They fund tours directly by offering bands tour support, which is a financial payment made to cover the shortfall between touring expenses and guaranteed income from promoters. Record companies do this as playing live raises a band's profile and directly increases CD sales, which is where the real money is made. Record companies also fund tours indirectly by the production and distribution of posters, which are placed in major cities and in the town where the band will play, in order to raise awareness of the CD, and by funding advertisements in the music and national press for the new release, which very often carries the tour dates as well.

There are other ways in which additional money to support the tour can be found. The sale of merchandise relating to the band can be extremely profitable. Although T-shirts are possibly the most purchased items, the larger bands sell a whole range of products which can include:

- hats
- shorts
- jogging bottoms
- posters
- cigarette lighters
- condom cases.

The only rule of merchandising is to sell as much as possible of anything. Everything which bears the logo or any image of the band is licensed by the band, who own the copyright, to the merchandiser, or is under a licensing agreement, which means the band receive royalties from the sales of all of these items. The merchandise can be manufactured by a professional company, such as Acme, which undertakes to produce the items as required and which provides the tour with a member of staff known as the *merch man*. He joins the tour and, upon reaching each venue, sets up a stall in a place where the majority of the paying customers must pass. He is responsible for all the goods, and before and after each show he does an inventory of the products and has to account for every sale. Alternatively, the band can purchase merchandise direct from a manufacturer and provide a *merch man* who is then responsible to the tour manager for accounting for all sales. It is then the job of the tour manager to provide a float each night, to check the items sold and to balance this against income. The sale of merchandise can be extremely lucrative and it is true that some bands, especially at stadium level, make more money from the sales of merchandise than they do from their live show.

Another way of raising funds for the tour is to employ one or more support bands who buy onto the tour; that is, they or their record company pay money to the headlining band in order to be their opening act. They will do this in the belief that they are guaranteed to play in front of an audience who may not have previously heard of them. It is important that the music they produce complements that of the main band. They recoup some of the cost of the buy-on from fees paid by promoters, but they also have to cover fuel, accommodation and living expenses. Most bands have probably been a support band at some point in their careers and it is surprising how many bands become bigger stars than the bands they originally supported!

Once the band, the manager and the record company have finalised their arrangements for product release, the agent is instructed to begin making the tour arrangements. At this stage a first-draft budget is drawn up and submitted to the record company. Decisions have to be made about the number of shows the band can afford to do, which is balanced against the number they actually want to do. The manager and agent will also discuss the amount of money they wish to see as a guaranteed income from each show. Some bands and their managers have an unrealistic view of the current market place and their value within it. It is the role of the agent to balance this difficult decision, based on the needs of the band and the promoter.

Bands at different stages in their careers have varying decisions to make on their tour. When a band first sets out around the country, they rely on local promoters in each town to provide them with PA and lighting systems, sound and lighting engineers, a local crew, and catering. Each promoter is contracted to provide these items by the agent in the rider to the contract. As their career progresses, a band can demand better-quality riders. Bands reach a point when they can choose to carry their own production and catering. This means the band choose the PA and lighting company which best meets their requirements and truck the equipment from show to show. The advantage for the band is that they retain total control of how they sound and look on stage and work with a regular, settled crew who know how to bring out the best in the band's performance. The obvious drawback is the costs, which include hire for equipment and trucks, hire of sleeper coaches for crew members and the wages of the travelling crew. On occasion, bands also have a sleeper bus which they live on for the duration of the tour, rather than using hotels. If the band choose to stay in hotels, then there are specialist travel agents who can arrange accommodation as required. Very often, extremely good nightly rates are acquired by booking into a chain of hotels across the country.

The key to a successful and smooth running tour and individual shows within it is the choice of tour manager. The tour manager is responsible for the welfare and well-being of the band and the co-ordination of each event as far as the artist is concerned. The tour manager is employed several weeks prior to the tour starting and one of his first tasks is to aid the band's manger and agent in making decisions regarding production, i.e., PA and lighting equipment and catering requirements. On larger tours where production is carried form venue to venue, it is quite likely that a production manager will be employed. The role of the production manager is to ensure that the crew employed with the equipment and the local crew employed at each show have everything ready and in place, fully operational, by the time the band and tour manager have agreed to arrive at the venue. The production manager liaises with the venue and/or the promoter regarding any technical matters or matters relating to health and safety rules, venue regulations, etc. He will motivate and manage the crew to get the best performance out of each person on the day. The production manager travels with the crew and is viewed as head of the production team.

The tour manager assists the band's manager with the setting of budgets and the production of the tour itinerary. The tour itinerary is a book issued to every person on the tour and is a detailed breakdown of each day's show with details, such as venue address, telephone numbers, hotel details, distance form previous venue, town map. In order to complete the itinerary, the tour manager needs to telephone each venue individually and speak to the manager to gain details such as:

- contact names and telephone/fax numbers for the venue.

- size of the stage.

- amount of electrical power on stage available for use.

- details of local crew.

- parking arrangements.

- times (doors open and curfew time).

- capacity of venue (the number of people allowed in the building).

- dressing room facilities.

- catering facilities.

- access for equipment (e.g., whether there are any stairs to negotiate).

This initial contact with the venue serves as an introduction to the people the tour manager will be working with on the day of the show.

Once all the information needed has been obtained, the tour manager has the requisite number of itineraries printed and bound ready for the start of the tour. Laminated passes are made, which are issued to each person on the tour to enable them to move freely around venues and to gain access to areas not open to the public, e.g., the dressing rooms, catering facilities.

Figure 10:1

Figure 10:1a   Costs of Angry Chair show at The Arena

THE ARENA

EVENT: Angry Chair   DATE: _____

ADVANCE TICKET PRICE: £9.50   DOOR TICKET PRICE: £10.50

% BREAK DETAILS		EXPENDITURE				PYT
		BUDGET	ACTUAL			METHOD
		NET	NET	VAT	GROSS	& REF.
MAIN ACT	ANGRY CHAIR		6500.00			
Supports	1. Support 1		100.00			
	2. Support 2		50.00			
Promotion	Tickets		96.00			
Expenses	Posters		50.00			
	Press ads		260.00			
	Handbills		70.00			
Staffing	Security		425.00			
Expenses	Stewards					
	Stage Crew		280.00			
	Electrician		50.00			
Equipment	PA		499.00			
Hire	Lighting		320.00			
	Misc.					
Rider	Food		650.00			
Clauses	Buy Ins					
	Misc. laundry		12.80			
Misc.	Box office commission		478.63			
	Performing Rights 3% net income		393.93			
VENUE HIRE			200.00			
PROMOTOR BUILT IN PROFIT			600.00			
TOTAL COST OF SHOW			10936.36			
TOTAL TICKET SALES			13131.06			
NET REMAINDER			2194.70			
% PAYMENT TO PROMOTER			438.94			

Figure 10:1b   Box Office Statement for Angry Chair show at The Arena

THE ARENA

BOX OFFICE STATEMENT

ADVANCE SALES	NO.	GROSS	VAT	NET	BO COMM. RATE	NET COMM.
The Arena	672	6384.00	950.81	5433.20		
Rock Records	112	1064.00	158.47	905.53	7.5%	67.91
Tourist Information	67	636.50	94.80	541.70	5.0%	27.08
Local college	74	703.00	104.70	598.30	10.0%	59.83
Next Town box office	132	1254.00	186.77	1067.23	10.0%	106.72
Records Galore	34	323.00	48.10	274.90	7.5%	20.62
Vinyl Heaven	62	589.00	87.72	501.28	7.5%	37.60
Pig in Muck Records	43	408.00	60.84	347.66	5.0%	17.38
Reel Records	32	304.00	45.28	258.72	10.0%	25.87
Big Chain Records	143	1358.00	202.33	1156.17	10.0%	115.62
TOTAL ADVANCE SALES	1371	13024.50	1939.82	11084.68		
DOOR SALES	229	2404.50	358.12	2046.38		
TOTAL INCOME & SALES	1600	15429.00	2297.94	13131.06		478.63

I CERTIFY THIS TO BE AN ACCURATE AND TRUE RECORD OF TICKET SALES

FOR _____   AT _____

ON _____ 20 ____

SIGNED _____

Figure 10:2a – j   Part of the itinerary for Angry Chair's European Tour, Spring 200X

Figure 10:2a   Dates and venues

ANGRY CHAIR EUROPEAN TOUR: SPRING 200X

Mon	27 February			Travel
Tue	28 February	Windsor	England	Old Trout
Wed	1 March			(tba)
Thu	2 March	Portsmouth	England	Pyramids
Fri	3 March	London	England	*The Scam* TV Show
Sat	4 March	Northampton	England	Roadmender
Sun	5 March	Norwich	England	University
Mon	6 March			Press
Tue	7 March	London	England	Radio 2 Session
Wed	8 March			(tba)
Thu	9 March			Press/travel
Fri	10 March	Glasgow	Scotland	Garage
Sat	11 March	Manchester	England	University
Sun	12 March			Off
Mon	13 March	London	England	Forum
Tue	14 March	London	England	*Most Hated* (DTV)
Wed	15 March	Amsterdam	Netherlands	Paradiso
Thu	16 March	Cologne	Germany	Live Music Hall
Fri	17 March	Hamburg	Germany	Docks
Sat	18 March	Copenhagen	Denmark	Grey Hall
Sun	19 March			Off
Mon	20 March	Oslo	Norway	Sentrum
Tue	21 March			Off
Wed	22 March	Stockholm	Sweden	Palladium
Thu	23 March			Travel/off
Fri	24 March	Berlin	Germany	Huxley's Neue Welt
Sat	25 March			Off
Sun	26 March	Munich	Germany	Charterhalle
Mon	27 March			Off
Tue	28 March	Zurich	Switzerland	Volkshaus
Wed	29 March			Off
Thu	30 March	Milan	Italy	Factory
Fri	31 March			Travel
Sat	1 April	Madrid	Spain	Revolver
Sun	2 April			Travel/off
Mon	3 April	Lyon	France	Transbordeur
Tue	4 April			Off
Wed	5 April	Paris	France	Elysee Montmartre
Thu	6 April	Nancy	France	Espace de Seichamps
Fri	7 April			Travel

Figure 10:2b   Tour personnel

TOUR PERSONNEL

Band

Paul Jones	Drums
James Rain	Keyboards
Paul Kelly	Bass
Billy Dement	Guitar
John Dutton	Vocals

Crew

Tom Surman	Tour Manager
Peter James	Production Manager/Monitor Engineer
Bruce Dickens	House Sound Engineer
Charles Leg	Lighting Designer
Jonty	Drum Technician
Simon Feind	Bass Technician
Slim Thomas	Guitar Technician (UK)
Roger Cure	Guitar Technician (Mainland)
George Ramis	Merchandiser
Charlie Wright	Bus Driver (UK)
Ian Wright	Bus Driver (Mainland)
Tom Sutcliffe	Minibus Driver (UK)
Jon Ericson	Truck Driver

Bandit

Karl Humus	Bass
Phil Card	Guitar
Ian Long	Drums
John Tuskie	Guitar/Vocals
Gerald Peterson	Manager
Nick Rose	Sound Engineer
Thomas Green	Backline Technician
Ken Paulinus	Bus Driver

Figure 10:2c Tour related offices

Company names, addresses, telephone numbers (including the international dialling codes) and contact names for the following:

- **Management**
- **Pre-production**
- **Agency**
- **Record Company**
- **Bus Company**
- **Travel Agent**

Figure 10:2d   Other addresses

Company names, addresses, telephone numbers (including the international dialling codes) and contact names for the following:

- **Accountant**
- **Merchandising**
- **Sound Hire**
- **Trucking**

Figure 10:2e   Telephone information

TELEPHONE INFORMATION

Calling from	Co. name	Tel. No	Country/City	Time difference	
U K	AT&T Direct	08008 90011	LA	Minus	8 hours
	MCI	08008 90222	NY	Minus	5 hours
	Sprint	08008 90877			
Netherlands	AT&T Direct	06022 9111	LA	Minus	9 hours
	MCI	06022 9122	NY	Minus	6 hours
	Sprint	06022 9119			
	BT Direct	06022 9944	UK	Minus	1 hour
Germany	AT&T Direct	01300 010	LA	Minus	9 hours
	MCI	01300 012	NY	Minus	6 hours
	Sprint	01300 013			
	BT Direct	01308 00044	UK	Minus	1 hour
Denmark	AT&T Direct	80010 010	LA	Minus	9 hours
	MCI	80010 022	NY	Minus	6 hours
	Sprint	80010 877			
	BT Direct	80010 444	UK	Minus	1 hour
Norway	AT&T Direct	80019 011	LA	Minus	9 hours
	MCI	80019 912	NY	Minus	6 hours
	Sprint	80019 877			
	BT Direct	80019 0044	UK	Minus	1 hour
Sweden	AT&T Direct	02079 5611	LA	Minus	9 hours
	MCI	02079 5922	NY	Minus	6 hours
	Sprint	02079 9011			
	BT Direct	02079 5144	UK	Minus	1 hour
Switzerland	AT&TDirect	1550 011	LA	Minus	9 hours
	MCI	1550 222	NY	Minus	6 hours
	Sprint	1559 777			
	BT Direct	1552 444	UK	Minus	1 hour
Italy	AT&T Direct	17210 11	LA	Minus	9 hours
	MCI	17210 22	NY	Minus	6 hours
	Sprint	17218 77			
	BT Direct	7200 44	UK	Minus	1 hour
Spain	AT&T Direct	90099 0011	LA	Minus	9 hours
	MCI	90099 0014	NY	Minus	6 hours
	Sprint	90099 0013			
	BT Direct	90099 0044	UK	Minus	1 hour
France	AT&T Direct	19 0011	LA	Minus	9 hours
	MCI	19 0019	NY	Minus	6 hours
	Sprint	19 0087			
	BT Direct	19 0044	UK	Minus	1 hour

Figure 9:2f Currency information

APPROXIMATE EXCHANGE RATES
(As at 24.02.200X)

United Kingdom		One day's Per Diem at $ 35 = £23.33
$ 1.00 = £0.66		Dollar purchase rate: 1.5 ($)
$ 1.5 = £1.00		

Netherlands		One day's Per Diem at $ 35 = FL56.00
$ 1.00 = FL 1.60	£1.00 = DM 2.30	Dollar purchase rate: 1.6
$ 0.63 = FL 1.00	£0.43 = DM 1.00	Sterling purchase rate: 2.8

Germany		One day's Per Diem at $ 35 = DM 49.00
$ 1.00 = DM 1.40	£1.00 = DM 2.30	Dollar purchase rate: 1.4
$ 0.71 = DM 1.00	£0.43 = DM 1.00	Sterling purchase rate: 2.3

Denmark		One day's Per Diem at $ 35 = DM 192.50
$ 1.00 = DK 5.50	£1.00 = DK 9.00	Dollar purchase rate: 5.5
$ 0.18 = DK 1.00	£0.11 = DK 1.00	Sterling purchase rate: 9

Norway		One day's Per Diem at $ 35 = NK 217.00
$ 1.00 = NK 6.20	£1.00 = NK 10.00	Dollar purchase rate: 6.2
$ 0.16 = NK 1.00	£0.10 = NK 1.00	Sterling purchase rate: 10

Sweden		One day's Per Diem at $ 35 = SK 245.00
$ 1.00 = SK 7.00	£1.00 = SK 11.40	Dollar purchase rate: 7
$ 0.14 = SK 1.00	£0.09 = SK 1.00	Sterling purchase rate: 11.4

Switzerland		One day's Per Diem at $ 35 = SF 41.30
$ 1.00 = SF 1.18	£1.00 = SF 1.91	Dollar purchase rate: 1.18
$ 0.85 = SF 1.00	£0.52 = SF 1.00	Sterling purchase rate: 1.91

Italy		One day's Per Diem at $ 35 = L 53,550
$ 1.00 = L 1,530	£1.00 = L2,480	Dollar purchase rate: 530
$ 0.0007 = L 1	£0.0004 = L1	Sterling purchase rate: 480

Spain		One day's Per Diem at $ 35 = Pts 4,270
$ 1.00 = Pts 122	£1.00 = Pts 197	Dollar purchase rate: 122
$ 0.008 = Pts 1	£0.005 = Pts 1	Sterling purchase rate: 197

France		One day's Per Diem at $ 35 = Fr 171.50
$ 1.00 = Fr 4.90	£1.00 = Fr 7.90	Dollar purchase rate: 4.9
$ 0.20 = Fr 1.00	£0.13 = Fr 1.00	Sterling purchase rate: 7.9

Figure 10:2g Itinerary for Monday 27 February - arrival in UK

Date: Mon 27 Feb   **Place:** London England   **Status** OFF

TRAVEL
From: USA
To: UK
Distance: A long way

CREW ITINERARY   **BAND ITINERARY**
6.30am   Bob arrives London Heathrow
6.30am   Charly arrives Heathrow
6.55am   Tom & Tony arrive Heathrow

                                                8.00am   Band arrive London Heathrow

                        On clearance, transfer to hotel by minibus

TBA   Truck loads at SSE
TBA   Truck loads at Peavey
TBA   Truck loads at Marshall
TBA   Truck loads at Meteorlites

VENUE
Name:
Address:
Telephone:Fax:
Production office:
Capacity:

PROMOTER
Company:
Telephone:Fax:
Contacts:

HOTEL
Name: Mayfair Inter-Continental
Address: Stratton Street
                         London W1A 2AN
Telephone: (+44) 207 629 7777   Fax: (+44) 207 629 1459

AFTER SHOW TRAVEL
To:
Distance:
Travel time:

ADDITIONAL DRIVEL:
Welcome back to Europe, distinguished foreign chappies!

Figure 10:2h Itinerary for Saturday 4 March - a UK venue

Date: Sat 4 March   **Place:** Northampton, England   **Status** Showday

TRAVEL
From: London
To: Northampton
Distance: 66 miles

CREW ITINERARY

8.30am	Crew Wake-up
9.20am	Lobby call
9.30am	Crew drive to Northampton
11.00am	Load-in
4.30pm	Angry Chair sound check
6.15pm	Support soundcheck
7.30pm	Doors open
8.15pm	Support on stage
8.45pm	Changeover
9.15pm	Angry Chair
11.00pm	Curfew

BAND ITINERARY

2.20pm	Band lobby call
2.30pm	Band drive to Northampton

VENUE
Name: The Roadmender
Address: 1 Lady's Lane
           Northampton
           NN1 3AH

Production office:
           Fax: (+44) 604 603166
           Capacity: 900

PROMOTER
Company: The Noise Factory
Telephone: (+44) 604 604503
Fax: (+44) 604 603166

Contacts: David Walker-Collins/Tim
Telephone: (+44) 604 604503

HOTEL
Name: Mayfair Inter-Continental
Address: Stratton Street
           London W1A 2AN
Telephone: (+44) 207 629 7777   Fax: (+44) 207 629 1459

AFTER SHOW TRAVEL
To: London
From: 66 miles
Travel time: 1.5 hours

ADDITIONAL DRIVEL: Another non-large establishment, but at least this one has enough mains power to run the sound and lights simultaneously.

Figure 10:2i   Itinerary for Tuesday 14 March - a TV show

Date: Tue 14 March   **Place:** London England   **Status:** TV Show

TRAVEL

From: Hotel
To: DTV Studio
Distance: 20 minutes

ITINERARY

TBA   Lobby call
TBA   Check out of hotel

4.00pm   Load in to TV studio
6.00pm   Band call time
8.30pm   *Most Hated* broadcast begins
10.00pm   Broadcast ends
                              (All timings to be confirmed)

VENUE   PROMOTER

Name: DTV   Company:
Address: Old TV-AM Building   Telephone:
               Hawley Crescent   Fax:
               Camden NW1   Contacts:
               Telephone: 0207 284 7777
Production office:
               Fax: 0207 284 7711
               Capacity: Fleur or Eve

HOTEL

Name: (None)
Address:
Telephone: Fax:

AFTER SHOW TRAVEL

To: Amsterdam
Distance: 307 miles
Travel time: 10 hours

ADDITIONAL DRIVEL:
Live-to-air TV show. Another exciting opportunity to emulate L7 and embarrass your road
crew in public, followed by an oh-so-popular overnight bus/ferry/bus journey to Amsterdam.

Figure 10:2j Itinerary for Wednesday 15 March - a European venue

---

Date: Wed 15 March   **Place:** Amsterdam Netherlands   **Status:** Showday

TRAVEL
From: Hotel
To: Venue
Distance: 400 yards

CREW ITINERARY		**BAND ITINERARY**
On arrival check in to hotel		On arrival check in to hotel

11.00am	Crew wake-up	
11.50am	Crew transfer to venue	
12 noon	Load-in	4.20pm Band lobby call
4.30pm	Angry Chair soundcheck	4.30pm Band transfer to venue
6.30pm	Support soundcheck	
8.00pm	Doors open	
9.00pm	Support on stage	
9.30pm	Changeover	
10.00 pm	Angry Chair	

(No curfew)

VENUE   **PROMOTER**
Name: Paradiso   Company: Double You
Address: Weteringschans 6-8   Telephone: (+31) 15 159555
             1017 SG Amsterdam   Fax: (+31) 15 138680
Telephone   (+31) 20 6237348   Contacts: Marjolein Zonneveld

Production Office: (+31) 20 6268790
            Fax: (+31) 20 6222721
            Capacity: 1250

HOTEL
Name: American Hotel
Address: Leidsekade 97
             1017 Pn Amsterdam
Telephone: (+31) 20624 5322   Fax: (+31) 20 625 3236

AFTER SHOW TRAVEL
To: Hotel
Distance: 400 yards
Travel time: Er...........

ADDITIONAL DRIVEL:
Tempting though it may be to find an excuse to not bother doing the gig, we are at least staying over tonight so there will be time to indulge in various categories of unspeakable naughtiness after the show.

There are different types of tour manager:

- Those who have grown up with the band and who work exclusively with them.

- Those who are professional and available for hire and work for any band who will contract them.

There is a direct parallel with the background of bands' managers, as discussed above. Professional tour managers soon become well known within the live music industry and gain reputations based on their personalities and methods of working, which soon spread amongst bands and agents. Agents are often called upon to select a tour manager for a band and they will have regular tour managers to work with their bands. Many tour managers, if they do a good job, are requested by individual bands every time they tour and their reputations and workloads can increase as a band's career grows within the industry.

The tour manager's next job is to meet the band and he will probably be invited to pre-production rehearsals. Much will depend on how he and the band get on together, as they will be spending a good deal of time with each other over the following weeks. Many tour managers have been sacked and replaced even before the first equipment has been loaded on the truck. Immediately prior to the tour starting, the tour manager will meet the rest of the crew and production personnel if the tour is carrying PA and lights. He will have final meetings with the band's management where he will receive copies of every contract for each event, details of wages to be paid to crew, a tour float (money), and any final information regarding last minute changes. The day before the tour starts he will probably collect a tour bus and will carry the band from venue to venue and hotel to hotel. If the band are living on a sleeper bus, the tour manager will be shown his bunk. The tour begins!

On the day of any show it is a team effort that makes each event come together and work. If the tour manager is travelling on a sleeper bus, then he always wakes up outside the venue at which the band is to

218

appear that day. But, if the tour manager is driving the tour bus, his day will begin in a strange hotel bedroom. He will spend the day acting as guardian. After ensuring that everybody has had breakfast and has gathered all their belongings together, he will drive the band to the next town where he will book into the next hotel. Leaving the band to their own devices for a short time, he may visit the venue to meet the promoter and familiarise himself with the place. He will liaise with the promoter and the production manager to ensure that everything is running to agreed timetables. He will get an estimated time for soundcheck, when the band will need to be present to check all the equipment and to set sound levels ready for the show. The first deadline of the day is the time at which doors open to the general public; this can be particularly important to a venue which is hoping for bar sales to people attending the event. If everything is going according to plan, the tour manager will collect the band and bring them to the venue ready for soundcheck, usually at around about 4.00p.m. Soundcheck can take anything between an hour and forever! A lot of this comes down to the attitude of the band members and the skill of the sound engineer as well as the quality of the equipment. A small technical problem can hold up the whole process and throw the whole schedule into disarray, causing much anxiety amongst everyone working on the show.

Whilst the band are soundchecking, the tour manager will view the dressing rooms to ensure that catering agreed with the promoter is present. This will include such items as the provision of towels, glasses and eating utensils. If the band are to eat on the premises, then the tour manager will liaise with the caterer about the time that the evening meal is to be served. Alternatively, if the promoter is paying the band a sum of money for meals, then the tour manager will collect this and, when soundcheck is complete, take the band from the venue for a meal. With luck, there will be some time left for the support band to have a soundcheck but this is not the main band's tour manager's responsibility as the support will have their own tour manager. Before leaving the venue for the evening meal, the tour manager agrees with the promoter the length of time that his band will be on stage. This is usually specified within the band's contract. Most bands like to return to a venue at least half an hour before they are due on stage and it is the tour manager's responsibility to ensure that they do so.

When the band are on stage, the tour manager meets the promoter to settle financial arrangements relating to the band's performance at the show. He will see all the tickets printed for the event and he should be given a full box office statement indicating all the tickets sold and their value. Income is defined as the total ticket sales, less the VAT. This amount is then set against expenditure net of VAT, which is used to calculate any percentage payment to the band. VAT is then added to this at the end of the calculation. The tour manager then asks the promoter to furnish him with a list of all the costs incurred, backed up where possible with receipts and invoices. It is the tour manager's responsibility to double check all the figures to ensure that they are correct. Some tour managers, if they are wary of the promoter and their honesty, stand at the doors to the venue counting punters as they come in. Thankfully, this is not done often as mutual trust between promoters and bands is necessary for the industry to function. As soon as the tour manager is happy that the figures for income and expenditure are correct and corroborated, he collects the band's guaranteed fee and any income from the percentage break agreed on the contract. An element of the money collected is VAT and he issues the promoter with a VAT invoice. It is usual to be paid in cash and it is the tour manager's responsibility to count the money and check that it is correct. The percentage payment is a share of the profits made over and above all the expenses, including the band's guaranteed fee and some contractually agreed profit to the promoter, and is usually split with the highest percentage going to the band, normally 70 or 80 per cent. Most promoters use a fairly standard form which documents the box office income and their expenditure and allows them to calculate easily any percentage payment to the artist. The tour manager should ask for a copy of such a document to take away with him.

One skill which all tour managers must have is numeracy. They are completely responsible for the control of all money coming in and all money going out. It is normal for tour managers to bank all event income at least every two days, with the exception of a small float which they will have been provided with at the start of the tour. Any money taken out of event income to subsidise the float must be accounted for very carefully. The tour manager is responsible for paying PDs (*per diem*)[1] to both the crew and the artists, amounts of which are set before the tour and taken into account with the wages bill. PDs are given in cash on a daily basis to cover any expenses which are not covered by the tour manager or promoter, such as extra food and drink. Those receiving PDs do not have to account for what they are spent on. The tour manager must also have enough cash to cover emergency replacements of equipment and petrol. If the band are staying in hotels, then these bills are usually covered on account prior to the tour starting. But, the tour manager is responsible for paying for any extra accommodation charges or for settling additional bills which may have been incurred, such as damage to property. He should keep all receipts and invoices for any money paid out in this manner. After the tour, there will be a full financial breakdown of all money spent and the tour manager will be expected to be able to account for every penny which came out of petty cash. Many tour managers use laptop computers with basic accounts packages to maintain accurate tour records. With or without the aid of technology, tour managers must have a basic knowledge of accounting procedures, especially working knowledge of petty cash and analysis systems.

Now that the show is finished, the punters have gone home and the crews are reloading the truck, the tour manager has completed all his business with the promoter and his next task is to get the band back to the hotel. This can often be harder work than it sounds as artists that have just left the stage after an exhilarating performance in front of an enthusiastic crowd can be excited and ready to party when all the tour manager wants to do is get some sleep. Extricating the band from a dressing room full of fans, hangers-on and local press can be a delicate task. At the hotel, the tour manager may spend some time going over the accounts for the day, filing invoices and receipts, and checking money into the hotel safe. In the early hours of the morning he will finally manage to get into bed with the final thought of the day being

---

[1] A *per diem* allowance, strictly meaning *for the day*, is a payment, usually in cash and in local currency, to cover out-of-pocket expenses when travelling.

that he will be doing it all again tomorrow in a different town and a different hotel room.

Conclusion

Now that we have dealt with the final element of managing the live event, we will look at several areas that impinge on management of the live artist. The first of these is the outdoor event.

Chapter 11

Music Event Management Outdoors

by Dr Robert Carpenter

Introduction

Why put on an outdoor event? With all its problems of weather, bringing in of services and so on, an indoor venue, or a large temporary structure such as a big top or the Kayam (a purpose built theatre tent), is less of a risk as there are fewer variables to consider. This is a question that an event manager should keep in constant review until he is committed to the event.

There are obvious attractions to being involved in large outdoor events. When someone thinks about it, they probably envisage a larger high profile event. Because outdoor events are perceived to be larger, and to attract bigger artists or more high-profile performers, they are also seen as being more exciting to be involved in. But, the majority of outdoor events are single concerts with all types of music genre, from jungle music to brass bands, and heavy rock to light classical.

An outdoor event is in general very similar to one indoors. The topics covered in Chapters 1, 3, 4 and 6 apply equally well in both situations. But, the topics covered in Chapters 5, 6 and 9 are more relevant for larger events or for those that could be called one-off events in unlicensed venues.

At the start of any planning process the event manager needs to bring together all those people who will have an impact on the event. At the earliest stages, probably better defined as pre-planning, there will just be the manager and the client, but others should be involved too. The

223

conduct of these meetings is important as the manager wants to impress each person concerned with the event. It is also extremely important to ensure that detailed notes are kept and that members present at each meeting agree to these notes.

There are many reasons for choosing a particular site. One reason may be that the promoter owns the site. For example, the owners (or their agents) of stately homes, such as Sandringham, who have asked event organisers Performing Arts Management to organise an evening of classical music with fireworks and lasers, or farmers, such as Michael Eavis who hosts Glastonbury festival.

Another reason for the choice of venue is that the event is subsidised in some way. For example, it may be funded by a local authority which wants a particular type of event brought into the area. The same might apply with corporate sponsorship or hospitality – or for many more reasons. Whichever reason, if the site is chosen for the event manager, his main planning roles in the early stages are to make sure the site is suitable and, if it is not, then he must plan to make it so. Perhaps, just as important, he should plan to convince those concerned that he has the means to make it so, both practically and financially.

With the luxury of starting to plan with no predetermined venue, the event manager has an opportunity to choose a site that provides many of the services and facilities he prefers.

Some important considerations on choosing a site are:

* Geographical location. Transport to the site. Is it served by good public transport or a good road system that is easily accessible to the target audience?

* Site properties. Is the site served by good routes of access and egress for the audience, the bands and the crew, or for any site services required or for the emergency services? Does the site offer good security (gate crashers)? Does it provide a good natural auditorium?

- Site services. Is there easy access to the services required for the event (e.g., power, water, sewerage, access roads). If not, can they be brought onto the site within your budget?
- Local population. Will there be significant objections to your proposed event? Will the owner object?

Another early step is to determine the type of event that will be organised.

Again, this is often chosen largely for the event manager. For example, if he is offered an artist of the calibre of Britney Spears, he already has his event – the problem is one of venue. If his remit is to put on an event for the people of a small sleepy village, what does he do?

There is a great variety of event types to chose from and the dividing lines between them are vague, but they include: festivals, religious, music, eisteddfods, garden shows, ballooning; concerts of any description, though distinguished from other events by usually being a single entertainment genre; parties; Green Fairs, May Day, strawberry fairs; raves etc. The choice of event links in with the choice of music type and performer appeal and also with the target audience.

The rationale behind these choices are discussed in Chapters 1, 5, 6, 8, and 9, as are choices of artist, PA and stage lighting.

Once the event manager has selected a date, venue, type of event and has probably decided upon the headlining band, he needs to get an entertainment licence and, if required, an alcohol licence for the proposed event. This can be a time-consuming exercise but, if done properly, it will make the rest of the planning less arduous.

Planning

The main differences between an indoor event and an outdoor one are the processes involved in the planning stages.

Under the Local Government (Miscellaneous Provisions) Act 1982, Schedule 1, paragraph 6, wholly or mainly open air premises used by the public on one or more occasion for public dancing or public music (and also sporting events where the public watch and any other public entertainment of a like kind), must be licensed by the local authority. Other relevant legislation includes:

- Schedule 1 to the Local Government (Miscellaneous Provisions) Act 1982 (as amended by Part IV of the Fire Safety and Safety of Places of Sport Act 1987).

- Schedule 12 to the London Government Act 1963 (as amended by Part IV of the Fire Safety and Safety of Places of Sport Act 1987).

- Section 41 of the Civic Government (Scotland) Act 1982 (as amended by Part IV of the Fire Safety and Safety of Places of Sport Act 1987).

- The Licensing Act 1964 (as amended by the Licensing Act 1988).

- The Licensing (Scotland) Act 1976.

- Private Places of Entertainment (Licensing) Act 1967.

- Relevant local authority regulations.

The application for a licence will probably be required on the authority's standard form and will is likely to require the event manager to submit outline site plans showing major structures and facilities, and also showing proposed positions for emergency services and control points. He may also be required to show more detailed plans giving descriptions of electrical layout, emergency lighting, water/sewerage, or emergency services' access and egress.

As it is essential to have these plans for the safe and smooth running of the event, I strongly suggest that site plans are prepared at this stage and submitted as proposed plans. These can always be changed, if needed, during the consultative stages of the lead up to the event.

Many local authorities have additional requirements under their own Regulations and conditions. This can be very variable nowadays, with some authorities, particularly those who became sensitised to the idea of outdoor events during the pay party boom of the 1980s, going over all applications for a licence very thoroughly – frequently charging large amounts for the privilege of doing so.

The reason why some authorities do take such care is because, when they licence an event, they are saying that it will be a safe, well-run event and that there will be someone in the departments involved who has ultimate responsibility in the event of an incident. This will involve the local Chief Constable, the Chief Fire Officer, the Environmental Health Department, and, increasingly, the Building Control Department. Sadly these departments tend to be guided by different regulations, laws and guidelines but, with good planning, the event manager should be able to pre-empt every need. This is also essential in the case of an incident, as it will guard the event manager from accusations similar to those that the local authority personnel are guarding themselves from. In the case of an adverse incident, he may be guilty, unless he can prove he took all reasonable care to avoid the incident.

Licences are granted by a panel made up from these interested parties, together with a number of elected officers of the local authority. Thus, it is important for the event manager in his application to demonstrate that the event will be both safe and well run, and that the event will be appreciated by the community, in order for the elected officers to give approval.

A good licence application will foresee any problems and will have planned to prevent them or, at least, will have contingency plans should problems arise. It is good practice for the event manager to talk to the local authorities early and to ask them what they would require him to provide if he were to make an application. If the application is likely to be contentious, an approach to the local police and fire officers is also sensible. It is also good practice for him to talk to the community where the proposed event may take place. For this, some idea of the size of the event will be needed in order to recognise the correct community. It is useful to talk to the community before the application is made because part of the application process may be to advertise the intentions of an event and it is important that there is some control over any rumour that may start up in opposition to the plans. This will give the event manager higher chances of getting the local community on his side.

Currently, there is a very varied approach to event safety: some authorities leave it up to the event manager, while others want to have and to check every detail well in advance. As safety of events is rightly becoming a greater concern throughout Europe, more and more authorities require evidence that the event manager has made every attempt to ensure that the event will be safe. Equally so, it is now becoming evident that the industry wants to police itself. Therefore, it is important for the event manager to be able to convince potential clients of his ability to manage the event properly.

Early research will show which points to pay particular attention to in the application, but in any case a good application will give due consideration to all of the following:

- Desirability
- Feasibility
- Risk Analysis
- Statutory requirements
- Environmental Health Officers and Environmental Health regulations
- Site supervision
- Crowd control
- Security
- Stewards
- Police
- Fire safety and rescue
- First aid and rescue
- Parking coaches/cars
- Water supply
- Electricity supply
- Main and secondary lighting
- Toilet facilities
- Hygiene facilities
- Welfare services

- Rubbish disposal
- Noise control
- Stages
- Marquees
- Fireworks
- Lasers
- Other entertainment
- Catering facilities
- Corporate hospitality
- Merchandising
- Accident log reporting system
- Disability access
- Fire points
- Information point
- Lost property/persons
- Mechanical handling
- Meeting point
- Message system
- Emergency message system
- Security fencing
- Telephones

You need to bear in mind the requirements of the law, any local variation of the law, the safety of punters during the event and safety of the crew, before, during and after the event. Not all of the above are required for every event, but it is worth the time to check to see if they are required, as an event manager.

A good application will demonstrate that the event manager is capable of running his event properly, successfully and safely. A good application has the effect of inspiring confidence in the people from the authorities, and, therefore, the event is more likely to proceed.

Guide through the planning application

When a local authority receives a licence application, what happens is that a desirability study, a feasibility study, and a risk analysis on the proposal is carried out. (The local authority also charges the applicant a lot of money.)

Desirability study

The local authority looks at a proposal and decides whether or not the event is the right sort of event for that area. This means that the licensing panel ask themselves that question, and it will also depend upon any comments received from interested parties other than themselves who have become aware of the proposed event, either through any advertisements submitted as part of the application procedure, by word of mouth or by any advance publicity. If the event manager feels there may be opposition to his event, it may be worthwhile mounting his own campaign in support.

Feasibility study

The event manager will already have done this, both as part of the application and on his own behalf, before he decided to invest significant effort, time and, by now, money. Presumably he has convinced himself that the event is feasible and it is now up to him to similarly convince the licensing panel. Part of this study may look into the financial security of the promoter and may involve lodging deposits or guarantees.

Risk analysis; The law, standards and guidelines
(See also Chapter 6.)

Legal duties Together with the various legislation covering public entertainment licensing law (*vide supra*), the main Acts which are relevant to the event are:

- The Health and Safety at Work Act 1974. This Act says that you – as a promoter, an event manager, a licensee, a venue owner, or a subcontractor – have a statutory duty to protect the health and safety of your workers, your audience, the artists and performers and any other person who may be affected by your work. The event manager needs to assess the physical risks to any person caused by the event. This will necessarily involve assessing the type of audience he is expecting and any risk they impose on themselves. For example, will they be likely to abuse alcohol or drugs, will they be aggressive, or naive, will they be likely to form a stampede to see the artists or when the speciality Thai food bar opens? He must also assess any risks there may be during the build-up and breakdown of the event to those involved and to passers by.

- The Control of Substances Hazardous to Health Regulations 1994 (COSHH). This Act sets out clear regulations for the control of any material that may have an immediate or long-term effect on personal health or the environment, and is particularly relevant to the methods chosen to dispose of such waste products from the event.

- Manual Handling Regulations 1992. These Regulations require that any unnecessary manual lifting that may result in injury is avoided. Consider the use of forklift trucks or tractors and trailers, for example, to make load carrying safer, provided there is adequate ground support to use them safely.

- Other laws that may have an affect on the event are listed at the end of the chapter

As each aspect of the event is looked at, the event manager must also do a risk analysis of it.

Guidelines

The most relevant set of guidelines to the planning and running of an event is the *Guide to Health, Safety and Welfare at Pop Concerts and Similar Events* (HMSO). Although this was meant as a set of guidelines, some enforcers are using them very strictly, mainly because if anything does go wrong and they were shown not to follow them, they would be taken to task. There are also a number of specific guidelines issued by HMSO covering such activities as bungee jumping, paintball war games, agricultural shows and brewery deliveries, which may impinge on the activities of your event. All suppliers should be aware of these.

Do they affect you, as an event manager? It is important for you to know the types of questions and certification that you should require your suppliers to produce. It is important also for you to keep aware of changes in guidelines as they may jeopardise your event. For example, proposed changes to the Primrose Guide (Chapter 13 of the *Home Office Guide to Fire Precautions in Existing Places of Entertainment and Like Premises*) would require any site marquees to have a documented history of their fabric showing their date of manufacture, the original fire safety certificates, together with repeat fire safety certification every five years. If this were to come into effect, and your supplier was unable to produce the documentation, the local Fire Officer can stop your event – and it would be your fault. This is where trade associations come into their own. A good trade association should both keep you informed of potential changes and help to fight against any unfair (or fight for any fair) proposals for change.

NVQs are mentioned briefly here because it seems likely that, in the near future, everyone will need a qualification to swing a sledge hammer. In line with other industries and European harmonisation, NVQs are in the process of development or are already in operation for the leisure industry as a whole, including leisure and tourism, and hospitality and catering. Trade associations should be able to supply information on all developments.

Site inspections

It is usual for authorities to require the event manager or his representative to be available, both for site visits before the event and to be available during the event to any of their authorised officers. Health and safety inspectors have statutory powers to enter and inspect any event at all reasonable times. These inspectors have enforcement powers which enable them to stop an event or to take samples or photographs and it is a criminal offence to obstruct or fail to comply with the inspectors' instructions.

Environmental Health Officers

Event managers come into a lot of contact with Environmental Health Officers (EHOs) before, during and after an event. Although an EHO has the power to stop an event at any time, I have always found them extremely useful and helpful, if treated with respect, and if I have acted on what they say. If you, as an event manager, feel that something they have asked you to do or to provide is unreasonable, they will listen to your reasoning with understanding and may sometimes change their mind.

The areas of interest to EHOs include all aspects of the Health and Safety at Work Acts, COSHH regulations, public health, sanitation and water supply, standards of food preparation and pollution control.

Site supervision

Overall site supervision is the event manager's responsibility. Even though he may have delegated others to supervise various areas, even the whole site, he should be aware at all times that the event is running as he would wish.

Crowd control

The concept of crowd control is a bad one. A crowd will only get out of control if it is badly managed or made more dangerous by insufficient or inappropriate provision for their demands. This means that the event manager has to analyse any potential needs of the audience, both during the normal running of the event and if any incident occurs. This does not mean that he has to plan for every eventuality, but fire and explosion, or electrical blackouts, for example, should be foreseen.

These risks should be assessed during the many pre-production meetings with police, fire, environmental health and any appropriate subcontractors. Pay particular attention to to bottlenecks in access and exit routes, and to any 'pressure points' that may form during the event. The most obvious crowd pressure point is in front of the stage during a rock concert or exit routes in the event of an emergency.

Stewards and security

Stewards and security are the front line of crowd management. Though it is possible for the event manager to organise this himself by, for example, bringing in the local scout pack dressed in bright yellow overjackets, for an event of any reasonable size a recognised and recommended security firm is advisable. Properly-accredited firms supplying stewards and security, give training to their crew and enable them to be easily identified from the general audience and from each other, usually by the use of identity cards and numbered jackets. The various responsibilities given to stewards and security personnel, ranging from car parking attendants, to traffic marshals, crowd marshalling, seating assistants, safety stewards and security staff, require different types of people and training. In the case of a serious incident, it is the stewards and security team who will be in the front line of crowd management, so all people with this responsibility should be given appropriate training.

Police

If the event is for more than a few hundred people, it is likely that the police will want to have some involvement in crowd management, starting with traffic control at the event entrance. As police involvement increases from more than just a presence, they may want to charge the event manager. This is a costly addition to the budget as their charges can start in the region of £20.00 per hour. Although they may perform a very useful service, at this stage they are competing with security and stewarding companies charging from £6.00 per hour. Nevertheless, it may be considered a worthwhile expense. The organisers of Glastonbury Festival pay hundreds of thousands of pounds to their local police force for attending their event. The cost of policing events has risen dramatically. Many promoters have had disputes with local police forces over the costs. In two recent cases these disputes almost caused festivals to be cancelled but, last minute revisions of police costs, enabled them to take place.

Fire safety and rescue

You must take care at all times during the tendering stage of planning that the suppliers of all equipment and services brought in know about and comply with the legislation governing their equipment or service. It is usually worthwhile asking the provider to guarantee that they do comply and to produce copies of any relevant certification.

Other than that, guidance can be sought from the County Fire Officer. I have always found him to be extremely keen and helpful, but do listen to and heed his advice because the county fire officer is one of the people who have the power to stop your event if he considers it unsafe.

Some major points you should consider before seeing the Fire Officer are the means of giving warning in case of fire and the means of access and egress for fire-fighting vehicles.

The usual means of giving warning about fire is through a public address system, probably through the main stage PA, which should automatically cut off the stage sound and play a recorded or other message, though this is usually accompanied by a backup public address system around the whole site, allowing the warning to reach those places the main PA is not able reach.

It is essential that unobstructed ways in and out for emergency services' vehicles are located that, if possible, are separate from those used by the audience. They should be good, hard-standing roadways or an appropriate temporary roadway.

All fire exits from any temporary structure should be marked with a lit emergency exit sign which has battery backup lighting in the event of failure (a maintained exit sign).

First aid and rescue

The event manager is required to supply a properly equipped first aid point or points, supplied by a recognised first aid provider, such as Medcall Ltd or St John's Ambulance Brigade, and to keep records readily available for inspection of all persons treated. Advice can be sought from the service provider about positions and numbers required. Access for ambulances can be provided using the same route as for fire emergencies.

Major incident emergency procedures

Written emergency procedures must be provided, which have been agreed to in advance by persons concerned, which may involve the first aid team, fire, security, stewards, police, any local emergency planning officer and the event manager. These procedures will involve the event manager in detailing incident control, chain of command and areas of responsibility.

Site security

Overall site security means that the site should be suitably equipped to avoid gate crashers. The anticipated nature of the target audience will enable you to determine the lengths they may go to in order to try to obtain unauthorised entry to the event. From this information, the event manager will know what must be done to deter their unauthorised entry. Entry controls vary from existing fencing or hedges to heavy duty double fencing, with security staff patrolling the 'no man's land' between, together with high-security ticket printing with holograms, fluorescent inks and embossed paper to deter counterfeiting of the tickets.

Communications

For events of any size, good communications between core personnel are essential for a well-run event, and good communications between those involved in emergency procedures are essential if there is an emergency. Appropriate communications should be arranged early in the planning process.

Stage barriers

There may be a tendency for the crowd to push towards the front of the stage, and it is likely that some form of front-of-stage barrier system will be required. These can range from simple crowd control barriers to heavy-duty crush barriers with internal access areas that allow stewards to extract distressed members from the crowd and take them to a place of safety or care. Just as one barrier system may be too weak for some requirements, to go for the strongest system each time is inappropriate and will detract from your event. It is up to the event manager during the pre-planning meetings to determine the correct system for the event.

Signs

The use of signs is an important means of directing the punters, both within and outside the event. Within the event, signs can be used to inform and to direct people to the attractions, service points, emergency controls etc. Outside the event, signs can be used to both direct people to the event and to car parks, and also to advertise the event.

Care should be taken not to contravene any local legislation that may control the use of signs. The local planning authority usually administer this.

Organisations, such as the RAC and AA, provide an efficient sign service and are used to working with local legislation where it occurs.

Parking coaches and cars

You need adequate parking for the event. This can either be provided on site or provided off site, with transport arranged to and from the event. Whichever method is used, there should be appropriate signs and any need for services or control at the car parks should be met. If car parks are to be used at night by a significant number of people, they should be lit, and probably include toilet facilities.

Water supply

Apart from the water supply required for the toilet blocks and for fire fighters' use, additional water outlets may be needed. This can range from a single outlet for the caterers' use, to that sufficient to cater for the campsite. The Environmental Health Officer will probably notify the minimum number of outlets required. The water provided must be clean and potable.

Electricity supply

Generally it is sufficient to say that all electrical services, temporary or permanent, should comply with the current Institute of Electrical Engineers (IEE) wiring regulations. There may be other considerations that the event manager may want, or may have, to make. Can he put up with a sustained lack of power during the performance? Does he need a backup power supply in case the primary supply fails? If generators are used, they should be sited with due consideration to any fire hazard caused by their fuel supply, or to any noise nuisance caused to the event or its environment. The method of power distribution is also worth reviewing. There is a power loss between the source of power to its end point of use. The greater the distance, the greater the power loss in the cable and, also, the greater the likelihood for the need to fly or to bury the cable: so, even if the site has its own power supply, it may be more cost effective or safer to bring in generators distributed throughout the site as primary and as backup sources of power.

Main and secondary lighting

Any parts of the site intended for use after dusk and before dawn should be correctly lit for their intended purpose and any route of access or egress should have backup emergency lighting. This should be in addition to any back up power arrangements that have been made and is usually in the form of battery-powered lighting with a specified duration of battery reserve. The term *correctly lit for their intended purpose* obviously involves a value judgment and the local authority will have the final say on this. Unless they are concerned about light pollution (I have not heard of this as being a problem for one-off events) the authority's concern will be that there may be areas that are too dark for safety. If an event requires particularly dark areas for any reason, the event manager must be prepared to provide a reasonable explanation and probably a greater level of emergency lighting.

Toilet facilities

The question of sanitary accommodation is emotive, evoking memories of poor and too few facilities with long queues, encouraging people to water (or worse) the bushes. The Health and Safety Commission has published recommendations which should be regarded as a minimum. Many local authorities insist on more. It is probably best for the event manager to consult the authorities in the event's area to see what they require, then to see if he prefers a greater number for the comfort of the audience.

Generally, you need two WCs per 100 women up to 200, then one per 100, and one WC and 0.5 m length of urinal per 200 men. This allows for a reasonable length of queuing at an eight hour event – though some authorities consider these provisions to be too little. The number of WCs and length of urinal can be reduced for shorter events. The event manager should make an assessment of the likely number of disabled people present at the event and provide the appropriate number of facilities. These should comply with BS 5810:1979 (Access for the Disabled to Buildings – General Recommendations) and a similar number of WCs as for women should be supplied. Appropriate WCs should also be supplied for the staff/crew.

The toilets should be well lit at night, both for safety and to avoid fouling, and they should be regularly maintained and cleaned. Where possible, the toilets should be sited close to mains drainage, but this should not be at the expense of their adequate distribution around the site to avoid congestion in one area. Self-contained units can be used provided they are appropriately serviced. Toilets should not be sited next to catering outlets.

Hygiene facilities

With the exception of catering and first aid facilities, the type of washing facilities required depends very much on the length of event.

Events of less than eight hours' duration really require just the basic hand washbasin in the toilet blocks. The number depends upon local guidelines and the event manager's own taste. I have seen recommendations vary from one hand washbasin per WC to one per block of 8 WCs. All basins should be regularly maintained, provided with bactericidal soap and adequate means of drying (and of clearing up the litter, if necessary).

For events lasting for more than eight hours and with people camping on site, more extensive washing facilities are needed. Ideally facilities should be provided according to the legislation regarding public access to camp sites. In practice, this is usually far too expensive and impractical and the local authority has the power to grant exemptions for short-term sites. If you, as an event manager, are proposing to do this, speak to those concerned at a very early stage in your plans.

Welfare services

Penny Mellor of Festival Welfare Services recommends that no open-air event with an expected attendance of 10,000 people or more, or where people are on site for 24 hours or longer, should take place without the full range of welfare services.

When planning such an event, people concerned with welfare and the health of people both working and attending your event should be included in relevant pre-planning meetings. These meetings should consider provision for the following:

- Information point – for both information of the event itself, usually in the form of large site plan and programme details, and general local information, transport after the event.

- Message system – where personal messages may be left, e.g., a notice board.

- Meeting point for missing people – a designated area for people to reunite.

- Befriending service – such as the Samaritans.

- Health Promotion Service – such as drug and youth counselling and advice.

- Lost property/left luggage – a secure site, clearly marked on the site plan.

- Telephones – if there are no telephones near the site, or if there is no pass-out system, there should be some telephones on site, if possible both coin and card operated, and an operator connection facility for making reverse charge calls.

Rubbish disposal and site cleaning

The cleaning and tidying of the site, both during and after an event, is often put at the bottom of the priority list. It is an essential part of any event. Even for a two-hour, low-profile event, the event manager's image will be enhanced if he is knowkn to have arranged to leave a clean site. More realistically, people will not notice if he has cleaned up after the event but will create a fuss if he has not! For events of longer duration, arrangements should be made to clean the site during, as well as after, the event.

Methods of collection and disposal are well worth giving serious thought and may go as far as the event manager specifying to caterers and bars the type of containers they should provide. Catering outlets are a major source of waste and arrangements should be made with the caterers for correct and regular disposal of their rubbish.

With the increasing awareness of the desirability of reducing, reusing, or recycling waste, proper thought about this will be good PR both with the audience and the local community. Given the correct target audience, a feature could be made of recycling and may enhance the event, with separate collection points for each type of recyclable product.

The Environmental Protection Act 1989 is the main piece of legislation governing the management of rubbish at outdoor events and requires that all waste is handled in the correct manner, by trained staff who are aware of the environmental and public health risks.

Noise control

The local Environmental Health Department will probably set noise levels at various points around the site, which must not be exceeded, either at all or for more than a pre-determined short time. It is also common for the noise limit to reduce after a certain hour, usually 11 p.m., 12 midnight or 2 a.m.

During the planning stage, the event manager should consult with the Environmental Health Officer and decide how and where monitoring positions will be placed, together with the arrangements should the sound limits be exceeded. This could be anything from a complete shut down of sound to a warning telling the event manager that he has exceeded the imposed limit.

Stages

Most outdoor music events require some form of staging area and it is likely that the stage itself will be a feature of the event. The stage chosen should be capable of doing the job required of it. There is no point in having a 36 m² PAGODA stage (6 metres across) for a 60-piece orchestra (more suited to a 14 m² GEODOME with a 15 metres stage width). The stage system chosen should be one that the event manager likes the look of and one that becomes part of a feature of the event. A stage made by the local scaffolding firm with scaffolding board stage and rusty tubes, supporting a makeshift tarpaulin cover, which will probably leak or blow off in inclement weather, will detract from the event, whereas a 12 metres POLYGON, with shiny aluminium framework and clean white sheets fed into keder grooves will be safe, water-tight and attractive, becoming part of the event.

The guidelines about the design and construction of stages for outdoor events are quite precise. The event manager should make sure that the company supplying the stage is both aware of the guidelines and follows them. He should also be aware of the requirements of the lighting and effects companies for flown equipment from the stage roofing system and should ensure that the equipment he is bringing in can cope with their requirements or that alternative arrangements are made.

PA and lighting

The choice of stage PA and lighting is very much the same as for indoor venues. There are a few further considerations when organising an outdoor event.

If there is a large or spread-out audience, one or more *delay towers* will reduce the need for extreme sound pressure levels from the main PA wings. The event manager may prefer to have a large number of delay towers, reducing the volume from each, and from the main PA, to give a uniform spread of sound level. A delay tower is a speaker tower set some distance in front of the stage. Its PA is linked to the main stage PA by a delaying device, which ensures that sound is emitted from the delay tower at the same time as the same sound from the stage reaches the tower. Remember that any structure used to support the PA system must be sound and conform to the appropriate regulations, also that structures in front of the stage may interfere with sight lines of the audience.

An event held during the day should allow for the effect of daylight or bright sunlight on the show. If the stage is between the audience and the sun, there may be problems upstaging the performance of the sun. Wherever the stage is positioned for a daytime show, and the event manager wants the show to have any reasonable lighting effect, he will have to increase the power of the show. Again, he should take care that any structure supporting the lighting is capable of such support within the guidelines.

Marquees

It is likely that the event will require some form of tentage, be it just for the first-aid area or as a major part of the event – for holding the main stage, catering, or concession area with stalls for merchandise etc.

Tentage in this country can be divided into two main types:

- Traditional pole marquees, with central poles holding them up and guy ropes to hold them down.

- Frame marquees, generally of aluminium construction, requiring no central poles or guy ropes.

Which is chosen is up to the event manager, and there is a wide choice of each type. The traditional marquee's use of guy ropes can be a problem in certain situations as the guy ropes cause trip hazards but, apart from that, they are often the cheaper of the two types. They can come in very large structures, for example, big tops or the Kayam can hold 10,000 people.

Fireworks

Fireworks can provide grand eye-catching displays or finales for the event and are a feature or selling point. It is possible for the event manager to organise his own display and if he is prepared to spend time and money learning the safety aspects and how to do it, he would probably produce a reasonable effect. The Department of Trade and Industry (DTI) has published a leaflet *Safer Displays: A Guide to Fireworks Safety*. There is also a video available from the Firework Makers Guild.

If you choose to use professionals, seek references about which company is best this year. Costs of firework displays vary enormously but, as a rule of thumb, the more it costs, the better the show – as long as a good company is chosen. From a safety point of view, the company should be a member of the British Pyrotechnics Association or The Event Suppliers Association (TESA) and should comply with their guidelines and, more pertinently, the Environmental Health Officers and Fire Officers should be happy with their procedures.

Lasers

Lasers are another form of high-profile visual effect which often form part of displays. They can produce spectacular effects. They are versatile as they can be pre-programmed to produce any image and, with a good operator, can adapt to variations in live events, but they are best suited to indoor events with stable and controllable environments.

Special effects lighting, such as lasers and strobes, usually require licence approval and the event manager will be required to provide relevant documentation to demonstrate their safety. The Health and Safety Executive (HSE) and British Standards Institute (BSI) have both produced guidelines for laser safety, which have been excellently summarised in TESA's guidelines on laser safety. Well-regulated supply companies are used to supplying such documentation, which the event manager should collate at the tendering stage.

Other entertainment

There is a great variety of other entertainment available either as main attractions or as side shows. Some examples are a water ballet, medieval jousting, a street circus and participation events. By reading the trade magazines listed at the end of the chapter, you, as an event manager, will soon discover these and many more. Again, the suppliers of such acts and services should be well versed in relevant legislation and appropriate certification should be collated at the tendering stage.

Income Generation

A large part of income generation (for example, from ticket sales) is discussed in Chapter 9. But, probably more than for small indoor events, the following offer possibilities to increase the income from large ones held outdoors:

- Radio.
- Television and media.
- Sponsorship.
- Catering facilities.
- Licensed bar.
- Corporate hospitality.
- Merchandising and concession sales.

Catering facilities

Good catering is a major part of any event lasting more than a few hours and can in itself become an enjoyable feature, if there is quality and variety to choose from.

Catering facilities are also a source of income for the event through the rental of space to mobile caterers, though this should not be abused. It is very easy to attempt to increase revenue by having too great a number of caterers for the number of people at the event. It is a hard balance to strike as it creates a bad impression if you have too many or too few outlets. If there are too many, the caterers have to charge too great a price for their product and the customer is not happy. If there are too few, the public is not provided with the service it deserves and potential income is lost. The event manager should not be carried away with over-optimistic and unrealistic expectations of audience numbers.

The Mobile and Outside Catering Association recommends that there should be one general and three specialist caterers per 4000 people, with increased specialist mix as the numbers increase. This recommendation is probably about right for a short event of less than six hours' duration. For any event longer than six hours, the numbers should increase accordingly. For multi-day events, where the bulk of the audience remains on site, the three main meals per day for most of the audience should be catered for.

The choice of type of mobile catering outlet is as varied as the choice of restaurant and take away retailers. You need a good mix, again taking into consideration the tastes of your target audience.

The Food Safety Act 1990 and subsequent revisions regulates mobile food outlets very well and it is essential that all your outlets conform to these regulations. Most Environmental Health Officers are very strict about this. One important aspect of food hygiene at longer festivals is the disposal of waste which should be done in consultation with the waste management company.

Event managers should also be aware of the fire hazard involved in heating food and liaise with their fire officer to ensure the mobile food outlets are safe.

245

Licensed bar

Another potentially good source of income is a properly-managed bar. Licensed bars often offer an outlet for sponsorship; many events are supported by brewers keen to see their product given exposure to particular target audiences.

Corporate hospitality

If you can segregate an area which has good visibility for the show and which can also be serviced from the bar and catering areas, you could offer corporate hospitality. This is where space is sold either directly to a company, so they can entertain their clients and sustain a favourable relationship with them, or to specialist corporate hospitality companies who act as middle men for the service.

Merchandising and concession sales

These are further, potentially very lucrative sources of income, supplying anything from band memorabilia, tapes and CDs, to eggs and bacon or leather belts.

Some contracts with bands preclude the sale of their merchandising other than through their own agents. The event manager can enter into negotiation over this during the pre-contract stage.

Insurance

Apart from employer's and public liability insurance, insurance against theft or damage and against adverse weather should be considered.

From the terms and conditions of suppliers, the event manager will be aware of any liabilities he may incur should equipment be lost or damaged. It should be simple to determine whether to be insured against theft or damage and for how much.

For adverse weather you can insure against many factors that could affect the success of your event. It is even possible to insure against making a loss. But, the more that is insured, the higher the costs; you will have to make a value judgment which, if any, type of occurrence you would like to insure against.

Some examples of the more common events that can be insured for are:

- The main attraction not turning up.

- Adverse weather.

- Marquees falling down.

Insurance against rain and bad weather comes in two forms:

- Adverse weather, which pays out if an event is cancelled.

- A *pluvius policy*, which pays out if a certain amount of rain falls in a certain place within a time period.

There are advantages and disadvantages with each type. Pluvius is a good policy if the event is dependent upon a high *walk-up* (people buying tickets at the event on the day) for its success, where a relatively small amount of rain can dramatically affect the walk-up numbers. Rain all day on the day before the event, which leaves the site totally waterlogged and unsuitable for use, is covered by adverse weather insurance. If it rained only a little the day before so that the event could be held but would need considerable expense – laying extra trackway, moving the car park to a site a mile away and arranging for extra transport for your audience – the choice is not straightforward.

After the licence application has been submitted

Getting a licence approved takes a long time, so long that you will probably need to start organising the event before you have the licence. You should inform everyone involved that all negotiations are subject to licence approval. Once this has been achieved, you must confirm with you have agreed to date.

Management of the lead up to the event, from basic agreement to the first real site day

The process is similar to any music event. Just as for an indoor event, you need to choose a venue, artists and catering suppliers, or to put services out to tender. You need to approve and to book artists, to plan for the PA, lighting, publicity, advertising and ticketing. The differences are, on the plus side, that the venue is already lined up, but, on the down side, there will almost certainly be a lot more additional services to put out to tender and probably on a larger scale.

Having gone through the licence application process, the event manager will have a reasonable idea of which services she requires and, therefore, the additional decisions, going out to tender, approving and booking processes should be a matter of routine. With both indoor and outdoor events, timetable planning is essential to overall success . You really cannot start the process too early in order to give plenty of warning to those companies and key personnel you wish to use.

Key personnel include the designated person from each of the service providers, key representatives from the local authority and any person to whom you have chosen to delegate aspects of responsibility and work.

There will need to be many meetings with representatives of all or some of the key personnel, both on and off site. In these meetings procedures and timetables will be agreed with the key personnel. Any problems should be foreseen and worked out here.

Towards the end of the planning procedure, if she has not already done so, the event manager needs to discuss the detailed timetabling of what is due to arrive when and where with the site manager. The event manager or the site manager also needs to contact any other site personnel required, from general crew to stage managers and catering managers, if the event is large enough to warrant these. A date will be fixed with the site manager for his arrival on site and his planned finish day after the event.

Site management

Apart from a few planning meetings, the site manager's role starts from the day the site is marked out to the day the last contractor leaves and the last piece of litter is picked up.

The site manager should have planned the arrival of all site services and equipment both in good time for the event and for its intended use. There is little use having the stage builders come on site and then getting bogged down in their vehicles because the temporary roadway will not arrive until a day later. Equally, the work to be done should be timetabled to avoid congestion.

If the site is large, the event manager should further delegate responsibilities. Common tasks for delegation include appointing stage managers for each of the stages and crowd management, usually to the designated foreman provided by the subcontractor.

The event

On the day of the event, provided all has gone smoothly, the event manager should be in a position much the same as for smaller events, as discussed in Chapter 8. He should continue to oversee the event, ensuring that all is running as it should be, and that his delegated personnel are functioning correctly.

After the event

Once the event is over, it is the site manager's responsibility to ensure the smooth return of the site to its normal usage. Usually this involves retracing the steps undergone during the build up of the event, for example, by ensuring there is no congestion and that the temporary roadway is not removed before the staging contractor has left the site.

Ideally, after the event, a passer-by should not be able to tell it took place. All the contractors should have left, together with their debris and all the litter and rubbish should have been thoughtfully disposed of. In practice, though, there is at least a bald patch of grass from areas of most use and the event manager may, depending upon the sensitivity of the area, have to instigate a programme of reinstatement.

After the site is cleared and the event manager has had time to catch his breath and collect his thoughts, it is a good idea for him to arrange a post mortem with all interested parties in order to evaluate his procedures and to see how he could improve on them for his next event. The following lists are intended as a guide and as a good starting base. They are not intended to be exhaustive.

Conclusion

Relevant laws, published guidelines, trade associations and journals are listed below to help you if you wish to know more about managing outdoor events.

Laws and guidelines

Health and Safety at Work etc. Act 1974

Schedule 1 to the Local Government (Miscellaneous Provisions) Act 1982 (as amended by part IV Fire Safety and Safety of Places of Sport Act 1987)

Schedule 12 to the London Government Act 1963 (as amended by part IV Fire Safety and Safety of Places of Sport Act 1987)

Section 41 of the Civic Government (Scotland) Act 1982 (as amended by part IV Fire Safety and Safety of Places of Sport Act 1987)

The Licensing Act 1964 (as amended by the Licensing Act 1989)

The Licensing (Scotland) Act 1976

**Figure 11:1   Phil Windsor checking electrical cabling and
components at an outdoor event**

Private Places of Entertainment (Licensing) Act 1967

Relevant local authority acts
IEE Regulations for Electrical Installations (Institute of Electrical Engineers wiring regulations, 16th edition, 1993) HFC Guidance note G550 Electrical Safety at Places of Entertainment and the Memorandum of Guidance on the Electricity at Work Regulations 1989

Guide to Health, Safety and Welfare at Pop Concerts and Similar Events, HMSO

Code of Practice for Outdoor Events, National Outdoor Events Association, 1993

Managing Crowds Safely, Health and Safety Executive, 1992
Control of Substances Hazardous to Health Regulations 1994

Code of Practice for Environmental Control at Open Air Pop Concerts, HMSO, 1993

NVQs - as and when they appear

Trade associations

ABTT   Association of British Theatre Technicians, 47 Bermondsey Street, London, SE1 3XT

ACES   Amusement Catering Equipment Society, 86 Pullman Court, Streatham Hill, London, SW2

ARTSLINE   London's Information & Advice Service for Disabled People on Arts and Entertainment, 5 Crowndale Road, London, NW1 1TU

BALPPA   Showman's Guild of GB, Guild House, 41 Clarence Street, Staines, TW18 4SY

BECA   British Exhibition Contractors Association, Kingsmere House, Grantham Road, Wimbledon, London, SW19 3SR

FMG   Fireworks Makers Guild, 1 Hill View Road, Hatch End, Pinner, Middlesex

FWS   Festival Welfare Services, 61b Hornsey Road, London, N7 6DG

IEHO   Institute of Environmental Health Officers, Chadwick Court, 15 Hatfields, London, SE1 8DJ

MOCA   Mobile Outside Caterers Association, 1301 Stratford Court, Ham Green, Birmingham

MUTA   Made up Textiles Association, Heath Street, Tamworth, Staffs, D79 7JH

NOEA   The Outdoor Event Association, The General Secretary, 7 Hamilton Way, Wallington, Surrey, SM6 9NJ

NR   Network Recycling, 10 Picton Street, Bristol, BS6 5QA

PLASA   Professional Lighting and Sound Association, 7 Highlight House, St Leonards Road, Eastbourne, BN21 3UH

PSA   Production Services Association, 6 Durham Street, London, SE11 5JA

PSE   Portable Sanitation Europe, 722 College Road, Erdington, Birmingham, B44 0A5

TESA   The Event Suppliers Association, 29 Market Place, Wantage, Oxfordshire, OX12 8BG

Journals and other literature

Access All Areas   Greetlake Services Ltd, 65 North Road, St Andrews, Bristol, BS6 5AQ

Applause   Applause Publications Ltd, 132 Liverpool Road, London, N1 1LA

The Enos Guide   P O Box 96, Rotherham, S66 0GZ

Events (year)   Outdoor Events Publications Ltd, Unit 8, Fordwater Trading Estate, Fordwater Road, Chertsey, Surrey, KT16 6HG
The title of this publication changes annually to *Events (year)*

Kemps   International Music Book, Showcase Publications Ltd, 12 Felix Avenue, London, N8 9TL

Live!   Pro Light & Sound, 35 High Street, Sandridge, St Albans, Hertfordshire

Showman's Directory   Brook House, Mint Street, Godalming, Surrey, GU7 1HE

White Book   Published annually by Birdhurst Ltd, PO Box 55, Staines, Middlesex, TW18 4UG

Chapter 12

The Record Company

Introduction

This chapter examines the workings of record companies. It starts with a look at the configuration of major record labels and their departments. The main body of the text is concerned with reputedly the largest independent rock label in Britain, Music For Nations (MFN). I felt that because MFN worked so much like a family, it would be easier to get across the main points of record company management in a smaller unit than through looking all the massive departments of a conglomerate. Since the first edition of this book was published, the way in which the major labels are configured has changed a number of times and may do so many more times in the near future. A number of major labels have combined, been bought up by other companies, de-merged or have been reincarnated as new companies.

The major label

A label is a marketing identity. Just as a chocolate manufacturer may make 15 types of chocolate bar, each with its own separate identity, a major record label consists of other labels each with their own identity. When this book was originally written, Polydor was one of six music labels owned by the parent company Polygram. The other five labels at the time were Phonogram, London, Island, Go Discs and A&M. The multinational not only concentrates on the production of records but also has expanded into other areas of leisure, including film, video, promotions and product development as well as music publishing. Other companies, such as Sony and EMI, have also expanded into the production of hi-fi, lighting equipment and toys, to name but a few of

255

their other interests. But, recently Thorn and EMI demerged. Making records and CDs takes up only a minor, but significant, part of their income and expenditure and a fair element of their profitability. At the turn of the year 2001 there are five major entertainment organisations which incorporate record companies: Sony, Warners/ADL, BMG, Polygram/Universal and EMI. EMI and Warners/ADL were due to merge, but this is currently on hold. This picture changes all the time and will continue to do so.

Many of the major labels, within the five major entertainment organisations, are split into a number of departments. Typically these are sales, production and stock control, artist and repertoire (A&R), marketing, legal, finance, press, promotion, manufacturing, distribution and their supporting business such as royalties and accounting.

Many people feel that those persons working within the A&R department are basically glorified talent spotters. Their job is three-fold:

- To find the band.

- To make records and CDs with that band, which results in a finished album or single – on time and when it is needed.

- To work the record or CD within the company.

Their job also entails seeing bands live and listening to tapes, albums and CDs sent by prospective bands and artists. The A&R department decides upon a band or artist and whether they feel that they will sell in today's unstable market. The company sometimes looks for gaps to fill in the market, although there is some artistic integrity within this process. It takes foresight, especially in today's changing music climate, for a company to sign a band and then wait for a year to 18 months before a CD is released by them. Once everyone agrees that the band or artist is right for the company, contract negotiations start. This process is conducted by the legal department.

There are two types of deals commonly made with artists:

- A recording deal, where the artist receives a lump sum of money on signing the contract; the record company pays the recording costs and administers the payment. This deal is commonly used for up-and-coming artists who will receive another lump sum on completion of the album.

- A fund deal, where the artist receives money to cover the cost of the advance and recording. The advance is the amount of money that the record company has paid to the artist as part of their contractual agreement or signing-on fee. Artists administer the recording of the album themselves.

Once the artist has been found, the next step is two-fold. Firstly, a product needs to be manufactured and, secondly, the artist or band needs to be marketed. Somewhere, between manufacture and marketing, lie production and stock control, sales and distribution.

Manufacturing the product is extremely complicated and, owing to the nature of this book, will not be discussed in detail. It is sufficient to say that the manufacturer needs the capacity to produce the product in time for when the customer needs it to be delivered.

Production and stock control are the middle men between the record company and the manufacturer/distributor. It is the production department's responsibility to turn the raw material into a product that can be sold. The production department needs to ensure that the label copy, art work, photographs and production tapes are in the right place at the right time. This department also works with the sales division, ensuring that the stock is monitored and that the correct quantity of product is available. It is their responsibility to monitor the sales and demand patterns and, thus, ensure that the company has enough stock to deliver for call off, release date and for the life of the record. This is done by dialogue and research. It is the production department's job to tread the fine line between out-of-stock and overstocks, which are discussed at greater length later in this chapter.

The job of a good distributor is to be able to cover the market with the right amount of supply for the customers' demand. This is a tricky job even an impossible one, especially in today's changeable climate.

Distribution is carried out in two areas: new releases and, the backbone of any record company, the catalogue, which contains all the releases of the company still in stock or not deleted. Major record companies are extremely efficient at distribution today. A major company, like Polygram or Warners, have trucks in the high street every day. Many have a 24-hour call down to any area within the UK.

Each product of a record company has to be launched and marketed properly. Again, a whole book could be dedicated to this complex and, at times, cut-throat skill. The territories marketed expand with the longevity of an artist. International, national and regional areas are all important in marketing and have to be approached in their own special way.

Types of record company

There are three different types of record company:

- The most prolific is the privately-owned record company, known as the independent company, or *indie*. Such a company usually records one or two very specific genres of music and is dealt with specifically in this chapter.

- The major record company, which usually has a number of departments and other businesses and so is termed a *conglomerate or multinational* company.

- A subsidiary company of a major company which acts like an independent company but is part of a multinational.

The smaller private companies have to use record distributors, such as Pinnacle, to get their product out to the public, whereas the multinationals have their own distributors. One important point that most people do not realise is that each record company has two areas to which it promotes. The first is the general consumer or the record-buying public. The second is the retail industry concentrated in the major chains and independent high-street shops. The second part of this chapter concentrates on both of these important outlets.

258

It may seem strange that there are only six[2] multinational, major labels, but there are thousands of independent labels, from those run in a front room, to companies like Music For Nations which has built up a great reputation over the last ten years.

Music for Nations, a case study

Birth and development

Music for Nations (MFN) started off as a heavy-metal label; their first signing was Ratt. The company then signed Metallica, Anthrax and Megadeth, three of the most influential Thrash metal, and now mainstream, rock bands around today. Most of MFN's early product was licensed from America. As things started to develop, the company began to sign bands from other labels and to take on bands in other genres of rock-related music. The Under One Flag label was started specifically for bands in the Thrash metal and death metal genres. Another label, Food For Thought, originally the forerunner of MFN, was specifically tailored to suit the more muso (competent or over-competent at playing an instrument or instruments) type of artist. Both Joe Satriani and Stevie Vai produced albums on this label. Over a period, the company also licensed complete labels, such as Metal Blade from America. The company has currently licensed the Continuum label from America, which broadens their genre base by giving them artists like Charlie Watts and Ron Wood. This label also includes dance and rap acts, which again diversifies MFN's product portfolio. Although MFN were first known as a metal label, they have branched out over the years. The Devotion label started in 1990 and specifically caters for industrial bands. This label also licensed the Wax Trax label in America and has now blossomed into a happening alternative/industrial label.

MFN soon began to keep its bands longer. When new, with no track record, the company found it hard to keep bands for any period of time, because of the large investment needed to promote, market and distribute highly-successful bands. Getting the bands to sign contracts for long periods of time with a new label was impossible, but now that MFN has established itself, with a good reputation throughout Europe, it tends to be offered a lot of rock product first. This is a good situation to be in. Rock is going through a small recession at the moment, yet MFN does not see this as a bad thing but rather beneficial – whilst the majors are not actively involved in the signing of new rock acts, it means that MFN can take the pick of the crop. Over the last few years, there has been a lot of rock product chasing the same currency. It is now felt that this has evened out a little, and maybe the quality of the music has also improved.

MFN is a company that gives its artists time to develop. This allows the artist time to write, time to mature and time to develop both an audience and a following. Production costs, art work and other product-related costs have risen since the company started, and the sales of products have reduced, but these facts have to be faced and new ways of production and distribution tried. Although people complain about the price of CDs, MFN have not put up their prices to the wholesaler for a long time. Things at the moment are quite healthy on the rock front and a bright future for the company looks likely.

Managing Director, Martin Hooker, formed MFN, and Gem Howard has been there since the beginning. I talked to Gem in depth about the company and its prospects and pitfalls. The results of that interview follow.

Staff structure and development

MFN is a small company. One of the great advantages of a small company employing a small workforce is that employees tend to become involved in a lot more aspects of the business than they would in one department of a major record company. In a large company someone could stay in the same job for a long period and get to know very little about what other people do in other departments. One of the biggest bugbears when telephoning a conglomerate is that, if you cannot contact the right person, then no one else can help you. In a small company there is usually someone who can give you an answer immediately. When working for some larger companies, you can experience rejection when you try to look at the workings of other departments, especially if you try to get involved with other people's specialist areas. But, in MFN, as an example of a small company, one member of staff started in production, went into sales and now deals with the licensing agreements. It was a natural progression over a period of years.

When MFN started there were four members of staff, now there are 12. At the outset everyone helped in every area but now the roles of each member of staff are a lot easier to define. Each employee feels that one of the benefits of working for a small company is that they still tend to get involved in everything and have an idea of how most things work, from putting the band in the studio to the demo of the track. They can even gain knowledge of how the product reaches the racks in the shops. Not only do the staff understand a little bit about the other aspects of the company, but also they have a good understanding of its general running. If the managing director is away, the other directors can look after the company in his absence. They are not foxed by enquiries and regularly deal with royalty demands, tour supports, signings or a licensing enquiry. The directors have been involved in all of these queries so they can take an enquiry through from origin to completion.

The nature of the company means that Music For Nations has a very strong promotional side, and there are always between two and three press people within the company at any given time. Artists are assigned to the person whom the management feels will deal best with that particular act or that particular project. This is a satisfying way to assign artists as the people dealing with the act seem to relish taking on any new work. There are times, of course, when outside promotional people have to be used. For instance, when one of the bands make it in a very big way, outside promoters are used to get the band the best possible profile in conjunction with the work being done on the inside of the company. One area where outside promoters are used is in the promotion of rap music. This is an area with which the company is not yet familiar and a firm of outside promoters has been appointed. There is no real point in trying to sell something yourself that you are not familiar with. The best way to approach this is to get involved with

261

people who do know what they are doing and to learn from them. The rap genre is an area that a few MFN employees have become very interested in lately, as it is new and growing. In the past, the company knew nothing about this type of music; the interest developed, and it became fun being involved with a different type of music.

Figure 12:1 Tigertailz in full swing at the Pitz
during a warm up gig, Woughton Centre, Milton Keynes.
© Chris Kemp photograph

Talking to the employees of MFN, it soon became apparent that there is a great feeling of fun within the company, and a bonding between people that keeps the company buzzing. The staff feel that metal genre can become a little insular at times – it is not all the staff members' favourite kind of music, but it is something they do and do well. It keeps the interest going to have a variety of artists on different labels within the company, or it could end up just dealing with *Kerrang* and *Metal Hammer* every day of the week which, to the staff, would be extremely boring.

One of the major artists that MFN looked after in Europe was the late Frank Zappa. MFN exclusively handled Frank Zappa's catalogue on Barking Pumpkin Records all over Europe until the end of March 1995. Although deceased, Frank still has lots of material sitting in the vaults that may never see the light of day. It has always been a slow process with the Zappa family because they are so meticulous about their work. Based on the Zappa family's past history with other record companies, MFN have done well to keep the relationship going for over six years, and Frank seemed very happy with it; MFN had trebled his income from European sales over this short period. Whilst alive, Frank Zappa had total control over what MFN did with his work, when it was put out and what it looked like. MFN were happy for him to do this. It may have been frustrating at times, but the kudos of having such a major artist with such a great catalogue with their company, far outweighed the downside. There are very few people, apart from the likes of Diana Ross, that have such an extensive catalogue. There are not many artists that have such longevity. MFN is still selling *Sheik Yerbouti*, which is getting on for twenty years old, in huge amounts: 200,000 have been sold on CD alone. MFN has been selling that particular album for only four years, which shows the level of interest in the artist. New people are becoming interested all the time.

The managing director has his own personal assistant and deals with the royalty element and much of the contractual paperwork. His PA has major label experience. The production manager used to work for a subsidiary of a major label and has been with MFN since 1989. The production manager deals with all day-to-day manufacturing and production. He produces the sleeves, CDs and booklets. He organises art work and film work, briefs the repro houses, organises masters or directs finished masters, and the cutting of records or CDs. This is a full-time job with the number of releases that the company produces per year, currently between 50 and 70. Timing is very important and the company has to react quickly, especially when competing against release dates in other territories. The import/export business is so cut-throat that it relies on beating other people's release dates. Obviously MFN has to try to ensure that it can always have new releases out on time, especially before American releases, which arrive in Britain very quickly.

As already stressed, timing is important. New releases must be shipped out in time so that they have simultaneous release dates in as many territories as possible. This is a full-time job as products are shipped out every day. All orders must be received in time and different freight companies have to be appointed to make sure that the product is shipped to various countries at the right time. At MFN the directors oversee the staff responsible for shipping and deal with the international side of the business. The directors travel to different countries to make sure that everything goes according to plan and to sort out any hassles, and there are many. Generally they want to sell more records and CDs. The directors attend MIDEM and the New Music Seminar every year. These are the two main music get-togethers which are important to MFN as an independent company. The directors are able to look for licensing product, keep in touch with other licensees and generally have a visible presence there. It is certainly important for MFN, as a small company, to be represented, although it is not felt as important for the majors. The company does a lot of business there – a lot of people offer the company product – and MFN comes out with something good every time that the directors attend.

Licensing and retail

Another director's assistant helps with the various day-to-day problems with licensees, making sure that they have pre-release tapes, for instance, or photographs, biographies and posters. Communication is very important. You must put together a good campaign and convince people that you are behind an artist, otherwise it gives people the excuse not to do the work. This goes right down the line to the retailers who almost want you to guarantee them a chart position or a punter walking in on the day of release and asking for the record, before they are interested in stocking it.

This is a big problem because people tend to assume, whether bands, managers or the general public, that if you have a CD coming out then it is going to be available in every shop worldwide. They do not understand that a sale is a sale; the retailer has to buy the product and stick it in a rack and pay for it in 30 days. In today's financial climate the retailer has to be very careful with stock control. There has to be a good reason for the retailer to stock the record or CD, and it is one of the hardest things in the business to be able to give that reason. It may mean less releases, working things properly, working things up front, and giving a product good lead time but, in the end, this will ensure greater quality. In conjunction with this, the company's marketing machine must be in tune with the release. Advertisements must be in magazines at the right time so that promotion for the product hits the newspapers, magazines, radio stations and billboards at the same time as the CD. All these things are becoming more and more important.

In the past, some releases sold themselves on reputation, while other bands' releases sold for varying reasons. It was easier in the mid-1980s to sell product as punters had more disposable income, and record shops and punters were willing to take more chances. Today record companies have to be a lot tougher, a lot meaner and really think through the way that they work a release. Selling the finished product and dealing with the licensees all around the world really does mean a lot of work. Getting everything to happen just at the right moment at great distance can be a nightmare. For example, in Germany, nearly all the music magazines are monthly and their lead times are at least six weeks prior to their street dates. Thus, it is absolutely vital that everything is in place at the right time.

It is not so bad in Britain because most magazines, such as *Kerrang* and *New Musical Express* (*NME*), are weekly and there is more time for planning. But, Germany is such an important territory for rock and metal that you must make sure that everything you do is exactly right and you have all the right information. For instance, your company may have a band touring in six months' time. This may sound a long time in advance, but your company must have the dates today to give to the licensees in Germany, who in turn feed them to the magazines. This is done so that the tour dates are included in the advertisement in the correct month. This also stops the agents quibbling and claiming that they have not put the tour together yet, because agents are the first people to complain when a record company is not promoting their shows very well. Agents, the record company, the licensees and marketing departments all have to mesh together smoothly. It is difficult to comprehend just how far back you have to work to make sure that you have everything running to plan. But, it is not always possible to do this and agents and record companies do not meet deadlines. The results are albums and CDs which are released without tours and tours which go ahead without product, sometimes irreparably damaging the artists' reputation, or even the record companies' or agents' reputations.

There have been cases where a company has an artist who it is due to sign but has not yet done so. The artist has an album or CD, but no release date, and a tour is already booked. The company knows that it will not be able to do a perfect job on the artist, so it takes a different tack and promotes the artist in more of an American style. This style means putting out a release and then doing the work on it. (It is very difficult explaining to Americans that, in Britain, record companies work an artist up front. The Americans tend to put out a release and then to work it. In America there seems to be a lot more time to work on musical projects.) If you release a record or CD in Britain and it does not work in the first two weeks, it is very difficult to stimulate more interest in it. You cannot go back into a shop and say that you know the release was out two weeks ago and no one has been in to buy it but the band will be coming over to tour next month.

A company like MFN does not have the facility for sales reps to go back into shops after they have sold a new release, because they have such a large volume of new releases to handle. The company cannot possibly work the whole catalogue, which contains all their releases. To work each one of these releases for long periods of time would be impractical and incur large amounts of time and money. From MFN's point of view, once a release is out, it is out. It is very rare that any company would have the facility to work a catalogue. Obviously, there are employees who go into shops to make sure that their company's stock of big-selling artists is topped up, but it is difficult to get more stock out once it has been sold to the shops. This is why its so important to be able to convince the retailer, at the right time, to take enough stock, without taking too much. It is also important to have a good spread of retail outlets so that, when people go out to buy the release, it is readily available and they can find it.

This is a difficult area and causes hours of meetings, culminating in decisions that the directors hope will be the right ones. It is frustrating, when you are working a band and you are several albums or CDs down the line, that the only thing that shopkeepers remember is not how many they sell but how many they have left over. For instance, a shop might have taken 1500 copies of a release, done a special campaign on it, but returned 400. When you go back in with the band's next album, the shop staff will remember the 400 they had to return, completely forgetting the 1100 that they sold. It is a constant battle to make sure that enough product is available, but not too much produced.

A major company can always get more stock out. Because of the way the majors work, they are used to putting out 10,000 units, selling 7000 and having 3000 returned. Retailers are under pressure to stock major label artists; they will get favours on other releases for doing this. It is certainly true that you can do a lot of damage by putting too much stock out that does not sell through.

Staff specifics

A&R look at talent and sales potential with licensed product. This is particularly relevant because you are basically buying a master tape and a set of films for a certain amount of money, as opposed to putting a band in a studio. There is also no chance of the production over-running and the cost budgets escalating. With licensing, the directors look at the bands as how many units they can sell, while others look at it more artistically. At MFN the directors hear of things and these are passed on to Martin Hooker for a final decision. Positions in the company are somewhat irrelevant; there is a UK and International marketing manager who calls himself the General Manager. In a big company, some sort of demarcation is needed but, in a small company, this sort of demarcation would cause a certain friction. Gem Howard is an all rounder; he has a lot of experience on the live front because, many years ago, he was a road manager. Gem has probably visited most of the venues in Europe at some time or another, so he has got a good knowledge of touring relevant to a record company for developing artists and getting sales to having the artists profiled live. He deals with agents, promoters, posters, flyers and those areas pertaining to live acts. Gem deals with the management aspects of putting together budgets for tours, something that MFN does a lot. But, record companies do not help with the administration of tours. This business is quite complicated, especially with foreign bands, for example, the obtaining of carnets (inventories of stock required by border controls for tax and equipment verification purposes), booking sleeper buses, getting good deals for ferries, and many other details. Record companies tend to sort out all the logistical problems which saves money and helps to cut corners. Gem knows a great deal about this. In addition, Gem deals with all the video material, sell through and promotion. He knows a little bit about everything.

The production and shipping departments work very closely together when getting orders in, putting on initial quantities and dealing with re-orders. Stock must arrive at the right time and there must be enough stock on order for the new releases. Someone is employed by MFN to deal with mail order and general enquiries. Mail order is very important at the moment because, with vinyl being deleted rapidly, there are many requests for vinyl by mail order. There is also a receptionist who deals with visitors and telephone calls. In major companies everyone is watching their backs very carefully and no one wants to take any decisions. In a small company the employees can react faster and any query or emergency can be sorted out quickly.

There is a big difference between corporate culture and that of the small company or family firm. The situation at MFN is such that a band or management representative can ring up and say that he has a chance of doing a set tour, supporting a certain major artist, and it will cost this much, can MFN do it? Martin gives them an immediate answer.

International perspectives

Many British subsidiaries have no international base and it is difficult to sell an artist well with this limitation. For instance, there are not many of the major British rock artists' records in Norway. One of the things that MFN is good at is selling records everywhere, week in week out; the company is still selling records that it brought out eight years ago.

When Iceland, Portugal and Finland are considered, together with Germany, the UK, France, Belgium and the other European countries, the number of records and CDs sold soon builds up. All the small sales in these countries added together make up a large proportion of MFN's sell through. The company has expanded slowly and they are not quite world wide. In 1994 they succeeded in selling to Brazil, Argentina, Uruguay, South East Asia and Australia. There is still Africa to conquer but it is difficult to find anyone who can pay for the product.

Figure 12:2 Little Angels playing a warm up gig at the Pitz for the Milton Keynes Bowl with Dread Zeppelin in Milton Keynes. *© Chris Kemp photograph*

Some European and Middle Eastern countries are very enthusiastic and easy to deal with, like Israel. Israel's record buying from MFN started when Gem went over there with Paradise Lost. After the tour, there was a very large number of people wanting to stock MFN product.

Much of it was based on the roll-on effect whereby, when one retailer buys the product, the competitors also buy it because they do not want to be left out. Half the population of Israel have got access to MTV (Music Television) and they watch *Headbangers Ball*. This is great because many of MFN's bands are featured on the programme. We are not really aware of it in this country, but the developing countries of the world really do know what is going on in the music industry. Half the population of Israel are of Western origin, which makes for an appreciative audience for MFN's products.

Selecting an artist

When selecting an artist, all the primary decisions are made by Martin, as the Managing Director; if he likes something, the company does it, provided that the price is right. Everyone in the company is able to go to Martin to give their opinion about artists and to suggest that MFN signs them on. If Martin agrees, then the company tries them.

The company receives tapes every day, but very few artists are signed from demonstration tapes. The majority of artists are signed through word-of-mouth or connections, from a buzz or are licensed from abroad. The only bands signed by the company from demo tapes were Acid Reign and Lionsheart, although Lionsheart had a history with their lead singer, Steve Grimmett, already being a vocalist of some note with Onslaught. Freak Of Nature's Mike Tramp was turned down by many companies. MFN took the band on and it is now working really well. Mike has toughened his image and gone back to basics, sleeping on the bus, no hotels, no nothing really. MFN does listen to all the tapes that come in.

Acid Reign were chosen because of the sense of fun in what the band did. In the end it backfired on them, but the initial vibe was very strong. They took the American Thrash theme and gave it an English lilt; the band did great business and it clicked in this country. Howard, the lead singer, was a great front man who made it all come together. Acid Reign had some friends, called Reanimator. MFN received two tracks on Howard's recommendation and signed them as well.

The life expectancy of a band that gets a recording deal is probably five years. If a band lasts for over five years, they are doing very well. In most cases, if the band survives over ten years, then there is a strong probability that the band will be playing for the next 25. Provided that it has some success once it has passed ten years, the band can keep going because it has built up a fan base. A number of bands on the label release one album a year. These albums sell in respectable numbers to a small fan base all over the world. It is good business sense to continue this policy.

Gem states that successful pop is 90 per cent fashion and 10 per cent talent. The right person, in the right clothes and with the correct musical sound, can be the next big thing but, if it looks bad, then forget it. A lot of rock and album-oriented rock (AOR) is 90 per cent talent and 10 per cent fashion. To the kids within this genre, it is not just the fashion but the music that counts. The best guitarist, the best stage show, etc. mean a lot to fans and this is shown in attendances at concerts.

Financial perspectives

The finances in a company like MFN work in the following way. There is no real norm within each of the various areas. An advance is given to an artist to allow them to live whilst under contract to the company. The size of the advance depends on the artist, from virtually nothing to a small fortune. The next financial outlay is on the actual recording, which costs as little or as much as the company wants to spend. Then there is tour support. This is to fund the artist to go around the country, or the world, and to perform the music that has been recorded, live, tempting the public to buy it. Initially tours are a promotional tool. A solo singer with a guitar playing to 5000 to 10,000 people per night is likely to make money. A band like Pink Floyd, building a wall across the stage every night, with all the technology they need, taking 200 people on the road, playing to the same number of people as the solo artist each night and charging a similar entrance fee, will make considerably less money or a loss. It all depends on what the tour gives people for their money. It could be that, even though you will lose money on a tour over a period of months, you will create enough interest to sell millions of albums or CDs.

How much is the cost of touring? How long is a piece of string? This can depend on how much you want to give back to the audience, how much you earn on the road and how many people you need to produce the end product. The big financial outputs of touring are transport, wages and hotel rooms.

Product costings

The costs of a CD were about £15 when the first edition of this book was published in 1995. Since then prices have remained about the same, some being even lower for special offers bought on the internet.

When the product is shipped out to shops, the costs can be attributed to the following main areas:

At the beginning of 2001, a standard CD on a major label costs about £14.99. The retailer buys the CD at a maximum dealer price of about £7.29 and will sell it at anything above £7.29. The dealer price varies from year to year, depending on the variable costs, such as raw materials. Most shops are on some sort of deal. For example, if they buy two singles they get one free. When a company is trying to break a band free, singles may flood the shops.

For MFN 25 per cent of the £7.29 is the distribution fee, which then brings their income per CD down to £5.46. Their distribution is by Pinnacle. Out of this they have to pay 8.25 per cent on publishing rights (dealer price + 31 per cent = £7.29 + £2.26 = £9.55) which comes to 79p. This brings the profit down to £4.67. Out of this have to be taken the costs to record it and promote it, and for the art work, the cover, the sleeve, photographs and films. A glass master has to be made for the CD, the CD has to be manufactured, and a number have to be given away for reviews and promotional purposes. This takes up the major part of the £4.67. It could cost £5000 for the art work. If 5000 copies are sold then each cover costs £1; if 50,000 copies are sold then each cover costs 10p. The more copies sold the less the proportional costs of manufacturing and producing the CD. The actual cost of the product is around 74p. Therefore, if one of MFN's CDs sells in a shop for £14.99 then that shop is making a profit of £7.70 on just that one CD. A lot of record shops buy a lot of independent stock and then sell it discounted to make their profit. A Warner's disc, for example, if it is sold to a shop for £8.84, is £1.50 more than MFN. The shop makes less out of the major companies than they make out of MFN.

Indie labels are often much cheaper in the shops. This can mean, not only the survival of the indie shops, but also the record label. The major labels are also distributed by themselves. MFN's major competitors are other independent record labels, such as Roadrunner and Earache. The company get on very well with the other independents. Earache, Peaceville and MFN are all in it together, whereas Roadrunner seems to be out on a limb. Sepultura was their main band and a lot of energy was put into promoting them. Earache records a lot of experimental music, but also has produced bands such as Carcass, Acid Reign and Lawnmower Deth. The Thrash genre was on its last legs and, during the recession, a lot of more marginal bands were dropped from the companies. During the first Thrash wave, companies had signed bands who were on their fourth album and were not going anywhere. They parted with these bands and gave space to developing bands to work, pushing them up and bringing new blood into the genre.

Agent-Record company relationships

Some agents do not deal with bands properly. They ask ridiculous prices when they know full well that the promoter will lose money. There are certain venues that people never get bored with, like the old Marquee. 25 years after first visiting the Marquee, there was still a buzz. Rock City is fun and everyone wants to go there. Managers of different venues communicate with each other and compare prices for bands. The Pitz in Milton Keynes had a 400 persons limit, and there was a maximum amount that could be paid for a band or charged for a ticket. It did not matter who the band were, the show had to be economically viable. Fees differ around the country as venue size and charges change. It is much better to play a venue on the 'wrong' night of the week, fill it and get £200, than to take the night off. If 250 kids see a band that should be playing a bigger venue, then the kids become excited and the reputations of the venue and the band are enhanced. Many MFN bands which play 1500 capacity venues also play the Pitz in Milton Keynes because it is mid-way between Birmingham and London. In some venues there is nowhere to eat or drink, the rooms stink and are badly cleaned but at the Pitz there are pool tables, a swimming pool and food and drink provided. At Wokingham Plaza there is a bowling alley. Bands like to go to venues where they have something to do during the evening. The bands love to wander around the pool, shopping in close proximity to the venue and getting no hassle. The Pitz is usually played as a first gig of a tour or the last before London – an easy gig which is usually packed.

MFN produces a video when an album or CD is finished and it is looking for a track to release as a single. MFN does not work in areas of music that are single-oriented, at least, not in the UK. Heavy metal never really has been single-oriented. Led Zeppelin, for instance, did not release a major single in this country. In this genre, if an item can be used as a lead track, a video is made of it. It may become a single with a video or just a promotional video. One of the major outlets for video is MTV. On the other hand, there is no point in spending a fortune on a band that is only sold live. In MFN, sell-through videos tend to be live shows, and promotional videos tend to be shot on location. Video seems to lose the dynamics of a live performance.

Sales management - Promotion - Manufacture – Distribution

The product production process has changed over the last few years. The end product used to be the album, but now it is the CD. The first CDs produced are sent out as promotional material. They are in a slim case with no inlay details or booklet. A sheet of paper, containing all the relevant information that the promoter, licensee or DJ will need, is included in the package. The licensees also receive a representation of the sleeve design and sales notes. The sales notes include information on the sort of album, type of music, track listing, who the band are, what type of advertising they need, what has been done before with the band and what will happen in the future. The licensee also gets information on the tour dates and any other relevant details that can possibly be given at the time.

The sales force form part of the promotion and distribution company. Every month the management presents to the sales force the new products coming out over the next one to two months, together with all relevant information. The sales representatives and telesales people can tell potential retail buyers what will be released shortly and suggest that they listen to it. Perhaps a band may not have been heard of but may contain members of other well-known bands. The reps need this information as well as tour dates so that, where appropriate, they can tell a retailer that a band will be playing in their area a week after the CD's release.

The shop manager is asked how many copies of the new release he wants. The band may be from the local area and the rep needs to know this so that he can encourage the shop manager to take more copies to satisfy the demand from local fans. Information given to the reps will be passed on to the shop manager. The national accounts manager will pass on this information to the retail chains, such as HMV, which buys centrally. All this is the initial sales stage and orders will build up pre-sales figures. These figures are sent to the record company which then knows the number of CDs that will be in shops on the release date. These figures are important for a number of reasons:

- The company must sell a certain number of units in order to be able to make the chart.

- To get a chart position, the record company needs to push those shops that it feels have under-ordered to take more CDs so that they might sell more. The company must keep the territory covered, constantly checking. If a product has a pre-sales figure of 5000 to 10,000, then the record company will want to sell even more of it. The demand for the product is there and the company must ensure that people who want to buy the product can get it. There is nothing worse than getting a low chart position because there was not enough stock in the shops.

275

- The record company needs to know how many CDs to manufacture.

The number of records or CDs manufactured has to be in direct relation to those sold. There is no point insisting that every record or CD must have 10,000 copies produced, if the total sales in Europe will be only 2000. There is also no point in manufacturing 10,000 copies of a record or CD when the record company knows that the licensee in Germany will order 50,000 copies. MFN manufactures in Britain for the whole of Europe, but the production department has to know the pre-sales figure before an CD is released in order to have enough copies in stock.

It is the same with many bands in this genre, right up to Iron Maiden, who go in at number one and then sink without trace. The major proportion of sales happens in week one, then sales tail off and stop. Although this is not always the case with the bigger-selling bands, most of their product sales are still in the first week after release and then slow down.

With many artists the record company has to guess what will sell. With experience it is fairly easy; the company knows that somewhere like Germany will always take the greatest amount and that somewhere like Finland or Iceland will never take more than a few hundred copies. It is rare for Finland to sell four-figure sums, the population of Finland being half that of London. The population of Iceland is similar to that of Croydon.

Other things reps must be told, and they have to tell the record shops, about any in-store displays and if anyone from the record company will put them in the shop. The rep has to find out if the shops will want to put the displays up and whether the shops will have street posters or flyers The shops need to know what advertisements are going in which magazines and when. Retailers do not think highly of magazine reviews but, if a band has, for example, a 5K review in *Kerrang* or a 10/10 in *Terrorizer*, then they have a wide profile and the shop is more likely to listen to the rep and to buy. If only one reviewer likes the product, it does not mean a lot but, if everyone likes it, then it does indicate a potential success.

Marketing and promotion

What marketing and promotional tools do MFN use? They use radio, not in terms of advertising, but for publicity. The company has a member of staff responsible for radio promotion as well as using radio pluggers who send mailings to all local radio stations, rock shows and whoever else they need to contact. All the releases are available for DJs to play. Everything that the company puts out will be played on radio at some time somewhere in the country, purely because someone somewhere likes that particular CD, even though no one else in the country may like it. Very often it may be that a record company is one of only a few supplying a radio station with CDs to play so that that company gets a lot of its products played. Radio, as part of media promotion, is important. If the artist has a high enough profile, the company will do radio tours. MFN have done one with FM where they went around the country doing interviews and acoustic sets with radio stations, either recorded or live, depending on what the radio station wanted.

Radio stations come in small groups, for example, the Chiltern Group, which contains four stations including Chiltern and Horizon. They have local and community programming. Often a company in London produces an interview with set questions, where the DJ in a local radio studio interjects at the correct point. Although this is a tape, it sounds like a *bona fide* live interview. Such a tape is sent to as many radio stations as possible and the DJs hold their own 'live' interview without actually having the band in the studio. This works very well because many of the radio stations are tiny and it is impossible to get two people in the room playing live, let alone five. On the tape it may say that the band are going to sing for the listeners, but the tape continues to be played and it sounds like the band are playing in the studio. The listeners think that the band are playing in their local radio station.

When bands are sent out to do live radio, the band rings the station to say that they are doing a gig in the area and the DJ may suggest that they pop in and do the show. The band then does a piece live in the morning which may bring a few more punters into the evening show.

Many of MFN's bands appear on video through MTV, mostly in Europe, but not in Britain. The company does reviews, CDs and media promotion. Flyers and posters are produced as part of the awareness campaign attached to the product. Poster sites are used, as well as shops and venues. The number of posters varies. To manufacture more posters is similar to the manufacture of more product – it is very costly. It is better to have 5000 and not need them all than to have 3000 and to be short; the print run-on costs are minimal. The run-on number is irrelevant; just add what you can get rid of. MFN have recently had printed 40,000 flyers for Paradise Lost. They needed 30,000 to take on the road, another 5000 for local promotion, and will probably have 5000 left over. But, should the band run out, then the contingency of 5000 will be used. This is cheaper than having a 35,000 printed then a further 5000 at a later date.

The promotional relationship between the band, the promoter and the record company is dealt with in more detail in Chapter 4.

For this chapter I am indebted to Gem Howard and Andy Black for their help and enthusiasm, the other members of the Music For Nations' staff, and to Jimmy Devlin and Darryl Franklin .

Thanks also to RIF raff, the BPI and the Arts Council for the papers sent from *On the Right Track*.

Conclusion

The record company contributes to the development of an artist. Part of this process is the production of the album. The next chapter deals with this in detail.

Chapter 13

Production in the Studio

by Tony Platt

Introduction

Music production is a creative process which straddles art, technology and business. As a result, it is never 'cut and dried' and a producer must be flexible. An open mind will open more doors in this industry than most other approaches – save that of your father owning the company!

Opinions differ greatly as to the best approach to music production but initiative, flair and individuality are important factors for success.

You can learn easily the technical aspects of the recording process, whether viewed from a musical or an engineering standpoint. No matter from which direction a producer enters record production, musical or technical, an appreciation from the other viewpoint will extend his options. For a musician wishing to produce for herself or others, the time taken to understand the basic engineering principles will help communication and make for a smoother session. For an engineer or producer, his flair with music will relate directly to his understanding of the fundamentals of rhythm and harmony.

What follows are guidelines which form the basis of most projects a producer will undertake for both demonstration (demo) and commercial purposes. You will see – and perhaps appreciate – that the variety and unpredictability of music production makes it simultaneously one of the most exciting and frustrating occupations to pursue.

Defining the role

Over the last 15 to 20 years the role of producer has changed dramatically. In the early days of recording, the technical difficulties were so over-riding that any 'production' had to be done beforehand, in rehearsal, by the musical director or arranger. One take was probably the most chance the musicians were allowed. Preparation is still an important factor in any production, though nowadays, coupled with a user-friendly technical environment, many more options are available. The development of independent, dedicated recording facilities has brought about the need for a proper liaison between the record label, the artist and the technicians, and the role of record and CD producer has taken on more importance.

Today record and CD producers are more akin to film directors, and record companies are progressively asking more of them. They are expected to participate in a wide range of decisions, from the choice of material through to preparing estimates for tape use in the studio. The record producer, or those delegated by him, need to organise everything from the technical specifications of the recording to the time that meal breaks are taken. At the same time, he needs to be fully accessible to the band for advice and direction on a variety of connected and unconnected subjects.

A creative working relationship with the band is of primary importance, whatever level of production the producer is contemplating. Different bands look for a variety of attributes and skills from him. Such is the way of creative collaboration that a 'chemistry' should be recognisably apparent from their first meeting. The producer will be wise to develop the aptitude quickly to create the conditions for this initial spark to be kindled into a close relationship of mutual trust and respect. In simplistic terms, the producer must understand the aspirations of the band so that he can create the right circumstances and conditions to make them a reality.

Levels of production

There are three main aspects to the levels of production:

- The level of artistic/creative enhancement.

- The level of technical requirements and quality.

- The size of the relevant bank balance.

280

The pursuit of perfection

Whether the producer is recording a demo or a full album for a major label, he must identify the genre of the artist, what personality they are seeking to project and decide how proficient they are at doing that. This will enable him to settle upon the level of creative enhancement he will need to provide. A good rule to apply here is, 'if it isn't broken, don't mess with it'. Remember, the word is *enhancement*: taking over and imposing only his ideas is not what production is all about. Examples A, B and C below show how this works and the subject is further discussed later in this chapter.

When recording has begun, the producer will need to make many decisions about how far to pursue perfection. One thing is certain, no song or piece is ever really 'finished'. It can, and should, evolve even after it has been released. The producer's job is to capture the best 'snap-shot' of the song at the best moment. Some producers will be happy with a take that has a few minor mistakes but which feels great, whereas others will retake and overdub to achieve musical precision. Some will spend months and even years obtaining the combination of perfect performance and feel. You, as a producer, must decide upon the approach with which you feel most comfortable and creative. Of course, in a multitracking situation, you will also have the luxury of deferring many final decisions, but they must be made eventually.

My personal philosophy on this can be best illustrated by the following story. The pianist Schnaebel was recording with Sir Adrian Boult. He played the introduction to a very difficult piece spectacularly wrong. Sir Adrian asked if he would care to take the piece again. He replied, *I might play it better but would it be as good?*

Example A

The artist is a singer/songwriter with a delicate haunting style who is still a little insecure about being signed to a major label and the prospect of recording. The demo is okay, but the artist is much more charismatic live. The musicians on the demo are not part of the deal and are probably not going to help the artist move forward much. The budget available is reasonable, but not large. The songs are good, but not quite mature enough to capture a wide audience.

You need to surround this artist with some creatively stimulating musicians who can either encourage song writing or collaborate in it. It may be best to start with one player and use him as a 'musical director'. Avoid musicians who are just 'doing the session', choose players who are prepared to become involved. If enough suitable songs are not readily forthcoming, cast around for extra songs from other writers. Spend a larger proportion of time arranging, rehearsing and fine-tuning the material until the artist and musicians are excited about the prospect of recording. The recording process is then the culmination of the preparation, rather than the focus of everybody's attention and you will be able to capture the performance and charisma of the artist. You will have held down costs by using the studio for the least time and, subsequently, will have surplus in the budget for any finishing touches, such as strings or guest musicians.

Example B

The artist is a group who work with sequenced material augmented with live brass and vocal textures. They are signed to an independent label with distribution through a major company so, the budget is tight, but the sound quality must be excellent.

The choices are simpler as the preliminary work can be done in a programming suite, the studio only being required in the final stages. The choice and arrangement of material is important and you should spend more on good-quality sound modules and a programmer, if needed.

Example C

The artist is a local, unsigned band who want you to help them record four songs to release on CD to sell at gigs and to use as a demo for record companies and agents. They have very little money but you have seen them play and you think they may have a future.

The first thing you must establish in your own mind is that, barring expenses, you are unlikely to make any money out of this. It has to be a joint investment by everybody concerned, whether they are investing time, money or both. Your dilemma is that the band will be keen to cover their costs by selling the CD to fans who really want a recording of what they have just seen live. You want to capture the spirit of the band live, but polished up enough for it to catch the ear of the artist and repertoire (A&R) fraternity; to rehearse and maybe tidy up the arrangements, but not to mess with them too much. Call around local studios and try to get a deal on some 'dead time' (unbooked). You may need to be prepared to call the session off if the studio gets a full booking, but flexibility costs nothing. Try to find a studio which is well looked after – it is better to book less time in a studio that works properly, but costs a little more, than to face constant breakdowns in a cheaper one. If everybody is fed up, the recording will probably reflect this. Make sure that you leave enough time to mix properly, even by booking a few hours to mix on a separate day, because mixes done at 3 a.m. after three 12-hour sessions are rarely your best work!

Level of technology

The technical requirements for a basic recording are decided by the producer's level of expertise or that of his engineer. Many top quality recordings have been made with minimal equipment but you, as a producer, must not skimp on the essentials and your equipment must be up to the job. No-one will thank you if a much-sweated-over recording is unusable because of clicks on the tape or rumbling background noise. The tape machine should be well-maintained and aligned. You need a good selection of microphones and some monitors with which you are comfortable and familiar. A room that you can talk in comfortably will give good recordings, but always take a cassette or DAT (digital audio tape) home after the first day's recording to get a perspective outside the studio. The console is important but can be patched around if troublesome, and so it is lower on your list of priorities. Saving a larger proportion of your equipment budget for the mixing is a good idea. You should make sure basic musical spares are available, such as drum skins and sticks, guitar strings and tuner batteries. It is frustrating to end a session because it is 11 p.m. on Sunday and the guitarist has broken his last string.

Level of funding

With record companies now influenced by accountants, it is easy for a producer to be dragged into protracted budget discussions. Budgeting is important, but the producer must not become obsessed with penny pinching and clock watching – both are counter-creative side-tracks. If you, as a producer, plan well and are clear in your mind which areas of a project will need what proportion of the budget, then you must stick to your guns. Most of the people you meet on the business side of record companies are only interested in balancing the books. The most persuasive arguments about creative integrity will be lost on them; so give yourself as much leeway in the budget as possible. There will be occasions when the A&R people ask you to submit a lower budget which fits the allocation and say that they will increase it later, if necessary. This is almost never done.

A seemingly infinite budget can be as much of a problem as an absurdly small one. The main difference between the two is that, with a small budget, a great many more decisions are made for monetary constraints. Somewhat ironically, therefore, you will often need to be more disciplined on a big budget production than a small one.

The art of juggling the level of technology, funding and planning without compromising or interfering with the creative process, can be the key to a successful production. Planning is very important.

Planning

The producer will have met the artist and made an assessment of the artist's expectations. He will have got some idea of the material to be recorded and how the artist wants it to sound. He will also have made some decisions on a possible venue (or venues) for the recording. It is possible, especially if the project is for a major label, that even before the producer is definitely hired he may be asked to submit a budget. In these circumstances nothing very much can be achieved until the budget has been approved. The producer must at least prepare an outline budget, even if producing a demo for an unsigned artist, as he (or his manager) will want some idea of the projected cost.

Any number of people will want to have their say in various aspects of the production and, once the producer has his ideas clear and can support them with viable figures, he can schedule a meeting with as many of them as possible. He must consult three main parties:

- The artist.
- The artist's manager.
- The record company.

The overlap of each party's involvement and responsibility will vary from project to project but Figure 13:1, below, gives a basic set up.

A growing number of major companies issue producers with a set of procedure guidelines which generally spell out, in plain English, what is contractually expected of them. The guidelines are helpful as they will clarify any specific requirements a particular company has. A résumé of these guidelines is shown in Figure 13:2, pages 286-7. Most of the requirements a producer will cover anyway in order to do a good job!

Figure 13:1   Involvement in a recording production

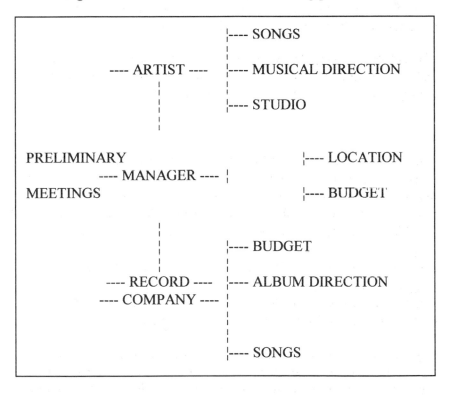

Figure 13:2 Producer Procedure Guidelines

Items shown in *italics* are those which vary greatly between different companies.

The following are procedures and information to help your recording projects progress smoothly and efficiently. A&R and A&R Administration are available to assist you with any questions or problems pertaining to financial or administrative tasks.

BUDGETS:
A detailed budget must be submitted and approved by A&R and A&R Administration prior to issuing purchase orders or the commencement of recording.

STUDIOS:
1) A detailed list of studios which will be used for this project should be submitted and approved by A&R and A&R Admin. You may place time on hold at a studio, but the company is not responsible for this time until the budget has been approved and purchase orders have been issued to the studio by A&R Administration.

2) Purchase orders are issued to the studios daily, weekly, monthly. Please make certain that at the end of each session, the work order is signed by you.

3) The company will pay the studio pursuant to standard dating policies (30 days from invoice date) unless otherwise approved in advance by A&R Administration.

MUSICIAN PAYMENTS:
1) *Here the producer will have specific instructions with regard to union agreements, tax and immigration authority requirements (work permits, etc.)*
2) Producers are responsible for the preparation of all musicians' Union returns or contracts.
3) Each management company will have time limits for the submission of these documents.
4) Compensation for rehearsals should be outlined in the budget, and discussed with A&R Admin. prior to making any agreements with musicians hired.
5) Producers who perform as musicians and/or vocalists should be aware that any advances paid to them also cover any union scale which would otherwise been payable for their performance. No additional payments

for a producer's performance will be made unless approved in advance by A&R Administration.

TRAVEL EXPENSES:
1) Airline tickets, accommodation expenses, per diems, and vehicle rentals must all be included in the submitted budget, and approved by A&R or A&R Admin. prior to incurring any travel expenses. The company will make all arrangements directly through our preferred travel agent.

2) Personal managers are responsible for their own personal travel and all other attendant expenses. The company will pay only for those persons directly involved in the recording of the project such as producers, musicians and engineers.

EQUIPMENT RENTALS & CARTAGE:
1) The company will issue purchase orders for all budgeted expenses and should be direct billed.

MISCELLANEOUS EXPENSES:
1) All miscellaneous expenses must be budgeted and approved by A&R Administration. This includes taxis and food billed through the studio.

TAPE INVENTORY & TRANSPORT:
1) Under no circumstances are master tapes to be taken from tunes not authorised in advance and in writing by A&R Admin.
2) On an ongoing basis the producer is required to maintain a full inventory of all tapes relevant to the project and their whereabouts. This list should be copied to A&R and A&R Admin.

SAMPLING:
1) The producer should keep a list of any samples used during the recording, noting the following information.

> TITLE OF SONG SAMPLED
> ARTIST
> COPYRIGHT OWNER
> LABEL
> PUBLISHER

This information should be noted at the time of sampling and include information about which final mixes contain it.

It should be noted that the artist, or the artist's representative, is responsible for obtaining sample clearances.

The budget

The level of attainable production will inevitably be influenced by the size of the budget available. However, by sensible and imaginative planning the producer can stretch out even the most frugal budget.

Figure 13:3, below, illustrates a typical budget plan. Not all items shown will be relevant to all productions. It is important to err on the high side with all costings in order to have room for manoeuvre and to account for any unforeseen costs. Nobody will be upset if the producer comes in under budget, but going back for more money is not easy.

Figure 13:3   Specimen album budget

PRE-PRODUCTION

      DAYS   @ £   /DAY   = £ ....

STUDIO
Recording and overdub

      DAYS   @ £   /DAY   = £ ....

Mixing

      DAYS   @ £   /DAY   = £ ....

TAPE
Analogue
    x 2" REELS @ £   /REEL   = £ ....
    x ½" REELS @ £   /REEL   = £ ....
    x ¼" REELS @ £   /REEL   = £ ....
    x CASSETTES @ £   /CASSETTE = £ ....

Digital
    x ½" REELS @ £   /REEL   = £ ....
    x DAT   @ £   /REEL   = £ ....
    x DISCS @ £   /DISC   = £ ....

        TOTAL STUDIO   **= £** ....

EQUIPMENT RENTALS
During recording approx.   = £ ....
During mixing approx.   = £ ....
                    TOTAL EQUIPMENT   **= £ ....**

ENGINEERING
Engineering fee   = £ ....
                    TOTAL ENGINEERING   **= £ ....**

MUSICIANS
Musicians fee   = £ ....
                    TOTAL MUSICIANS   **= £ ....**

TRAVEL AND LIVING
Fares   = £ ....
                                                                = £ ....
                                                                = £ ....
                                                                = £ ....
Car Hire   = £ ....

                    TOTAL TRAVEL   **= £ ....**

Accommodation
        DAYS   @ £   /DAY   = £ ....

Per diem
        DAYS   @ £   /DAY   = £ ....

Food
        DAYS   @ £   /DAY   = £ ....

                    TOTAL ACCOMMODATION   **= £ ....**

MISCELLANEOUS

                    TOTAL EXTRAS   **= £ ....**

ADVANCES
Producer advance   = £ ....
Artist advance   = £ ....

                    TOTAL ADVANCES   **= £ ....**

                    BUDGET TOTAL   **= £_____**

Organising the pre-production

The producer chooses the location for pre-production based on criteria dictated by the style or type of project he is working on. Some artists have their own home studio or rehearsal space. It is important at this stage not to be too finicky about this venue, for reasons discussed later. A location and a figure for the budget are what are needed now.

Choosing the studio

Most artists have some idea of where they would like to record, but their preferences are rarely based on technical or budgetary considerations. For example, they may prefer a favourite studio because of the people who work there. If the artist is based in another country or wants to record in another country, then the extra transportation and accommodation costs involved must be taken into consideration.

The producer's judgment must also take into account the type of distractions or encouragement a particular location may have for an artist. Some artists would be driven crazy cloistered in a country residential studio, preferring the excitement of city night life.

The recording medium used must be decided – multitrack, analogue, digital, sequenced – and how much 'live' recording will play a part in the production (see Studio Options, Figure 13:4, page 291).

Opinions vary as to the desirability of mixing in the same studio as the recording. I do not usually do this. On a creative level, I feel that a change of location at the mixing stage helps to restore objectivity, and technically my requirements for mixing are different to those for recording. You, as a producer, will be able to decide for yourself as you experience different alternatives.

The budget, location and recording medium are the key factors in drawing up a short list of potential studios. There are various listings of studio statistics, such as the *Kemps* and *Music Week* directories, and the Association of Professional Recording Studios has listings of its members. One or more of these should be available at the record company or management offices but, failing that, most large reference libraries have at least one of them. There are several 'studio factors' who will supply a list of studios from their database, given a basic specification of cost, technical requirements, etc. They will then negotiate a rate and confirm the booking. They receive a commission from the studio so, although the factor is not paid directly, the cheapest rate will be higher than if the producer booked a studio himself. Because of this, producers will be better off using this service only if they are working in an unfamiliar country. Also the factors' databases will contain only those studios which are willing to pay them commission, so the producer will not be offered all the alternatives.

Figure 13:4   Studio options

Recording medium	Facility Type	Suitability
Stereo analogue	Town studio	Pre-production
8 track analogue	Residential studio	Recording
16 track analogue	Mobile studio	Overdubbing
24 track analogue	Midi studio	Mixing
Stereo digital	Live venue	Sequencing
Multitrack digital		
Hard disc		
Midi based		

Studio specifications change frequently, so details should be checked. If possible, the producer and the artist should visit several studios on their short list because studio owners come second only to estate agents in imagination when describing their facilities!

Now you, as a producer, can make up at least a couple of rough 'game plans' and have the rates of studios involved to hand. At this time it is best to work with the quoted book rates for studio time, but also to have some idea of what discounts may be on offer from your preliminary choices. This will leave you some juggling space in the final budget. You will find that the process of negotiating a favourable studio rate is almost on a par with bartering in a Moroccan market.

Never accept the first rate quoted and be very specific about what you think the rate includes. Your budget can take a severe knocking if you suddenly find that all that wonderful outboard equipment you were encouraged to use was not part of the studio deal.

Factors which will affect the rate you pay include:

- The length of time you wish to book. Block bookings of several weeks always attract a discount.

- The state of the studio business. This will be affected by the number of studios in the market and the number of artists wishing to record.

- The status of the artist you are working with. It is an irony in the music industry that the more famous (and probably more solvent) an artist is, the cheaper things become. Free instruments, etc. may be provided in return for product endorsement.

- Whether you or your client are prepared to pay a proportion in advance. Studios generally welcome this as they often wait months for accounts to be settled. But, it is not always easy to arrange this with the business affairs department of major labels.

- Being specific about the extent of the facilities you wish to utilise. For instance, if a studio has both digital and analogue machines available they can hire out the one you are not using.

It is now fairly widespread practice to book studios on a daily 'lockout' basis which gives the advantage of picking up exactly where you left off. This generally is not much more expensive than the rate for a ten-hour day. If you find that the artist prefers to work shorter hours, then you can consider the hourly option.

Equipment rental

Proper control of rental requirements is an important factor in budget tracking. A log should be kept of equipment hired, noting down the day/s the hire commenced and ended and the rate expected for each item. With a little planning, large savings can be made. All the rental companies offer discounts for longer hire periods, making negotiation worthwhile. Some companies charge only for four days on a week's hire. The record company will undoubtedly have a discount deal with one or more of the rental companies. One of the benefits of joining the producer's organisation, Re-Pro, is large discounts with some rental companies. Many studios have a stock of extra equipment for rent. If you need any for the entire recording, it is worth trying to include it in the deal for studio time. Ensure that such deals are clearly understood and documented by fax or letter. It may be possible to rent equipment privately from other musicians, engineers or producers for better rates, but this can be false economy if the equipment breaks down.

Most record companies issue purchase orders for equipment rental (see Figure 13:2, page 286-7) and this is inconvenient if a producer needs to hire something out of normal office hours. He can plan for this eventuality by requesting an open purchase order, with a maximum limit, with the record company's preferred renter.

Musicians

This section of budget planning is dependent totally on the type of artist with whom you, as the producer, are working. It is essential that you leave yourself the option of using extra players, if this is appropriate. Sometimes it may be at quite an advanced stage in the recording when an idea for a guest musician comes up – and if you have a contingency built into your budget, this will not be a problem.

In America agreements with the Musicians' Union require a fee to be paid to all musicians on an album, even if they are also the artist. This can leave a large hole in the budget as the payment also includes social security contributions. Generally, this can be worked into the budget, by reflecting the *per diem* payments as the musicians' fees, but these calculations are best done in collaboration with the business affairs section or management.

It is now common practice to come to an arrangement with session musicians for an all-in fee, rather than calculating each piece separately. The promoter must be fair and offer a figure in keeping with the work involved. Musicians with large or unwieldy instruments will also charge for porterage.

Finding the right musicians for the job is often difficult. Great care must be taken, when introducing guest players to a project, that they are there for the right reasons. A producer may feel it is all right to put guests on an album solely for the publicity they will create. Whilst this ploy has paid off many times, it has also backfired on an equal number of occasions. Creative and musical criteria must be applied first before contemplating the commercial potential of such a move.

To book musicians when working abroad, or a large orchestra, the producer could use a session-fixer who will take care of all the booking arrangements and charge an all-in fee.

Engineering

If the producer is not capable or willing to undertake this aspect of the recording process, he will want to find someone compatible to work with him. He may develop a working relationship with a staff engineer at a given studio, so this will be a factor in his choice of location. Cost will play an important part and record companies are, in general, unsympathetic to hiring a freelance engineer for all of a project.

If the budget will allow an engineer for either the recording or the mixing but not both, which should it be? Again the answer is closely connected with the style and type of artist and the recording medium used. If you are recording an artist in a predominantly 'live' environment, it may be a wise move to be sure of the highest quality recording. The mix is then more a matter of blending the sounds and music. If you are building the recording with sequences in a midi context, then the engineer is best employed at the mixing stage.

Whatever the scenario, engineers, including assistants, need to be incorporated into the project. They should always feel that they are working with, rather than just for, the producer and the artist. Get this combination right and these people can make a big difference to the enjoyment and creative standard of the project.

If a producer is involved in a demo or very low budget recording, engineering options are irrelevant. Under these circumstances, motivation is the key word. The producer will want to work quickly and efficiently, so he must make clear to the engineering staff at the studio exactly is expected of them. In the cheaper demo studios, the engineers tend to make up in bluster what they lack in knowledge. This will be a test of the producer' people-handling prowess: he must assert his authority in such a way that the technicians and staff are aware that they are involved in a session with committed professionals. The irony here is that producers will often encounter more arrogance and incompetence in smaller studios (who should need the work) than they will in the larger, more successful facilities with outside funding.

Travel, accommodation and living expenses

It is hard to see how producing a record has anything to do with becoming an amateur travel agent, but travel and subsistence figures must be included in the budget. Normally, someone at the record company or management company will do the donkey work, but the producer must always check that people will be where he wants them, when he wants them. He must make sure that accommodation is suitable and convenient; unsuitable domestic arrangements can cause unbelievable problems with some artists. He must also try to incorporate a fair *per diem* payment for everyone concerned, which will go a long way to promoting domestic harmony.

Tape

This is another expense that can run away with itself, if not held in check. With multitrack tape costing hundreds of pounds, at 30 inches per second £1000 buys only about 2 hours of recorded time – only 20 takes of a six-minute song. If, at the start of any session, the producer instructs the engineer or assistant clearly how he wishes the tape usage to be managed, he will only have to monitor it occasionally. Controlling the use of DAT tapes and cassettes will also help and, on very tight budgets, they should be bought beforehand to avoid the studio mark-up.

Making the record

By now the producer will probably be fed up with administration and very ready to start the actual recording. It is unlikely that all the arrangements are finalised, but he will have been paying close attention to the mood of the artist and, if the creative urge is at a peak and enough of the basic organisation is in place, he will try to get things moving straight away.

Pre-production

In most cases valuable studio time can be saved by rehearsing and arranging the material beforehand. Once again, there are no hard and fast rules, but the producer must be prepared to seek the best alternative for the project. A pre-production period can give the producer and the artist an opportunity to settle down with each other. To produce well the producer will need to develop a close relationship with the artist and the value of pre-production time as a kind of 'courtship' should not be underestimated. The producer can apply various approaches to what can be termed as pre-production, but he must be careful not to 'over-rehearse' some artists, because this can lose the spontaneity.

In some cases, he may want to use this time for additional writing, either in direct collaboration with the artist or by introducing a third-party writer to the project. This can be an effective creative step and often will be welcomed by the artist. Some artists, though, may see such a suggestion as criticism of their writing abilities. During this period, the producer will want to achieve a good balance of material and start to establish the general tone of the album.

He must also develop a sense of the capabilities of the musicians involved and the best way to coax a performance out of them. This information will be invaluable later. In some extreme circumstances, he may find that a particular musician is not working out. It is obviously creatively and economically better to find this out before he starts recording, but he must decide how to deal with it and do so there and then. I have found on a few occasions where this has happened that the other players were aware of some incompatibility but were reluctant to broach the subject. This is the producer's job – he must not shirk the responsibility. If the project does not work musically, it is no good blaming one of the players. Conversely (nothing is cut and dried remember!), he may decide that the circumstances do not warrant such an upheaval and he will have to be satisfied with 'damage limitation'.

This may take various forms. If, for instance, he finds that the drummer is a bad timekeeper, he could trigger samples of his drums from a sequence. Keyboards can be dubbed as midi-recordings and edited on computer screen. (Most music today is digitally remastered, which means it is electronically timed so that each change and track ending is perfect.) If the producer takes the time and trouble to understand the options available in recording, he will be able to find a way to solve most problems.

If the recording is to be midi-based then the pre-production time also becomes pre-programming time. There are now numerous programming suites available at a cost considerably less than normal studio time. But, if neither the producer nor the artist are capable or willing to cope with the technical aspects of programming, the producer must include the cost of a specialist programmer in the budget.

It is possible to programme almost all of the music beforehand, but I would advise that you, as a producer, avoid becoming side-tracked with the almost infinite options of which sounds to use. Use the time to perfect the performances and make notes about the most appropriate sounds for each part. When the music is ready, hire a studio and all the best-quality sample modules you can afford and transfer it to tape. On a technical point, transferring to tape may strike you as unnecessary when working with sequences, but I have always found it preferable than descending into 'midi hell' just as I am ready to take a mix!

I cannot overstate the importance of making notes whilst the pre-production is going on. Even the most retentive memory can forget small details and, by the end of the project, tiredness will not help either. Be constantly listening for ideas. Your receptiveness to ideas at every stage will help to strengthen your relationship with the musicians, but forgetting to incorporate a good idea is inexcusable. Also during the pre-production, you will need to make notes about your technical requirements in the studio.

The recording

If the producer has not yet needed to be too flexible in his approach, this is the stage where the change occurs. It is now most important for him to establish a basic pattern and momentum for the recording stage. To a certain extent, a pattern will have emerged during pre-production or programming, but it is up to him to carry this through the change of venue and emphasis. The first day is always somewhat chaotic and the producer must not allow himself to become too stressed by this. For this reason, it is never advisable to have everybody turn up at once. As a producer, arrange for the equipment to arrive the previous day, if possible, and arrive yourself at least an hour before the first musician. This will give you the opportunity to introduce yourself to the people at the studio and gently establish your preferences and ground rules. This will also give you time to sort out any crisis of misunderstanding or misinformation that may have occurred. It is always better to handle any early difficulties out of the artist's sight/earshot because, though it may not be your fault, even tiny problems can be blown out of proportion and damage the artist's confidence in you or the studio.

Establishing a good workable sound is obviously the first priority. You should avoid fine tuning the sounds too much at this stage. The overall sound will be affected by many things such as confidence of the players, the correctness of the arrangement and the engineering technique. As a general rule of thumb, if after much microphone changing and moving of instruments etc., the sound still is not right, then look at factors other than just the technical ones.

Even at this stage you must be prepared to adapt or develop the arrangement. As the full glory of the sound appears in the studio many new ideas should start to flow. These ideas can suggest changes in the arrangement and those changes can help to develop the sound. Once again you must place yourself in a position to juggle these influences with the minimum of compromise. You need to make sure that the engineers are staying alert to what is going on and are in a position to capture the take. Nothing is so soul destroying to an artist as playing what he considers to be the finest take in his life only to find that the assistant has missed the first four bars!

In practical terms you may feel that you want to record all the backing tracks before embarking on the overdubbing procedure. There are advantages and disadvantages to this approach. If you are recording

12 songs, this may be a daunting prospect for the drummer, but if he is 'in the groove', so to speak, it would be counter-productive to break the flow. It is important to involve all the players in the recording as soon as possible. Apart from the creative advantage of this, there are some practical gains. Leaving all the vocals or solos until last puts an unfair pressure on those musicians to perform to a time limit and so should be avoided wherever possible. This particularly applies to the vocals. It is useful to have the melody (vocal) in place early on in the recording in order to correctly frame the arrangement and orchestration. Additionally, this will give the singer the chance to evaluate and tidy up any rough parts of his or her performance.

Your approach to vocal production needs to differ somewhat from the rest of the music. Whereas a guitarist can change strings or guitar or amplifier to achieve a desired effect, a singer has to rely solely on his or her one voice. This can lead to a great sense of insecurity in the singer, which can manifest itself in a variety of ways. You will need to be appreciative of this possibility and react positively and supportively. It would be impossible to discuss all the varied scenarios this can bring about but, giving the singer a reasonable amount of time to perform, will go a long way to avoiding most difficulties.

Any repairs to or re-takes of other instruments you intend to keep with the backing track should be done as you go, whilst the musician has the same 'feel'. I am of the opinion that players should never be encouraged to think of their part as just a guide. For instance, it cannot be very encouraging for the drummer if he feels the guitar player is just going through the motions. Most particularly, a positive playing approach is more likely to encourage a naturally dynamic performance and to inspire greater interaction between the performers.

Once again flexibility is the key; do not be afraid to change the approach if spontaneity is flagging. If the energy levels are dropping, then take a day off.

In a demo situation a great deal of this becomes irrelevant. Time will be at a premium and the resulting pressure can be extremely counter-productive. Additionally, you may well be dealing with musicians who are inexperienced in recording techniques. Note how the approach in Example C above applies.

Mixing

Now you are at the point where you need to summon all of your objectivity. If at all possible, you should try to take a few days' break between recording and mixing. This will enable you to recover and to clear your head for this next important step.

It can be argued that the mix is the most important stage of the recording process. I cannot agree that any part is fundamentally more important than another. A bad recording will never mix well, uninspiring arrangements will not record well and a bad song is always just that. Of course, in keeping with the nature of music as an art form, opinions on what is good and bad are always subjective.

Suffice to say that if you have got this far with a project you will, hopefully:

- think the music is good.

- have made your best effort to choose and arrange the songs well.

- inspired great performances in the artists.

- made or commissioned a quality recording.

Your overall approach to the mix will depend on certain factors. If you are engineering the mix yourself you will not have to explain what you want to someone else. But, it can be difficult to maintain objectivity over the course of a long mix and, naturally, your hearing will not stay sharp. This is a good case for working with an engineer on the mix regardless of your own capabilities as an engineer.

The way that you have recorded will be relevant now. If you have recorded mostly live instruments, you will have on tape an ambient connection between the various musical events. This will provide the catalyst with which to blend the instruments. Furthermore, if you have recorded certain instruments simultaneously, such as drums, bass and guitar, their relative balances are naturally present.

300

If you have recorded one instrument at a time or triggered samples, you will have to create a common ambience artificially. It is most important that you achieve this: if the music sounds as if it was performed at the same time, it will be more coherent to the listener and probably more enjoyable.

Whatever your approach, you will find it worthwhile to do several versions of the mix containing, within reason, any alternative balances that may apply, the most common of these being a louder vocal mix. As you listen in the studio over the course of a few hours, your perception of the vocal balance will change as you become more used to it. As a result, when you play back the mix later, the vocal may not be as loud as you thought. Better to be safe than sorry by doing an extra mix whilst the equipment is set up.

Mixing computers of varying sophistication are found in nearly every studio. To fully exploit the advantages offered by this technology, whilst avoiding the many pitfalls, you should clarify your attitude to and relationship with computer-aided mixing. Remember that, whilst computers are heralded as time-saving devices, the expected level of achievement from computer-assistance is so much higher that you will find this 'saved' time is swallowed up quickly and easily. You should base your decisions about the level of computer-assistance on creative criteria rather than just labour-saving ones.

Mastering

This is the last process before manufacture. During mastering you can really consolidate the work you have done. Insist on attending the mastering session yourself and choose the mastering location carefully. Most especially, find a mastering engineer you can work with and who is able to interpret what you want to achieve. If you find that a particular mix really does not sound right within the whole concept, it is worth considering a re-mix of the song (if the budget allows). This is your last chance to get it right! A mastering suite is generally very unflattering acoustically, so you will need to take away a reference copy before allowing the record to go into manufacture. The most accurate and convenient reference would be a CD and these are now just as cheap as any other copy.

If you are producing a demo, then the duplicating plant will work from a DAT master which you should label clearly as being an equalised production master, requiring no further changes. Production masters for manufacture by the major labels will be 1630 U-Matic Digital and similarly labelled.

Strictly speaking these details are slightly outside the producer's remit but, as your responsibility to yourself and the artist is to deliver the best result possible, you need to at least maintain a watching brief.

Tying up the ends

It is the producer's responsibility to provide the record company with all the label information pertaining to studios, musicians, writers, engineers and guests. You must provide these in writing and ask for a full label copy, when assembled, so you can check no-one has been left out. Additionally, you will have seen, from the producer's guidelines, (Figure 13:2, page 286-7) the requirements with regard to the use of samples. You must be very conscientious about adhering to these guidelines otherwise all sorts of litigation can result.

Styles and professionalism

As a producer, your overall style of production will depend very much on the music you are producing and the kind of person you are. There is plenty of room for expression of all kinds within music production and it is up to you to find your own level. If you should find yourself involved in a production that eventually proves not to be your style, then the most honest and prudent production decision would be to bow out. Obviously this may not be possible, but shows the importance of choosing the right components to do the best job. This could, in some circumstances, involve hiring another producer for songs more suited to him. The point is that your professionalism must extend to objectivity towards your own performance too.

You should always be prepared and interested to learn from every project with which you are involved. You will learn new ways of dealing with difficult people and situations. You will learn new techniques by working in different countries and studios – do not be afraid to experiment with them. Your best album should, preferably, be the last one, and the most enjoyable the one you are currently working on.

Spotting raw talent

Producers will not often be involved in talent spotting from a record company stance. But, it is just as important for them to be able to recognise where the particular talent in an artist lies. This will help them to evaluate their own contribution to the artist and eventually enable them to produce that artist well. A producer's overall worth to an artist is greatly enhanced if he likes and appreciates what they are trying to do.

As it is most likely that a producer's first direct experience of an artist with whom he may work will be in live performance, it is worth remembering that his perception of a live performance will always be affected by the circumstances. A fun night at a good venue will always leave a better impression than a wet, winter Wednesday in Walsall! Conversely, any artist who manages to uplift such a potentially negative situation is definitely worth a second visit.

Audience reaction is a good measure of the particularly successful aspects of a performance, but beware the 'partisan' crowd who will get excited just because they know the bass player. A second or third visit to different venues will enable a producer to evaluate all these factors.

There can be no formula for spotting potential and so often talent is impossible to quantify or describe. If a producer can develop in himself an instinct for good commercial music, he can avoid the pitfalls of merely following trends and fashions. In this way, he is in the privileged position of helping to realise the talent in an artist – a reward in itself.

The business of production

As a producer, there will be various aspects of your professional life which you will have to get organised. The business of music in the 1990s is much more corporate than ever before and, therefore, needs careful handling.

Contracts

It is impossible to discuss all the legal and business ramifications of your role as producer. Producer contracts are complex and lengthy documents which require specialist knowledge to interpret correctly. But, I will deal with some of the fundamental factors of which you will need to be aware.

All payments to a producer are considered to be advances against royalties earned from the sale of the recording. You will receive a lump sum as an advance and it is normal for this to be paid 50 per cent on commencement and 50 per cent on delivery of the completed project. When the figure attributed to your percentage of the sales exceeds your advance, you will receive further royalties.

After the preliminary negotiations on your behalf, you must ensure that you put in writing the outline points of the agreement and post or fax it to the record company. The record company will then present you with their standard form of contract. You must have this checked by your legal representative. There will undoubtedly be clauses included which are not necessary or acceptable and, inevitably, there will areas of ambiguity in the terms. You must make sure that the contract contains all the negotiated factors, including *per diem* payments and the company's responsibility for travel and accommodation costs.

In the early stages of your career as a producer, you will probably handle the basics of this business yourself. Inevitably, you will have to take some risks when dealing with smaller companies or individuals. This probably means that you will do work for which you will never get your just reward. This is a fact of life in the music business and you will have to accept it. Bear in mind, if the quality of your work is creative and professional, you will be able to use it to promote yourself to other clients, so all will not be lost.

Promoting yourself

Two essential items are needed to promote you as a producer to potential clients and this holds true whether you are managed by anyone or not:

- A readable and informative biography and discography.

- A showreel.

Your biography should try to give an idea of your strengths and weaknesses and your preferred style of production. This may not get you considered for every project available, but you will be offered a higher percentage of suitable ones.

Your discography should include all the projects with which you have been involved – even the less successful ones; sometimes the most obscure connections will give that extra insight into your suitability.

Your showreel needs a different approach. Almost all potential clients will want to hear some of your work to help decide if you are the right producer for them. Obviously, if you have high-profile work riding high in the charts, then this will not be so important. But, this will not usually be the case and certainly not at the start of your career. Your showreel is your most important piece of promotional material. Considering that most potential clients will have several of these tapes to listen to, you would be unwise to send them everything you have ever recorded in its entirety. You should compile a tape (preferably DAT) with about a minute of each of your most recent and most relevant productions. If the company wishes to hear more, you can send them copies of the respective albums on CD.

Try to meet key A&R people by going to see them at the record company. It will always help if they can put a face to the name.

Most music business directories will give you a free entry in their listings. You should be informative, factual and brief – flippancy and verbosity never read well in a trade guide.

Take care to ensure that you receive the proper credit on the recordings you make when they are released. These credits are an important part of your self-promotion.

Management

As you progress up the ladder and achieve a track record, you will be wise to seek producer management. A good manager will make contacts on your behalf, negotiate advances and royalty rates, help with the budget planning and tracking, double check studio and travel arrangements and more. They are paid on a percentage basis so their services are performance related.

A good manager is worth his or her weight in gold, especially when you are dealing with international projects for the major labels. It is never easy dealing with major corporations, and getting paid by them within a reasonable time can be a nightmare. In these situations your manager will be able to 'play the bad guy' on your behalf, leaving you to concentrate on the creative aspects of the production. If you are doing a smaller production, for a smaller label with fewer staff, a manager will deal with acrimonious disputes, saving you from having to do so with the same people with whom you are discussing the music.

Covering your back

One of the less-endearing tendencies a producer encounters in the music business is the age-old game of 'passing the buck'. He can easily distance himself from this unsavoury practice by confirming all-important arrangements and conversations by fax or letter. Any instructions he gives to studios etc. should be confirmed by fax, as should any significant requests to the record company.

Conclusion

After the record has been produced, it has to be advertised. The next chapter focuses on one area of marketing, that of PR and promotion.

Chapter 14

The PR and Promotions Company

Introduction

Without the use of PR and promotions companies, the job of both the promoter in today's live music business and the record company and retailer would be much harder than it is. As the introduction of dance music has reduced middle-scale promotions and made it more and more difficult for live music promoters to attract audiences of around 2000 people to events, the PR and promotions companies are vitally important in the selling of artists to the public. The building of new audiences for small-scale artists is vital. The small live club scene and arena promotions are still very healthy, but those artists who fall in between these two find it hard to survive. The reason for this, as has already been stated earlier, is the movement away from the live music scene to dance music clubs.

The PR and promotion companies use a marketing system, which takes place in a number of ways, but its main elements consist of regional, club and student promotions. There are many promotions companies that service the live music and record industry and these include Wild, Renegade and Beatwax. But, the company used as an example here is Revolution, one of the country's leading PR and promotions companies.

Revolution's core business centres around regional and student promotions. The company services these club promotions by sending DJ's in alternative, rock, and specialist dance and student clubs new releases from established and new artists. The company's clients include Oasis, Fatboy Slim and Beck. Once the DJ's receive the product, they play it to their audiences to elicit responses. These responses are then fed back to the company so that it has some idea of how the product has been received. DJ's are also sent product release dates, tour dates, press, posters and videos of the band, depending on what sort of club the product is being played at.

Figure 14:1 Revolution Company Diagram

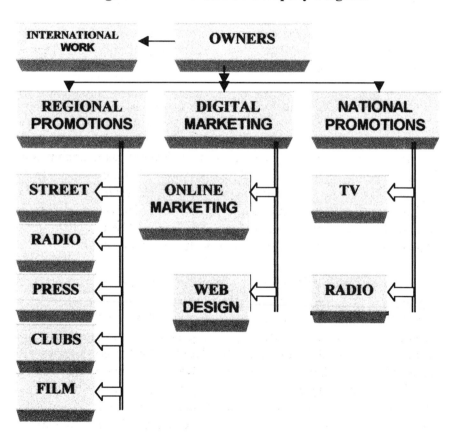

All of these elements are vitally important in providing the audience with information on the artists in question. Hearing new product before it is released enables members of the audience to spread the word to friends. The video enables the audience to get a feel for how the band look or how good the video is. Posters enable all sorts of information to be fed to the punters; for example, the posters may contain release dates of the product or live tour dates for the artist. Freebies attract punters to the club and often ensure their loyalty on other occasions. In a number of cases, launch nights may be held at particular clubs to ensure maximum publicity for an album or single.

There is usually at least one launch event or playback per week.

It is hoped that the information given to the DJ's translates into record and concert sales for the artist. This benefits retailers, record companies, venue managers and promoters.

Another area that Revolution concentrates on is press and radio. Regional and student press are important because the company earn their money from the quality and success of their promotions. Revolution is the number one student media Promotions Company and is, at the moment, working on Muse and Oasis. Feeding student press representatives with information and allowing them access to interview artists, is vitally important to the large number of individual university and college publications released each week. These outlets give students direct access to the artists through their local media.

Many clubs in the regions also have their own magazines, which act in a similar way. Many universities and colleges have either their own internal or small external radio stations and this is another way to spread the word about artists appearing at clubs and venues in the locality. In the past I have used Revolution a lot for press packs for some of the gigs that I have been involved with. This is often more beneficial than using a number of the press or record companies to secure product, transparencies, biographies, press and photograph. You only make one phone call to one company, instead of several phone calls, which does not always bring you what you want.

In some cases Revolution had already contacted all the local press in the area, which saved me the job of promoting the band to the regional and local press, and enabled me to concentrate on selling tickets through other means.

Revolution's regional promotions department has a street team consisting of 85 people around the country working for them on the street. The street team is vital to the Revolution ethos, as they constitute the face of the company in major cities and towns throughout the country. The team is run from Glasgow. They put posters and flyers in shops and clubs in city centres. They also visit clubs and collect addresses for mailings at gigs associated with product that Revolution are working on. The street team sets Revolution apart from other promotion companies as it enables the company to facilitate ideas that other companies find impossible to do. For instance, if a record company wish for a special poster campaign in selected cities, all Revolution has to do is to contact the team, mail out the posters and give instructions to the team of where and when the posters have to be placed. The campaign is then carried out. This team gives the company a base on the ground.

Revolution makes their money from the charges levied for their services. They are paid per job. The company overheads are high, therefore, they have to generate a lot of work. The work carried out by Revolution must be of a high standard, otherwise companies will not use the service again. The national radio department is a big earner. Revolution have a four-strong national radio and TV team, which has merged with other national radio and TV pluggers. The base business of this division is very strong. Revolution has also set up a digital arm to their business, which was the first online marketing company. A lot of PR companies service music websites but Revolution markets music websites online. The online company played a big part in Ian Brown's 'Dolphins' campaign. The company was finding it difficult to get the record played on the radio, but they had a big impact with their online campaign and the record went in at number five. Revolution are setting up a transatlantic website as the US see Europe as one territory rather than a number of separate entities. A US link is vital to the future of the company.

Film is one new area of promotion that Revolution has recently entered. Film is an important medium today because of a number of reasons. One of these is the popularity of soundtracks and the spin-off singles often associated with them. One of the reasons for their success in film promotions is their access to the student community and the success of their street teams in club promotion. Another reason is their fresh and interesting ideas that have not been used before in the promotion of film. The company has a pool of 16 creative and 85 reps across the country who can deliver on the marketing ideas. To date, Revolution has worked on campaigns with Buena Vista, Fox, UIP, Warner and Alliance. Revolution are usually involved in releases with either a strong youth or musical appeal. When the company was involved with 'The Beach', they organised 30 beach parties at key Universities across the country. The nights were branded with posters, slides, staff T-shirts and the Soundtrack to the movie was playing. There were also lots of give-aways.

The key to Revolution's success is that they are good at finding targets and then achieving them. They make their money by hitting the target well. Note that the aim of the company is to get people talking about the product by constant reminders that it is available, in concert or in the shops, or on the screen. These people then spread the message by word of mouth and this, in turn, generates sales. This matters in both the student and club communities where people discuss music and tell friends about great events. This not only creates a buzz around a product, but also ensures that students and clubbers alike return to the venue where they heard or saw the product. This closes the loop, as the audience is then captive for further promotions by the company.

> Martin Tibbetts, from Revolution, contributed useful material for this chapter – a long-time friend and perpetual nice-guy in the business.

Conclusion

This chapter shows that the marketing of a product or a live gig is not always down just to the promoter or Record Company. PR and promotion companies assist with the promotion. In the case of the live event, the promoter does not usually have to pay for the service, because it is an indirect benefit received from the record company paying the PR or promotion company to push the product. The playing of the product by DJ's, the placing of posters in clubs and the giving out of flyers with the concert dates on, are all part of the push to sell the product from which the promoter of the live gig indirectly benefits. But, the tour for an album or single is created to sell product. Therefore, the more people who hear the product or see the posters or flyers in clubs, the larger the potential audience for local gigs. Companies like Revolution often put flyers in clubs in cities near to the next date on a tour. It has been known for companies to put flyers both in local clubs and to hit clubs on the night that the band is appearing. The reasons for this are two-fold. Firstly, to procure names and addresses from people at the club so that when new product is released or the artist is playing in the locality again, people attending the club or concert can be directly targeted. Secondly, the club may be targeted because the band are either doing an in-store signing or appearance in the area or are playing their next date on the tour in the next town.

Bibliography and References

Access All Areas, Greetlake Services Ltd, Bristol June 1998

Applause, Applause Publications Ltd, London. August 1999

Collard, R., 1990a, *Total Quality*, Institute of Personnel Management, page 46

Collard, R., 1990b, *Total Quality*, Institute of Personnel Management, page 34

Collard, R., 1990c, *Total Quality*, Institute of Personnel Management, page 13

Diggle, K., 1984, *Guide to Arts Marketing*, Rhinegold, page 112
The concept of the 'Attitude Target' has been used to explain the way in which music fans behave in relation to concert attendance.

Events 2001, Outdoor Events Publications Ltd, Surrey 2000 (annual)

Health and Safety at Work etc. Act 1974, London: H.M.S.O.

Health and Safety Executive, *Managing Crowds Safely*, 1992

Hirsch, P., 1990, *On Record*, Routledge, pages 127-128

HMSO, *Code of Practice for Environmental Control at Open Air Pop Concerts,* 1993

HMSO, Control of Substances Hazardous to Health Regulations, 1994

HMSO, *Guide to Health, Safety and Welfare at Pop Concerts and Similar Events*, 1994

HMSO, Private Places of Entertainment (Licensing) Act 1967

HMSO, The Licensing (Scotland) Act 1976

REFERENCES

HMSO, Schedule 1 to the Local Government (Miscellaneous Provisions) Act 1982 (as amended by part IV Fire Safety and Safety of Places of Sport Act 1987)

HMSO, Schedule 12 to the London Government Act 1963 (as amended by part IV Fire Safety and Safety of Places of Sport Act 1987)

HMSO, Section 41 of the Civic Government (Scotland) Act 1982 (as amended by part IV Fire Safety and Safety of Places of Sport Act 1987)

HMSO, The Licensing Act 1964 (as amended by the Licensing Act 1989)

HMSO, Health and Safety at Work etc. Act 1974

IEE *Regulations for Electrical Installations (Institute of Electrical Engineers wiring regulations, 16th edition, 1993)* HFC Guidance note G550 Electrical Safety at Places of Entertainment & the Memorandum of Guidance on the Electricity at Work Regulations 1989

Kemps, International Music Book, Showcase Publications, London 2001 (annual)

Live, Pro Light & Sound, Sandridge, St Albans. June 1997

Milton Keynes Borough Council, *Schedule of conditions for theatres/indoor entertainment licences under the Theatres Act 1968 and Local Government (Miscellaneous Provisions) Act 1982*

National Outdoor Events Association, *Code of Practice for Outdoor Events, 1993*

Polhemus, T., 1994, *Street Style*, Thames & Hudson, page 83, quoting P. Toffler.

Showman's Directory, Brook House Press, Surrey, 1996

The Sanitary Installations Regulations (BS 6465)

White Book, Birdhurst Ltd, Middlesex, 2001 (annual)

Willis, P., 1990, *Moving Culture*, Calouste Gulbenkian Foundation, page 27

Index

The symbol – after a page number indicates
a lengthy section on the topic.

315

Q

R

S

V

W

Z